T0299019

THE CARDS

THE CARDS

The Evolution and Power of Tarot

PATRICK MAILLE

University Press of Mississippi / Jackson

The University Press of Mississippi is the scholarly publishing agency of
the Mississippi Institutions of Higher Learning: Alcorn State University,
Delta State University, Jackson State University, Mississippi State University,
Mississippi University for Women, Mississippi Valley State University,
University of Mississippi, and University of Southern Mississippi.

www.upress.state.ms.us

The University Press of Mississippi is a member
of the Association of University Presses.

First printing 2021
∞

Library of Congress Cataloging-in-Publication Data

Names: Maille, Patrick (Patrick H.), author.
Title: The cards: the evolution and power of tarot / Patrick Maille.
Description: Jackson: University Press of Mississippi, 2021. | Includes
bibliographical references and index.
Identifiers: LCCN 2020051284 (print) | LCCN 2020051285 (ebook) | ISBN
978-1-4968-3299-3 (hardback) | ISBN 978-1-4968-3300-6 (trade paperback) | ISBN
978-1-4968-3301-3 (epub) | ISBN 978-1-4968-3302-0 (epub) | ISBN 978-1-4968-3303-7
(pdf) | ISBN 978-1-4968-3304-4 (pdf)
Subjects: LCSH: Tarot. | Tarot (Game) | Tarot cards. | Magic. | Witchcraft.
| Secret societies.
Classification: LCC BF1879.T2 M324 2021 (print) | LCC BF1879.T2 (ebook) |
DDC 133.3/2424—dc23
LC record available at https://lccn.loc.gov/2020051284
LC ebook record available at https://lccn.loc.gov/2020051285

British Library Cataloging-in-Publication Data available

Contents

PART II

To Bonnie

When first we fell in love, it became possible to believe.
In the decades ever since, impossible to deny.
Love is genuine magic.
And ours is genuine love.

Acknowledgments

This book exists only because certain special people in my life made it possible for me to get here. I want to thank them in print and with sincerity, beginning with my wife, Bonnie Maille, who inspired and encouraged me in innumerable ways both emotional and practical while also doing an enormous amount of proofreading and making grammatical corrections as the project went from one draft to another. Both of our (adult) children played a role in developing this book. Their interests in Tarot allowed me to obtain perspectives and material that I drew upon in order to improve the quality of my research. The fact that my wife and kids loved the idea of this project fueled my love for the project all the more.

Many of the people at Oklahoma Panhandle State University are owed various debts of gratitude as well. From the support of my friends and colleagues at the library to the campus community in general, I found a great deal of encouragement in this endeavor. Chief among these supporters is Brad Duren, the dean of the College of Arts and Education, who introduced me to the community of scholars that make up the annual Southwest Popular and American Culture conference in Albuquerque, New Mexico. Professor Duren and the history students that we take to the conference every year have become a very special part of my life both personally and professionally. Participating as a presenter at the popular culture conference led directly to this book. The students who attended the conferences and participated in my classes have been a blessing, not only because I love being a teacher, but because they also served as a sounding board and a source of different perspectives and insights at various stages of research and writing.

Several people allowed me to interview them during my research and such people were invaluable to the final product. Among these were prominent members of the tarot community such as Mary K. Greer and Rachel Pollack. These interviews allowed me to learn quite a bit from some of the best minds in Tarot. They also showed me that the people I would be writing about were intelligent, witty, and an honest pleasure to associate with, even if it was just over the phone. I also wish to thank Deb Clark and Natasha Rice, proprietors of Sandalwood and Sage in Norman, Oklahoma, who allowed me to get a few insights into what it's like running a store that caters to customers who buy tarot cards and related paraphernalia. Dana Nemeth of Bowling Green State University's Browne Popular Culture Library deserves mention for her help with my research on comics. I appreciate her sending me source information that would otherwise have been impossible for me to locate.

My thanks go out to Katie Keene of the University Press of Mississippi, who reached out to me asking if Tarot and popular culture was something that I saw as a project going beyond presentations at an academic conference. Up to that point, I honestly had not considered writing a book on the subject. The University Press of Mississippi is also home to Mary Heath, who has guided me through the publication process. I thank her, too. I also wish to thank the anonymous reviewers for the Press that critiqued an earlier draft of my manuscript and gave me the opportunity to improve it at a point when I was ready to see it finished.

There are many people who helped to make this book possible or to improve its quality in various ways. They deserve nothing but credit and praise from me. Still, as with any other scholarly publication, proper criticism is to be expected, even encouraged. Whatever flaws or shortcomings may be found herein are, of course, the sole responsibility of the author.

THE CARDS

Introduction

Doesn't it seem as if everyone has seen tarot cards? They show up in movies, television, and comic books, and are sprinkled, here and there, across the landscape of popular culture. Yet, when it comes down to what we actually know about that "wicked pack of cards," as the poet T. S. Eliot famously called them, it isn't much, is it? That passing familiarity actually has the potential to add to whatever makes the cards mysterious and intriguing at the level of popular culture. Having said that, however, a more thoroughgoing familiarity with the cards will not likely cause them to become less interesting.

My first experience interacting with tarot cards came in my early twenties when a beautiful young woman, whom I was quite interested in, contributed to that interest by reading my cards. Although she was a novice in Tarot, she had *the* deck. That is, the most well-known deck and the one that has (as much as is possible) a sort of *official* status among tarot readers. I did not know at the time, of course, that her deck, first made in the early twentieth century by Arthur Edward Waite and Pamela Colman Smith, was the deck with the most cultural prestige. Nor did I know that there were a multitude of other tarot decks in circulation.

This same beautiful young woman from Texas, who ended up becoming my wife and the mother of my two children, also had a book which instructed her on how to read the cards. I have to admit that referring to a book while interpreting the cards makes the tarot reading a little less of a mystical experience. The book she had was called *A Complete Guide to the Tarot*, written by Eden Gray in the early 1970s. It turns out that that particular book, and that particular deck, might be the strongest influences on bringing Tarot into popular culture in the last hundred years.

Both have certainly been very influential in shaping the experience of becoming familiar with Tarot in American popular culture. Other than the fact that I fell in love with and married the person who introduced me to tarot cards, my initial experience would have had many similarities with the initial tarot experience of many other people in America over the last six decades. The most likely deck to end up in the hands of a tarot novice is that Waite-Colman Smith deck. One of the most likely books to serve as an introduction to a budding tarotist would be Gray's *Complete Guide to Tarot*.

The popularity of Tarot cannot compete with things like rock 'n' roll, television, or movies. Its presence in popular culture is nowhere near as pervasive. Tarot, however, has found a presence within all of these aspects of popular culture. I argue that, despite Tarot being truly familiar to only a small part of society, major elements of American culture have served as vehicles through which Tarot has established an important place in popular culture. These more significant parts of the popular culture—art, music, television, movies—serve, in turn, to make Tarot more popular still. And it would be fair to add that Tarot, in its own way, adds something to these core elements of popular culture.

One could certainly go beyond the four cultural areas to be explored in this book. For example, one could look at literature and find a wealth of references to Tarot. One could look at religious life, too, and find the subject of Tarot being treated (positively and negatively) as a significant topic. For the purposes of this book, I have chosen four areas that I consider to be important and interesting lenses through which to consider the cultural significance of Tarot. There is no need to rate their importance in any order. Nor is there a need to justify including or excluding other aspects of popular culture in which tarot cards might be found. This is not, of course, to suggest that exploring the place of Tarot in, say, American novels would not be worthwhile (indeed, it would). The four cultural areas to be explored here provide an adequate range of cultural touchstones through which to explore Tarot in popular culture while simultaneously keeping a manageable scope for the book.

This book will examine the place of Tarot in art, television, movies, and comics. Each of these subject areas is given its own chapter. The book will open, however, with a discussion of the history of Tarot. That topic will be explored a little more deeply than the others and will, therefore, require two chapters. One of those will be on the origins of Tarot and the other will look at Tarot from the twentieth century onward. The third chapter of the book will explore the community of people with an interest and attachment to Tarot. These will include a variety of people at various levels of involvement, making up a community.

I have also written a chapter on Tarot and art. Tarot cards, it can be argued, constitute an art form in and of themselves. They are also an inspiration for artists. Art has a place in popular culture, and consequently, such a chapter is merited. Art also shares something with the other three topics in that they are all visual media.

Some terms should be defined at this point because they will appear throughout the book, and since they might be understood differently by different readers, I will define my usage of the terms now. The first of these terms is "esoteric." By esoteric (and its related term, "esotericism"), I mean the traditions in Western civilization that are distinct from both traditional or official religious conventions and scientific rationalism. Sometimes referred to as the Western mystery tradition, esotericism encompasses a large number of beliefs and attitudes, most of which claim some degree of debated connection to (though not general acceptance of) both religion and science as social institutions. An important aspect of esotericism is that its various tenets are known to only a small portion of the population and truly understood by even fewer. The concept of esotericism was first articulated in the second century by Lucian of Samosata who used the word *esoterikos* in describing membership to an inner circle of people.

In some ways, esotericism is nearly synonymous with the term "gnosticism." Gnosticism usually has a religious connotation (particularly associated with early Christianity) but can be generally understood as referring to a particular group within a community that considers itself to have special and advanced knowledge beyond the conventional teachings of that community. They are likely to be viewed with suspicion by the community's mainstream members and further seen as challenging to the established leaders of the community.

The term "occult" should also be defined. In the parlance of popular culture, this word is often used to refer to the satanic (which may or may not be accurate, depending on the context). It will be used in this book with the more precise meaning of having knowledge of things that are hidden, with the specific connotation of those hidden things being associated with the supernatural.

Finally, let us consider a practical definition of the phrase "popular culture." This phrase can be more problematic than it appears at first glance. Indeed, a variety of scholars with backgrounds in anthropology, sociology, and history have debated the meaning and significance of the phrase, popular culture, for decades. Both words are value-laden terms with meanings that adjust based on any number of variables. For example, scholars of the Early Modern period commonly use the term popular culture when studying the witch scares of that era. The phrasing serves to underscore the distinctions between common people in villages and towns, on the one hand, and leaders in the church or judges in courts, on the other. The contrast between elite and popular is emphasized in that context.

In other contexts, the contrast between a social elite and the rest of society may be useful for examining a particular historical topic. A central underlying theme, however, is that different points of contrast are emphasized. This might involve minorities and majority populations. It might be beneficial in other contexts to consider tensions between social classes in terms of popular culture. In any case, it is often necessary to provide further context and to point out various nuances before the term can be consistently applied within the given discussion, article, or book.

Like so many other terms, "popular culture" is a useful construct despite the flaw (if it is a flaw) that the meaning can be a bit vague or flexible. Whether that is a strength or a weakness, the term continues to have value. Raymond Browne, who popularized both the phrase "popular culture" and the study of it as an academic discipline, took a broad approach in arguing that popular culture encompasses all that elite culture does not. For our purposes, the phrase will refer to widely held and commonly used values, beliefs, and modes of expression accepted by most members of society as well as the products of those values, beliefs, and modes of expression.

Tarot cards do not permeate the popular culture to the extent that fashion, movie theaters, or automobiles do. They are not commonly possessed nor are they even commonly seen. Although they are not part of the common experience of popular culture, many of the things that are part of the common cultural experience—art, television, movies, and comics, for example—can readily incorporate Tarot. It is along these lines that we shall explore the cultural significance of Tarot.

A brief note on capitalization of the word "tarot" should be inserted here. I will capitalize the first letter in cases where the word itself is being used as a noun, as in when it refers to a concept or an idea. In cases where the word is being used as an adjective (for example, as in "tarot cards"), I will not capitalize the first letter.

My personal interest in tarot cards, as I said above, came from my wife in our early adulthood. My scholarly interest in tarot cards came much later. I developed an interest in the history of magic while I was working on my doctorate in history. It was actually a secondary interest. My primary interest, the subject of my doctoral dissertation, was early Christian conversion. More specifically, I studied the attitudes of people in the early Christian period—both Christian and pagan—with regard to the supernatural. What some thought of as miraculous, others thought of as magical. What some saw as supernatural and good, others saw as supernatural and evil. In other instances, claims of the miraculous were viewed as deceitful con jobs. I found that one could not accurately dismiss or describe this divergence as one between pagan and Christian. The fact is, early Christians argued among themselves about what was real and what was false when it came to supernatural claims. They also argued among themselves about what was good and what was evil when it came to various claims associated with the supernatural.

That exploration into early Christian magic led me to further reading on the history of magic, and eventually, I began teaching a course on the history of magic. At that point, I still had little interest in popular culture. Also, my teaching fields have been in European history rather than American. Brad Duren, the chairperson of my university department (who is now my dean) had a long-standing interest in popular culture and involvement with an annual popular culture conference that he and members of our university's History Club regularly attended. Attending that conference with Professor Duren made me want to present papers there, and searching for a topic that could be pulled from my history of magic course, I settled on Tarot. That topic turned out to be increasingly fascinating to me and quite a good fit for the Southwest Popular/American Cultural Association which annually features numerous presentations related to television, movies, and comics.

When I was contacted by Katie Keene of the University Press of Mississippi to discuss Tarot as a writing project, it seemed clear that I had found a scholarly niche. The University Press of Mississippi specializes in the areas of film, television, and comics as key domains in the scholarly study of popular culture. Each of those three areas is a logical chapter topic within which to situate Tarot. I felt that art was an even more important cultural zone within which to situate Tarot and, therefore, included a chapter on the art of Tarot. What follows is the result of my efforts in this particular field of study. My intention is to appeal to those with an interest in popular culture or an interest in Tarot, and my means of doing so is simply by linking the two topics into a narrative.

Like many books on tarot cards, I begin with a history. The history portion of the book is lengthy enough to merit two chapters. Like any of the other chapters in the book, they could be read on their own and serve their own purpose. However, these first two chapters on history also provide useful background for a better understanding of the material to be covered in the remainder of the book. Names of important people, explanations of important concepts, and discussion of key events are all covered in the first two chapters. The later chapters could be read independently as stand-alone essays, but a greater depth of meaning and understanding is developed if the historical background is absorbed by the reader.

Having provided a historical review in the first two chapters, the third chapter looks at the contemporary tarot community. I wish to present a community of people with a very diverse set of beliefs and backgrounds as well as a range of places to stand within the context of a large community. There are all kinds of different people that make up the modern tarot community and that is, in itself, an important point for readers to understand. So, I will present a "flyover" view of America's tarot community to give the reader a sense of the people who make up this community. To push the metaphor a bit, I will also swoop down for a closer look at specific people who represent a certain place or type within the community. Thus, a bigger picture will be formed and simultaneously fleshed out with some detail where appropriate.

The two chapters on history and the chapter on a tarot community in contemporary American culture make up the first part of the book. The second part of the book will dive into particular aspects of popular culture and examine the place of Tarot within those areas. Part II will have four chapters: art, television, movies, and comics. Space would prohibit any attempt to treat these chapter topics exhaustively, but they are all treated extensively. What I have tried to do is to present key themes related to Tarot within the subject of these chapters as well as some of the most interesting examples. Another objective in each of the chapters of Part II is to demonstrate the ways in which Tarot can be applied to the subjects (art, television, movies, and comics) in ways that reflect or enhance the functions and goals of those media. There is an incredible synergy between Tarot and all four of those forms of media. These synergistic relationships will be explored in ways intended to shed light on both Tarot and these media so commonly associated with popular culture.

Finally, recognizing that the reader might wish to know the author's attitude about tarot cards, I will provide my opinion here. I do not believe that the cards have any supernatural powers capable of revealing future events or unveiling impossible-to-know details of the past. Nor do I believe that they have any preternatural powers that allow the reader to obtain information beyond what is available to anyone else. If this does not imply it, let me make it explicit to the reader that I do not consider the cards to be either bad or good in any inherently magical or miraculous sense. Just as the tarot deck should not be seen as a miraculous device, neither should it be seen as an evil. In fact, it seems just as silly to me that anyone would take religious offense at tarot cards as it would be for some other person to make a medical decision solely on the basis of flipping a card (or a coin for that matter).

Let us go a little further by considering a question I am occasionally asked: "Do the cards work?" When that question is put to me, I always respond by asking the questioner what the word "work" means. Defining the words up front is often important so that we do not make assumptions about implicit meaning. It is much the same with the word "magical." For me, falling in love with my wife and having children were both undeniably "magical" experiences. Yet, I see no place for wizardry, divine or semi-divine beings, potions, or spells for making such moments genuinely magical.

While I do rule out supernatural explanations when it comes to Tarot, I nonetheless think that the cards "work" in certain ways. The symbols on the cards have meanings that are psychologically and statistically likely to trigger thought and contemplation in any normal (another term with ambiguous meaning) person regardless of their disposition. The cards can represent types of people that are found in the lives of nearly everyone—authority figures, strong-willed women, helpful friends, and so on. Some cards suggest sadness, and others suggest adventure, caution, or any number of moods and circumstances. All of this means, with certainty, that various aspects of people's lives are reflected in the cards and, therefore, the cards will point to personal experiences and relationships (among other things) that have meaning and relevance in the life of anyone who uses the cards to stimulate thought, to meditate, or to explore their lives in ways that might not come to mind without some external prompt. In ways such as these, the cards work; and they work without question. They might work in ways that are humorous, unimportant, profound, ironic, or coincidental. But, they work because we use them. It's as simple and as certain as that, at least to me.

PART I

CHAPTER 1

The Origins of Tarot Cards

The First Cards

At some point after the Christian world of Europe obtained citrus fruits and algebra from the Muslims to their south and east, but before getting coffee and learning about how to distill alcohol, the Christian world of Europe also learned about, and imported, another product from the Islamic world: playing cards. These were the ancestors of the regular playing cards we use for poker and go fish. The four suits we are familiar with in America (spades, clubs, hearts, and diamonds) were actually a French variation made from suits that were originally swords, polo sticks, cups, and coins. The cards originated during the Renaissance. It was an era of great artistic genius and scholarly fascination with reviving the long dead intellectual gifts of ancient Greece and Rome.

The cards were drawn or painted with various styles, but the basic idea was that the number and suit were represented in a simple manner. The card number was represented by drawing the suit symbol the appropriate number of times. For example, the "Six of Cups" would have six cups drawn on it; the "Eight of Coins" would have eight coins.

The easiest comparison to make in identifying these transitions would be that of the club from the polo stick. They are both wooden objects that are intended for hitting something. The sport of polo is yet another creation of the Islamic world that would have been quite unfamiliar to the Christian world. Making the change to a more familiar yet similar object has an obvious logic. A comparable set of circumstances is connected to the transition of coins to diamonds. In addition to the fact that both items have monetary value, they are also both very basic shapes. The cups and swords are a bit harder to explain. The spade, as symbolized in a standard deck of cards, is not quite the same as the digging tool which shares the name. But it is sharp and pointed in a way that is only one or two steps removed from the shape of a sword that has been shortened and widened. The cups becoming hearts might be the most complicated of these evolutionary processes in card suits. Let us note that the cup as a vessel was identified as a symbol of emotion. The heart, too, represents emotion. That being the case, the transition is less of a physical shift and more of a shift from one symbol to another that is different in appearance but not in terms of representation. The court cards were a king, viceroy, and second viceroy. A king and two lieutenants might be a better way to characterize the cards. Europeans changed these by adding a queen and switched the viceroys to a knight and a page. Eventually, the knight and page cards of each suit were reduced to a single figure known as the Jack.

Muslims had playing cards in the late twelfth century. These playing cards eventually came to Italy from Egypt and Turkey. From there, they worked their way into eastern and southern France and up to Switzerland and Germany. Over a period of many years, there were many variations. Certain artists would wish to draw and paint much more detailed court cards, for example, while others might simply write the name of the card and draw the suit to which the card belongs. Some artists might be more elaborate than others in representing the suits. Regional differences also developed so that, for example, Spanish cards would look different than cards in France or in northern Italy.

Sometime before 1440, northern Italians had developed a new game, *tarocchi*, with completely different cards. The game was somewhat similar to modern games where one card trumps another to win a hand or score a point. But, the deck did not have suits or numbers. The cards were ranked, and only later were numbers put on them from zero to twenty-one. These twenty-two cards were later—much later—added to the earlier "regular" deck of fifty-six cards to create the seventy-eight-card tarot deck of modern times. That process, however, took a few centuries.

Tarocchi was an altogether different game than the game (or games) played with the cards that had been imported from the Islamic countries. This does not rule out the likelihood that, having learned about card games and the deck with four suits, northern Italians came up with a new game that borrowed and built off the earlier concept of a game played with cards. To put it differently, northern Italians seemed to have learned about card games from their Muslim neighbors and then made up their own card game—one so different that, while it did use cards, it used altogether different cards.

This cultural interaction between the Christian and Muslim worlds deserves just a little more attention in order to establish the global context from which card games emerged. The Islamic world of the Renaissance era was quite large compared to the Christian world. Islamic culture spanned three continents: Asia, Africa, and a large chunk of Europe. Christian culture was confined largely to Europe, despite a few outposts in Africa and the Middle East, until the Age of Exploration began in the late fifteenth century. The introduction of playing cards into the Christian world occurs just before the time of Columbus and the beginnings of Christian Europe's colonial expansion onto the global stage. The southeastern part of Europe was largely controlled by the Ottoman Empire, whose territory included modern-day Turkey, the Balkans, and Greece but extended beyond these large European territories. At the other end of Europe, Spain was also Muslim territory. Large areas of the Middle East, Central Asia, and much of Africa were also part of the Muslim world.

While the Christian world was smaller and not very spread out, it bordered the Islamic world in several different places, particularly, places along the Mediterranean Sea. Italy, where the story of tarot cards really begins, juts out into the middle of the Mediterranean Sea. Thus, to the east, Italy faced the edge of the Ottoman Empire's Balkan possessions. To the West, the Mediterranean trade routes connected northern Italian city states and the Papal States of central Italy to Spain (or, Al-Andalus, as it was known). To the South, Italians found themselves within easy contact of Mediterranean Islands populated by Muslims or even communities composed of a mixture of Muslim and Christian people. The entire northern coast of Africa, from Egypt to Morocco was also connected by trade and communication to Italy and the Christian areas of the Mediterranean world. The point is that the cultural contacts were important, well-established, and widespread. In such an environment, cultural artifacts such as cards could circulate easily.

Around the year 1450, an artist named Bonifacio Bembo illustrated a deck of cards for Francesco Sforza, the new Duke of Milan, and his wife, Bianca Maria Visconti, the daughter and only child of the previous duke, Filippo Maria Visconti. In 1966 Gertrude Moakley, a scholar employed by the New York Public Library, published a book about this Renaissance-era deck. She argued that the entire deck of trumps was based on the idea of a triumph (the ancient and medieval victory parades). The value of each card was associated with its position in the procession symbolized by the deck. There was a "juggler" who, in a real procession, would not stay in one place but rather move from front to back as the procession paraded through the streets. This card eventually became "the Fool" of the modern Tarot and has the number zero.

Moakley also compared the images in the deck to medieval and Renaissance literature, particularly, Petrarch's *I Trionfi* and Dante's *Inferno* (the first part of *The Divine Comedy*). This is an area worthy of a bit of attention from those with an interest in both Tarot and literature. Dante did, indeed, incorporate numerous elements of astrology throughout *The Divine Comedy*. All three books, *The Inferno*, *Purgatory*, and *Paradise*, make numerous astrological references and use the zodiacal signs. Each of the three books ends with a reference to the stars, and Dante is famous for describing the cosmos as powered in its motions through the love of God.

Moakley pointed out that "the Devil" is card XV. In *The Inferno*, Vergil and Dante are in Hell. "The Tower" card, which is number XVI, is also referred to as the Devil's House. The next card in the sequence (XVII) is "the Star." Moakley notes the significance of the tarot sequence as it aligns with Dante's story. Upon exiting Hell, the two characters see stars and it inspires in Dante a sense of renewed hope and faith. This is the meaning of "the Star" card, and it certainly does match up well with the poem.

Moakley is correct to identify a common sequence of symbol and meaning. And, it is worth mentioning that there is a Dante tarot deck sold by an Italian company, Lo Scarabeo. It was created in 2001 by Giordano Berti. However, I would argue that the symbols and their meanings had a widespread presence in fourteenth- and fifteenth-century Italy. This alone would adequately explain the presence of the symbols and their use in Tarot as well as Dante's poetry. There is, from what I can tell, no justification for claiming that the cards were designed on the basis of Dante's *Divine Comedy* being used as a guide. They are simply important cultural elements that are used as touchstones of meanings in any number of settings or circumstances, much as the archetypal imagery in some of the other tarot cards (such as "the Emperor," "the High Priestess," or "the Lovers") can be found throughout a variety of literary and cultural references.

Some of the imagery on the cards had importance that related to Milan and, particularly, to the Visconti and Sforza families. For example, one of the cards showed a man with a club striking a lion. It is likely that this represented the fight between Milan and their arch-rival, Venice. Venice took the lion as its symbol. The card would eventually be given the title "Strength" in future years, and the image was altered to show a woman gently controlling the lion's jaws.

Another change to the Visconti-Sforza trump cards and their imagery involves a religiously themed image. One of the cards is called "the Popess."

A female pope is a somewhat startling image. One possible interpretation is that it is presented as an amusement associated with the fictional tradition of Pope Joan who, in the Middle Ages, rose to the throne of Saint Peter disguised as a man before eventually being discovered a woman. Gertrude Moakley made an excellent argument, however, that the card was, in fact, a representation of Sister Maifreda da Pirovano. She was a member of the Visconti clan and a highly respected nun in northern Italy who participated in a movement in the later thirteenth century that was ultimately deemed heretical, despite the fact that they considered themselves to be a more proper version of the true faith. There was also a pope card in the Visconti-Sforza deck. In modern decks, "the Pope" has been changed to "the Hierophant," and "the Popess" has been changed to "the High Priestess."

In Milan, the Palazzo Borromeo has a fresco on one of its walls. This fourteenth-century image shows a number of women playing a game of *tarocchi*. They would have been using a deck similar to the Visconti-Sforza deck and in the same area of Italy during the same time period. These decks were used for playing a game that had no relation to divination or any form of magic. They would, however, evolve into what is known as the "Major Arcana" portion of the modern tarot deck.

In 1491, one year before Columbus, an Italian employed by the Queen of Spain, set sail on the first of his four voyages to the New World, another Italian, by the name of Nicola di maestro Antonio, painted what became known as the Sola-Busca tarot deck in northern Italy. He engraved metal plates so that the deck could be reproduced in outline and then painted by the artist. It is important for the fact that it contains both a numbered deck and the trumps of the *tarocchi*. The numbered cards, which would later be known as the "Minor Arcana," had pictures drawn on them that were more elaborate and intriguing than, say, seven swords or five wands or nine cups. Because the two different decks are found together in this case, one might see this as the oldest actual tarot deck, but the question of how it was used is unanswered. Is it possible that the two decks were combined, not to be used as one, but in a manner comparable to the way a single set might contain a board, chess pieces, and checkers? In other words, could this be two different games in a single set? If they were meant to be used together, it would still be a stretch to argue that they were used for divination or anything magical. The fact that the two decks are together in one set is fascinating, but it does not prove that the cards were used for fortune-telling or that they were even used together in one game.

The Sola Busca deck has minor modifications to the suits. The swords are the same but the coins are changed to discs and the clubs are more like wands or sticks. The cups are amphorae, which are more like jars than cups, and they have handles. Figures are painted on the numbered cards as one would expect to see on the cards associated with the *tarocchi* of Italian invention. That is, unlike the decks of cards that originated in the Islamic world, the Sola-Busca cards have figures or scenes whereas, traditionally, these cards only pictured their suit symbols. There are a number of historical, religious, and mythological figures painted on the Sola-Busca cards of both deck styles.

In 1995, a scholar named Sofia di Vincenzo advanced the argument that the imagery of the cards incorporate subtle references to alchemy. There may absolutely be some substance to that argument, but this could be understood as a tempting anachronistic projection of modern views about Tarot onto the cards' origins. Even if one accepts the premise that some of the images on the Sola-Busca deck(s) were inspired, to some degree, by alchemical imagery, this does not prove (nor even assert) that the cards are used in a manner that involves teaching alchemy, i.e., in the context of magical instructions. There are no obvious formulas, teachings, or rituals that appear in the cards. If such could be claimed with certainty, this would be the point in history where cards and magic are first linked (definitively). That cannot be demonstrated to be the case. One could just as easily assert that the use of historical figures, such as Alexander the Great and his mother, Olympia, who appear on the cards, is evidence that the cards were intended to teach lessons about family or politics. Biblical characters such as Nebuchadnezzar and Nimrod also appear on some of the cards, but one would not assert on this basis that the cards are intended to teach the Old Testament or to assert a particular religious doctrine.

It is fascinating to see alchemy linked to tarot cards in any way at all as early as the fifteenth century. Although one may speculate in whatever way they wish on the topic, in my view, instructions or teachings on magic do not seem to be associated with the Sola-Busca deck or, indeed, with any playing cards from the fifteenth century. It would be several lifetimes before cards and magic, cartomancy, was written about or practiced. Cards and belief in magic both existed during the era of the Renaissance. They do not, however, appear to be related or connected.

Mary K. Greer, one of the most widely known contemporary figures in American Tarot, and a student of all things Tarot, has made an interesting case for the claim that cards had an association with divination in the fifteenth and sixteenth centuries. She wrote a fascinating article on her blog (*Mary K. Greer's Tarot Blog*) entitled "Origins of Cartomancy." Greer examined several examples of artwork and texts from the period that do indeed suggest linkages of sorts. There are times where she found, for example, references that talk about cards alongside the casting of lots. These are comparisons such as using dice or drawing straws and then allowing a particular outcome to chance. In such cases, I would argue that the cards themselves are not necessarily seen as magical; by the same token, an agreement that a coin flip will determine who gets to make the first move in a game does not justify a belief that the coin itself holds magical (if you will) powers.

Greer also pointed to examples of art and literature from the period in which the topic of fortune is discussed and cards are also discussed in association. My perception is that these examples are comparable to the ones just mentioned, casting lots. All games of chance can be tied to fortune and fate just as any kind of contest that starts with an unknown outcome seems to reach a fateful conclusion once the outcome is known. It does not necessarily follow that the outcome can be supernaturally controlled, as with magic, while appearing to be left to chance or coincidence.

In spite of my skepticism, Greer's argument cannot be dismissed out of hand. I simply offer a different interpretation, not a refutation. There is room for debate on topics such as how one understands fate and fortune in relation to magic (loosely defined). Barring something more clearly articulated and definitively stated, I posit that the association between divination and cards is not clearly found in the Renaissance era.

Tarot Becomes Magical

During the Renaissance, a number of Italian scholars had great interest in magic, the occult, esoteric knowledge, and so on. Some of the greatest intellectuals of the Italian Renaissance—for example, Marsilio Ficino, Cornelius Agrippa, and Pico Della Mirandola—were exploring various aspects of magic. They studied, among other things, alchemy, astrology, theurgy, and other forms of what was called "occult philosophy." The most prestigious writings in the circles of Renaissance sorcery were those supposed to have been authored by Hermes Trismegistus, a brilliant sorcerer from early ancient Egypt whose writings had been preserved over the millennia and were written in an obscure, coded, symbolic form. Hermes Trismegistus turned out to be a fictitious figure, and the writings, though quite ancient, only dated to around the year 300 CE. A tradition known as Hermeticism developed among these Renaissance era *magi* and continued for quite some time after the Renaissance as it spread well beyond Italy.

It is important to note that none of the Italian Renaissance *magi* ever refer to the Tarot, nor do they explicitly refer to using cards, of any sort, as if those cards had a supernatural power of divination. We do not see it in the Hermetic writings even in off-handed, tangential, or metaphorical references. One must conclude that the predecessor of the tarot deck's Major Arcana and a tradition of Hermetic magic existed side by side but completely unrelated in Italy, the very birthplace of the cards.

As the Hermetic tradition spread throughout Europe in the sixteenth and seventeenth centuries, even after the Renaissance was over, cartomancy was not part of the magical repertoire of occult philosophers such as Paracelsus, the great German physician, or Isaac Newton, the great English physicist and alchemist. John Dee, the famous English mathematician and sorcerer, never refers to cards in his divination or occult philosophy writings. Giordano Bruno, the Italian occult philosopher who was put to death in 1600 for sorcery, is not associated with any references to cards, either. Thus, some of the most brilliant minds of the period were founders of modern science and practitioners of Hermetic magic—but were not familiar with cartomancy.

In fact, fortune-telling with cards cannot be documented in Europe before the seventeenth century—probably occurring in Bologna, Italy, before appearing in France (Farley, *Cultural History of Tarot*). Even so, Hermeticism, the idea that an ancient philosopher-magician provided a wealth of hidden knowledge to future *magi* capable of understanding it, became intimately connected to the evolution of the Tarot. Perhaps even more importantly, the iconography of the Italian *tarocchi* would be reimagined and reified into a potent set of symbols to be consulted for divination—not necessarily fortune-telling but insight in myriad matters both mundane and profound.

The card makers of Marseilles began to standardize the iconography of the Tarot (the French form of the word *tarocchi*) throughout the sixteenth century. They also added a written title for each of the trump cards. The game had become popular in eastern and southern France, Switzerland, and a few other areas of Europe but was not well known in many other areas of Europe including Paris and the rest of northern France. As Helen Farley noted in her *Cultural History of Tarot*,

> Though the symbolism of the tarot deck was readily understood within a fifteenth-century, Milanese context, the success of the game and its subsequent wide distribution, meant that the symbolism was no longer relevant or comprehensible to new users of tarot. Left to interpret the symbolism with little or no knowledge of the original meaning and sometimes the original use of the deck, several theories were formulated which described mysterious, though erroneous, origins, usually including some esoteric interpretation of the trump symbolism. (92)

The deck produced by the card makers of Marseilles includes a "Devil" card. "The Devil" card is not found in the Visconti-Sforza deck. It is quite possible that the card was added later, but it is also possible that the card was lost. Another card missing from the Visconti-Sforza deck (which is the fullest, as well as oldest, extant deck) is "the Tower" card. "The Tower" represents "the Hellmouth" or entrance to Hell. In early depictions it is referred to as "the House of the Devil," but in some instances it is referred to as "the Fire," "Lightning," or "the House of the Damned." It seems clear that the Visconti-Sforza deck served, at least to a significant degree, as the model for later decks. Therefore, the addition of "the Devil" and "Tower" cards raise debate. It is, again, plausible to suggest that the cards were original but happened to be lost. A deck known as the Gringonneur deck dates to (perhaps) 1475, well before the Marseilles deck, and contains both cards.

It is important to keep in mind, however, that the migration of the cards from northern Italy to Switzerland and France resulted in the cards coming into contact with, and being reproduced by people who were unfamiliar with the Milanese background of the symbolism. This migration resulted in changes that may have been deliberate or accidental. For example, the card that is familiar to people as "the Hermit" was originally "Time". The image on the Visconti-Sforza deck is of an old man with a staff, as is seen on later decks, but he was originally carrying an hourglass. The representation is recognizable as "father time." That hourglass was mistaken for a lamp by subsequent illustrators and the card has been known as "the Hermit" ever since.

Now we come to one of the most important moments in the history of tarot cards. It occurs during what is commonly referred to by historians as the Age of Enlightenment or the Age of Reason. This was a period in history where logic and reason were increasingly relied upon to answer questions of magnitude in life and society. It was a period where traditional beliefs about political and religious authority were called into question and expected, by many intellectuals, to be required to stand up to logical scrutiny. The status of the Church as a social authority of the greatest credibility began to be challenged. The idea of the natural "divine right of kings" was subject to criticisms which asserted that the "general will" of the people was needed to justify holding political power. It was also an era when science and technology were viewed as having the potential to revolutionize life in many ways and, indeed, so it was. The Stuart monarchy was ended with the Glorious Revolution of 1688 when the English people claimed the right to depose a ruler that they saw as (properly or not) unfit. It was an era when intellectuals such as Francois-Marie Arouet, known to history as Voltaire, challenged religious superstition, prejudices, and discrimination. The Enlightenment was a major influence on the political thinking that was foundational to the American and French revolutions.

As the American Revolution was being fought in 1776, a Frenchman in Paris happened to be observing some women from southern France playing a card game in a Parisian salon. The man's name was Antoine Court de Gebelin (circa 1719–84). Looking at the tarot deck of the card-playing ladies, Court de Gebelin became intrigued with the images and developed the hypothesis that each of the cards contained an image that was representative of something profound and, going further, that the sequence of these images represented an important philosophical teaching.

He connected the deck to the Hermetic tradition. The cards, it was claimed, were actually the pages of a secret book, *The Book of Thoth*. That title has stuck ever since. Thoth was an Egyptian deity whom the Greeks conflated with Hermes, the god who was also thought to have been a man (the various traditions are not entirely consistent) who once lived in ancient Egypt and was the greatest sorcerer in history. Court de Gebelin published his conclusions, and though they were erroneous, they were the first major step in the evolution of an esoteric Tarot.

The later eighteenth century was a period during which French intellectuals were fascinated with ancient Egypt (though not yet as knowledgeable about it, as they would become after Jean-Francois Champollion translated the Rosetta Stone in 1822). This helped to foster an environment that gave the cards a mystique which they have never lost. Court de Gebelin wrote a book called *Le Monde Primitif* (*The Primeval World*) in which he demonstrated an impressive knowledge of linguistics and symbology in arguing something along the lines that the ancient Greek writer, Hesiod, had argued many, many centuries before: that is, Court de Gebelin wrote about a Golden Age in the distant past, barely traceable in the footprints of history. His views about Tarot were merely a small part of the multi-volume *Le Monde Primitif*. In fact, he incorporated an essay on the cards by the Comte de Mellet who had further developed Court de Gebelin's ideas by associating numbers and letters with various meanings, claiming that doing so was an art which dated back to ancient Egypt, and further claiming that this was all connected to the Tarot. The book was read and respected in important social circles and gained a considerable amount of attention. John Adams, American revolutionary and United States president, owned a copy (and wrote comments as marginalia in it). Louis XVI, the king of France, also owned it.

Court de Gebelin's fascination with the cards and their symbology created a new window through which the world viewed these mystical cards that had seemingly found their way through the centuries from Egypt in ancient times to Italy during the Renaissance and, finally, to France during the Age of the Enlightenment. The mystique of Tarot continued to grow, building upon Court de Gebelin's work despite the fact that much of his understanding would eventually be discredited by future generations.

Shortly after Court de Gebelin's "epiphany," Tarot began to be seen as a tool for divination of the sort associated with fortune-telling. From this point forward, the original use of the cards, designed for a game of trumps, would gradually fade away while their association with fortune-telling would eventually eclipse the gaming purpose of the cards entirely. De Mellet's essay had suggested a way to read the cards; perhaps, the very first tarot layout for fortune-telling.

Jean-Baptiste Alliette (1738–91), who reversed the spelling of his last name and arrived at the alias of "Etteilla," had already published the first known instructions for using playing cards—not Tarot—for fortune-telling in 1770. It was called *A Way to Entertain Oneself with Cards*.

Alliette had claimed to have learned the art from an Italian, and this is quite possibly true because the oldest written evidence of using cards for divination of some sort is connected to Bologna, Italy, around 1750. Meanings for thirty-five cards are written down on a sheet for cards from a deck known as the *Tarocco Bolognese*. Although both the cards and their meanings are different than in Alliette's work, there is no reason to doubt that Alliette got the basic concept from Italy and developed it in another way.

Just five years before Alliette's *A Way to Entertain Oneself with Cards*, Giacomo Casanova, the famous womanizer, was in Russia where he had obtained a slave girl that he named Zaire. Zaire, according to Casanova's autobiography, *The Story of My Life*, had become a jealous young woman. She was also a card reader. According to Casanova, he came home one morning after a night of debauchery and was attacked by Zaire who, pointing to a layout of cards, said she knew very well what sort of sexual behavior he had been involved with. The truthfulness of the story is irrelevant for our purposes because—fact or fiction—it shows that divination with cards was being talked about (if not, practiced) in Russia in 1765. This little anecdote tells us that, while Jean-Baptiste Alliette may have been the first to write in any detail about how to use cards for telling a fortune, the idea was already familiar in Europe from France to Russia.

One can imagine Alliette's response upon finding out that a well-known, reputable scholar had published a widely read book in which cards were described as having an association with Hermetic magic. Alliette did not miss the opportunity to capitalize upon the moment (which is not to say that he was simply a con man with no faith in the product he was selling).

It is likely that he did believe in the mystical arts. Nonetheless, in 1783 he wrote *Cartomancy: The Art of Card Reading*. It used the tarot deck and added the Marseilles deck of numbered and court cards as part of a larger deck of Alliette's own design.

By incorporating the Italian-style Tarot into his deck of cards designed for fortune-telling, Alliette can be seen as capitalizing upon the attention that Court de Gebelin had generated toward the cards and simultaneously developing a new deck that could be used to claim to be a new standard for the market with an ancient pedigree in magic.

He even added astrological elements. This is something that neither Court de Gebelin nor Comte de Mellet had considered and it would become a significant development in the esoteric history of Tarot. We will return to Alliette's development of a system for using Tarot for divination in a moment, but let us briefly consider one part of the historical context of the first half of the nineteenth century.

The Elevation of Tarot and Eliphas Levi

During the Napoleonic period, cartomancy grew in France even though a cartomancer might find themselves jailed for a couple months for practicing the craft. The early 1800s was also a period when divination and clairvoyance gained a great deal of attention. In particular, Marie-Anne Le Normand gained fame as a clairvoyant and prophet. There are card decks (which are rather different from Tarot) associated with her, but she did not gain fame through the use of cards so much as through a repertoire of techniques for making predictions and, perhaps more importantly, publishing her claims of supposed previous predictions.

Le Normand, at a minimum, was taken seriously. She was arrested more than once. She made a lot of money. She was admired. She was ridiculed. She was known well outside the boundaries of France. There were claims that she advised the Empress Josephine, made prophecies about Napoleon, foretold the Bourbon restoration after Napoleon's downfall, and, in other ways, cultivated a reputation for divination. She wrote extensively. And, after her death in 1843, several biographies about her were written. Yet, as Ronald Decker and others wrote in their book on the origins of the occult in Tarot, *A Wicked Deck of Cards*, it is difficult to penetrate a fog of suspicious claims and get at the facts of her life (116–32).

An important point about Le Normand to make here is that she epitomizes the vogue for divination and fortune-telling in the first half of the nineteenth century in France. Cartomancy was a part of this that would soon grow. That growth would include a phase in which the use of many different card types (such as the playing cards with the suits of clubs, spades, hearts, and diamonds, or custom designed decks similar to the ones associated with Le Normand) would begin to narrow down and ultimately lead to the preeminence of the Tarot.

Jean-Baptiste Alliette developed his own deck a generation before mademoiselle Le Normand became famous—a deck that incorporated a significant amount of Egyptian-style imagery but also used the Tarot de Marseille and the trumps of the Italian *tarocchi*. Unlike Le Normand, he articulated a detailed system for reading the cards. This, in some sense, makes him more significant than her for the history of Tarot. He provided instructions on how to use the cards, but he also gave instructions on how to modify other decks to work with his system. He also linked the first twelve trumps (in his own sequence) to the signs of the zodiac, thereby establishing an astrological element on top of the numerological and alphabetical traits.

The *tarocchi* had traveled from Milan to Marseille and then to Paris, where it had become viewed as an esoteric device by Court de Gebelin. Like others, he was intrigued with the exotic imagery of the cards produced during the Renaissance but dislocated from their original context. Influenced by his interest in Hermeticism and a belief in a Golden Age buried in the distant past, he projected something esoteric onto the cards. Or, perhaps, the cards projected something into his mind, as they have done for so many others over the centuries.

At any rate, Court de Gebelin's writings, in turn, influenced Alliette to make some alterations to the Marseille deck before incorporating it as part of a deck of cards specifically designed for divination. This pack evolved into what came to be known as the Grand Etteilla and was being mass-marketed in 1838. It is still sold today by a French company called Grimaud. The interest that the famous mademoiselle Le Normand had cultivated in prophecy and fortune-telling probably had an indirect, yet beneficial, effect for Tarot. The late Ettielle's cards had become more popular than ever. The old Muslim playing cards and the Italian *tarocchi* were now combined into a single deck that no longer functioned as a game of trumps but served instead as a tool for divination.

The fascination with ancient Egypt in the late eighteenth and early nineteenth centuries gave an exotic appeal to the supposedly Egyptian Tarot. The false connection between ancient Egypt and the cards was significant. Although it was eventually uncovered as an artificial connection, that association could nonetheless be incorporated into the assigned meanings of the cards. Indeed, the process of doing exactly that had already been started. Consider some examples: "the Chariot" card originally had winged horses pulling the chariot, but these were soon to be permanently replaced by sphinxes. The woman on "the Star" card was identified by Court de Gebelin as the Egyptian goddess Isis. "The Popess" was changed to "the High Priestess" (which developed an Egyptian connotation associated with Isis).

In the early 1600s, a scholar named Isaac Cassebaum established that Hermes Trismegistus was a fictional figure by showing through linguistic, literary, and historical analysis that the Hermetic writings were nowhere near as old as they had been purported to be. The fact remained, however, that the tradition of a magical Hermetic philosophy was, indeed, genuinely ancient and had been developed further during the Medieval period. More to the point, the ambiguity of the cards and their imagery allowed Hermetic associations to be projected onto the cards. The same can be said for astrological and numerological concepts. Also, the Hebrew alphabet with its twenty-two letters could be applied to the cards and therefore link the cards to the mystical Jewish tradition known as the Kabbalah, an esoteric philosophy rooted in biblical interpretation but extending into metaphysics.

In the 1850s, Jean Alexandre Vaillant made the mistake of assuming the Gypsies (or, Roma) were historically associated with using the tarot cards as a fortune-telling device. This error was built upon another assumption—that is, that the Roma were descendants of Egypt (the word "Gypsy" is a variant of "Egyptian."). Consequently, Gypsies were linked to Tarot. The roots of the error went back to 1781 and the writings of Antoine Court de Gebelin and the Comte de Mellet. That association is one that has endured and even been embraced despite the problematic history.

Eliphas Levi (Alphonse-Louis Constant) (1810–75) is an interesting figure in tarot history. He planned on joining the priesthood, but eight days before he was going to be ordained, he confessed to an inappropriate romantic relationship with a young female student. He left the priesthood, but eventually became a deacon. When he was in his midthirties, he began a relationship with a woman named Eugenie, the headmistress at a girls' school. Alphonse-Louis Constant, who had not yet changed his name to Levi, had a son with the headmistress. Through her, Constant met a student named Noemie Cadiot and began an affair, leaving Eugenie and marrying the eighteen-year-old Noemie. The marriage resulted in a daughter who died at the age of seven, shortly after the divorce of her parents. Following that, he never married again or established a long-term relationship with another woman. It was around this time that Alphonse-Louis Constant became someone quite different, even changing his name to Eliphas Levi.

Levi's focus was never on Tarot per se. His interest was in magic, generally, and he was a prolific writer. Tarot was a part of that wider picture. Levi developed something of a "unified theory" of magic in *Dogma and Ritual of High Magic*, which he published in two volumes between 1854 and 1856. He considered a variety of types of magic, with Tarot being only one. Levi made the contention that all magical phenomenon tap into different manifestations of the same source of power in the universe which he called the Astral Light or the Great Magical Agent. Although he was not a significant advocate of the secret societies that would become popular in the later nineteenth century, he did stress the importance of initiation rituals. Within a short period of time after his death, Eliphas Levi seemed to have secured himself a place in the history of magic.

He also gave great emphasis to the distinction between low and high magic. High magic required an understanding of the philosophical and historical aspects of magic such as a knowledge of the Hermetic tradition, detailed astrological and alchemical knowledge and such things. He was also quite intrigued with the force of magnetism although it had been many decades since the work of Franz Anton Mesmer had fallen into disrepute. Perhaps, above all else, he was enthralled with the significance of symbology. Anyone who has ever really looked at a deck of tarot cards can quickly see that they are loaded with symbols.

The symbolism found in the cards excited Levi and he saw it as providing points of connection to various fields of what he considered high magic, the Kabbalah in particular. Levi also elevated the stature of Tarot by building off of the work that Court de Gebelin, de Mellet, and Etteilla had done in terms of supplying Tarot with an ancient pedigree that was suffused with a mysterious gnosticism of sorts. To define gnosticism in this context, I mean the sense that an elite few within a larger community have a greater depth of knowledge gained from privileged sources that the wider community is unaware of or fails to properly understand. Yet, whereas Court de Gebelin and de Mellet were scholars with a profound understanding of Tarot, Levi considered Etteilla to be merely a practitioner of "low magic." Levi claimed that the cards offered far, far more than simply a tool for fortune-telling and that Etteilla was nothing more than a fortune-teller, lacking the genuinely esoteric knowledge of the cards.

Levi used the Marseille tarot deck (which French people were then calling the Italian deck) believing it to be the true and original form. He noted, as Etteilla had, that the Hebrew alphabet contained twenty-two letters just as Tarot had twenty-two trumps and the book of *Revelation* had twenty-two chapters. Levi arranged specific correspondences between the Hebrew alphabet, matching the first letter, *aleph*, with the first trump, "*Le Bateleur*" (further modifying that card by placing the suits on the table in the picture), and ending with the last letter, *tav*, corresponding to "*Le Monde*." Each letter symbolizes a meaning. For example, *aleph* can mean "unity," and *tav* can represent "completion." These meanings, of course, are then tied to the corresponding card.

In the Marseille tarot deck, "the Juggler" or "Fool" card is not numbered. It does not even have a zero as in other decks. Levi chose to position the card second to last in the trumps, between "Judgment" and "the World." He then renumbered "the World" from twenty-one to twenty-two, and gave "the Fool" number twenty-one.

It was Levi who modified "the Chariot" card by changing the horses to sphinxes (which are not on the Tarot de Marseilles, giving it an Egyptian style). Similarly, he put a sphinx on the "Wheel of Fortune" card. He made a number of other modifications as well. Just as Etteilla had changed "the Juggler" to "the Magician," so, too, did Levi, adding that the magician has one arm raised and one arm down to indicate the Hermetic saying, "as above, so below."

It should be noted that Levi's understanding of the Kabbalah was developed from Christian, rather than Jewish, writers. It would be appropriate to refer to his form of the Kabbalah as Christianized. The most important of these writers was a Jesuit priest named Athanasius Kircher, who had lived in the seventeenth century. Levi, who was capable of reading Hebrew as well as Greek and Latin, used the esoteric symbol of the Tree of Life to create correspondences with the numerical cards. There are ten sections called *sephiroth* (each one representing a spiritual principle) on the Tree of Life. The aces represented the lowest of the *sephiroth* and the tens represented the highest level. His use of Kabbalah not only meshed well with the fact that the cards were numbered one through ten, but also with the astrological associations that were developing in relation to Tarot.

Some Christian symbolism was incorporated into Tarot in interesting ways that involved the Kabbalah, as Levi understood it. Here, it is worth noting that Levi once asked rhetorically, what are all the ancient talismans compared to a consecrated Host? The four suits, he argued, corresponded to four angelic beings called cherubim. In *Genesis*, the Tree of Life from the Garden of Eden is guarded by cherubim. The cherubim are more often described as angelic beings in the heavenly court of God. The word actually originates from an Assyrian term meaning "the near ones." One can readily understand how the Christian tradition would picture Jesus enthroned in heaven, surrounded by holy people such as the apostles, the Virgin Mary, and, of course, the four evangelists. It is in this way that Matthew, Mark, Luke, and John have been conflated with four cherubim: God in his heavenly court with angels has an equivalence with Jesus in his heavenly court with the Evangelists. This is not a particularly well-known aspect of tarot symbolism, but it is easy enough to see once it is pointed out.

Levi tied these four cherubim/evangelists to the four elements in ancient Greek philosophy and the four suits in the deck (fire for wands, water for cups, air for swords, and earth for coins). These cherubim are artistically represented as being winged and holding books. One is a man (or an angel), one is a lion, one is a bull, and one is an eagle. In traditional Christian symbolism. these represent the four evangelists (Matthew, Mark, Luke, and John), and the books that they hold are the gospels associated with their names. These figures appear on the "Wheel of Fortune" and "the World" cards.

Another correspondence that Levi pointed to was the Zodiac signs of Leo with the suit of batons (or wands), Aquarius with the suit of cups, Scorpio with swords, and Taurus with coins. The four elements of fire, water, air, and earth already had correspondences in place. Levi also added another correspondence to the suits. He used the four letters of the Tetragrammaton, the name of God/YHVH (Yahweh). Each letter had a Kabbalistic meaning that could be conferred upon the corresponding suit, thereby adding another level of meaning to the card as well as another level of magical tradition and mystery to Tarot.

Eliphas Levi was a nineteenth-century man who attempted to do what sorcerers had attempted throughout time; to tap into the divine or supernatural power and put it to work for himself (whether this was done altruistically or selfishly is always a separate issue). In that respect, he failed. Nonetheless, he had a very important impact on the history of magic in general and the history of Tarot in particular. He masterfully wove the two into the same complex fabric.

As Ronald Decker, *et. al.* wrote in *A Wicked Pack of Cards,*

> There was little originality in his ideas; but this very lack of originality was itself a strength. . . . He did not even expound seriatim the branches of the high magic of which he wrote, with separate chapters or sections on the diverse occult sciences and doctrines; he made a synthesis. In his writings, the Cabala [*sic*], alchemy, Hermetism [*sic*], astrology, magnetism and even a little black magic from the grimoires are inextricably intertwined. (169)

Another scholar of tarot history, Helen Farley, concurs, writing in *A Cultural History of Tarot*, "No one could say that his ideas were original yet his synthesis of Kabbalah, alchemy, Hermeticism, astrology, even magnetism (drawing on the work of Franz Mesmer) and black magic into a coherent tradition was original" (113).

In 1860, the same year Abraham Lincoln was elected president of the United States, Eliphas Levi published a *History of Magic*. He had been living alone in an apartment in France with his magical paraphernalia all around him, practicing his rituals and living the life of a nineteenth-century magus. He is not the Lincoln of magic, I suppose, but he did bring about an important shift in the history of magic. He had integrated Tarot into what we can properly call the Western tradition of magic. That is, Levi had fully integrated Tarot with the many ancient varieties of magic from astrology and incantations to alchemy, herbal remedies, and talismans. Furthermore, he did so as if Tarot had been there all along (a la Court de Gebelin). Tarot was not as old as any of these other magical categories, nor was it created to be a magical category in the first place. Remember, it was created as a game. Yet, perhaps more than his predecessors or successors, Levi gave Tarot a place so interconnected to the Western tradition of magic that it simply could not be removed any more than one could remove the flour from a cake once it has been baked.

Tarot and Secret Societies in the Later Nineteenth Century

The second half of the nineteenth century was a period of increased mysticism and belief in the supernatural. Levi and his predecessors had positioned Tarot to fit very well into this emerging cultural trend. The deck was now associated with ancient Egypt, Roma, fortune-telling, Hermeticism, secret societies such as the Freemasons (Court de Gebelin had been one), and a number of mystical or spiritual concepts, the most important of which was the Kabbalah. At the same time, an emergence of secret societies with interest in magic—ritually, practically, and philosophically—was developing in Western Europe and Great Britain.

The growth of secret societies with an interest in esotericism and the occult is critical to understanding the growth of Tarot in the historical context of the late nineteenth century. Such societies proliferated in the period from 1875 to the First World War (which began in 1914). It was in 1875 when the Theosophical Society began in the United States under the direction of the fascinating spiritualist, Madame Helena Petrovna Blavatsky and her associates, Colonel Henry Steel Olcott and William Quan Judge. Madame Blavatsky would gain international attention spreading her influence and organization to Europe and India.

Another group, the Rosicrucians, traced their origins back to a fictional figure named Christian Rosenkreuz who supposedly lived in the 1370s. The organization that bears his name is more properly associated with the Freemasons, and as such, it is part of a movement that emerged in the eighteenth century and developed more fully in the nineteenth.

Of these numerous organizations and societies with their secret rituals, questionable historical origins, ritualistic, esoteric, and occult interests, the one that might be of greatest interest to those exploring the history of Tarot is the Order of the Golden Dawn, which was founded in Great Britain in 1888 and had a brief but very influential existence. We shall discuss the Order of the Golden Dawn in a little more detail later, but for now, let me restate that secret societies with interests in the esoteric and the occult proliferated in the generation before the First World War in France, Britain, and America. Although these groups might have rivalries and disagreements, they reflected a cultural trend that reveled in social organization around ritual, esotericism, and the occult.

At one time or another, however briefly, a man named Gerard Encausse, later to be known as "Papus," was a member of all the groups just mentioned. Madame Blavatsky had established the Theosophical Society in Paris in 1884, one year after establishing a lodge in London. Encausse joined the Isis Lodge (as it was called) in Paris in 1887. The following year, he joined the Rosicrucians, and around 1889, he joined a group called the Hermetic Brotherhood of Luxor and later that year started the Independent Group for Esoteric Studies. In January 1894, the Order of the Golden Dawn opened the Ahathoor Temple in Paris and Encausse joined that group the following March. Eighteen ninety-four was the same year that he completed his medical studies, officially becoming a doctor and going into practice. By that time, he had gained a great reputation within these circles becoming quite well known by the name "Papus."

In 1889, Papus wrote *The Tarot of the Bohemians*. This was the first book devoted exclusively to the subject of Tarot. Eliphas Levi, remember, had written an extensive treatise on magic, *Dogma and Ritual of High Magic*, which incorporated discussion of Tarot into discussion of topics such as the Kabbalah, necromancy, black magic, astrology, and so on. Tarot did not have its own chapter nor was it a central topic. Rather, it was incorporated in various ways to elaborate upon and to develop other topics and the main theme of magic in general. What Papus did was to provide a full book-length treatment focused particularly on Tarot, using esotericism and the occult to demonstrate the centrality of Tarot to magic. The distinction is important.

Papus claimed (and likely believed) the Tarot actually dated back to the time of the biblical Adam. If it had been an unjustifiable leap of faith to assert that the Tarot went back to the time of the Egyptian pharaohs and the mythological Thoth (aka Hermes Trismegistus), Papus was now placing Tarot at the very beginning of the human story. The influence of Levi's *Dogma and Ritual of High Magic* is obvious throughout Papus's *Tarot of the Bohemians*.

The correspondence of the Tetragrammaton (YHVH, Yahweh) to the four suits of the cards is developed. One can see the influence of Athanasius Kircher's Christianized version of Kabbalah carried over from Levi to Papus. Papus also imitates Levi in the placement of "the Fool" as card twenty-one (instead of zero), in between "Judgement" and "the World." He also imposed a detailed numerological system on the cards which has (in modified forms) persisted.

Papus believed, mistakenly, that ordinary playing cards were derived from the tarot pack. He thought the trumps and the knights were removed. This, of course, demonstrates a lack of knowledge about the history of the two decks which were combined well after they were created and used independently of one another. Among his key points in *Tarot of the Bohemians*, Papus argues that Tarot has a principal and ancient place in the traditions of magic. Further, Papus says that Tarot is a lens through which all other forms, traditions, and mysteries associated with magic can be understood. Indeed, it is, just as Levi would have contended, the Book of Thoth.

Papus had a Swiss friend named Oswald Wirth, a Freemason and a hypnotist who contributed an "Essay on the Astronomical Tarot," to Papus's *Tarot of the Bohemians* in which Wirth claimed that the Tarot is "pre-eminently the sacred book of occult initiation." Wirth's essay contributed an extension of the use of astrology in Tarot by associating each of the twenty-two Major Arcana cards with an astrological formation, going beyond the twelve zodiac constellations. Elsewhere, Wirth would write about the numerological, alchemical, and divinatory representations associated with Tarot.

Wirth had designed a deck of trumps that incorporated Masonic symbols and Egyptian *motifs* despite his claims that the Tarot predates ancient Egypt. This deck was used by Papus to illustrate the *Tarot of the Bohemians*. Papus also used the cards of the Tarot de Marseilles to illustrate the Minor Arcana (the suit cards), embellishing them with Hebrew letters to facilitate the use of the Kabbalah. In the context of the Kabbalah and Tarot, Papus discusses the *Sepher Yetzirah* (the *Book of Creation*), tying its elements to astrological correspondences that had been given correspondences to the tarot cards. Interestingly (and tellingly), Papus's correspondences in this section of the book conflict with Wirth's correspondences in his essay elsewhere in the book.

It is important to note that Levi and Papus wrote with an intent to show that Tarot was of great significance in terms of ritual, symbolism, and hidden meanings that have nothing to do with divination. Their interest in magic was at the level of personal experience in the form of ritual and the Hermetic tradition. That is, they came to magic through these things first and, secondly, through Tarot, which they viewed as validating the Hermetic tradition and the rituals they held sacred. They did not begin with Tarot and then move to an interest in magic. They did not begin as fortune-tellers and find Tarot, nor did they seek out magic because of a preexisting effort to develop skills of divination.

Like Levi, Papus claimed the cards could tell the future. Both men, however, downplayed that claim by saying the Hermetic tradition and the ritual aspects of the cards were more important. Papus falsely claimed that the Egyptians and all the ancient writers used Tarot to predict the future. He then stated that, in the present, divination by tarot cards is mainly the practice of women whose intuitive nature makes them better suited to such things. Papus is also critical of Etteilla, as was Levi, for being a proponent of fortune-telling and lacking a more sophisticated appreciation and knowledge for the Tarot's philosophical stature.

By the turn of the century, Tarot had become a common topic in occult literature and that body of literature was, itself, experiencing a surge of interest. It was fortune-telling that many people cared about, not Hermeticism, symbolism, or ritual. Etteilla might have been relegated to the status of an uninitiated salesman in the minds of Levi and Papus, but if the cards were to be associated with an ability to divine the future, then that is what people wanted to read about and learn to do. No surprise, then, that in 1909 Papus published *Tarot Divination*, which put the focus on fortune-telling. He was reacting to, rather than driving, the form that interest in magic had taken. *Tarot Divination* was written twenty years after the *Tarot of the Bohemians*. It was a less researched book, probably written more quickly. It was largely derivative, even copying other works (including his own) at length. He even plagiarized Etteilla, whom he had been so critical of earlier.

Papus took the position that both the Major and Minor Arcana must be used. The cards that Wirth had designed, which had earlier been favored by Papus, were no longer useful because they only included the Major Arcana. Papus had an artist named Jean-Gabriel Goulinat (who was one of his patients) make a deck to go along with the book. His cards emphasized an "Egyptianized" imagery but also had very wide margins to allow for additional information to be placed on the card with the pictures. Numbers, Hebrew letters, hieroglyphs, zodiac signs, planets, and other information are written in these margins.

Five years after the publication of *Tarot Divination*, the First World War began. Dr. Encausse, now long known as Papus, was forty-nine years old and mobilized to the French army when war broke out in August 1914. His physical condition, deteriorating from tuberculosis, caused him to be demobilized in October 1915. He died one year later.

Late nineteenth and early twentieth-century France was the time and place where the occult Tarot developed into a quite sophisticated system with a written corpus that attached the cards (as they were undergoing a variety of visual modifications) to a tradition of magic that had only been adumbrated by the likes of Court de Gebelin and Etteilla. They were no longer two separate decks, with the first a game of trumps and the other the ancestor of the familiar playing deck of today. They were combined into a single deck and given a story, as well as a purpose, that asserted an ancient esoteric tradition.

They had always been intriguing, but now they were mystical and occult. It didn't matter—it still doesn't—that this story about telling the future and a past stretching back to ancient Egypt was demonstrably false. What mattered was that the cards conveyed a sense of wonder. That sense of wonder, felt by people who were enthralled with secret initiation rites and fortune-tellers, had become entrenched and would serve as a foundation for the mystique that the cards retain to this day. From France, the developing tarot community and its subculture would spread by crossing the English Channel through secret societies and bookstores. The works of Levi and Papus were soon translated into English and, by way of France, the cards themselves made their way from Renaissance Italy all the way to twentieth-century London. The word "Tarot" was borrowed directly from French to English despite the Italian origin, *tarocchi*. Indeed, the cards most likely to be found in England at that time were French decks such as the Tarot de Marseilles.

CHAPTER 2

Tarot in the
Twentieth Century

Bridges and Divides at the Beginning
of the Twentieth Century

If a country is quickly and brutally faced with the deaths of more than 600,000 people, you can be sure that it will result in some profound reconsiderations of the afterlife and of the connections between the living and the dead. That's what happened in America after the Civil War. That war ended in 1865. In 1914, an even larger war broke out in Europe and resulted in some sixteen million deaths by the time the Great War, the First World War, ended in 1918. In consequence of all these deaths, so many of them involving young people, it is no surprise that efforts to communicate with the dead increased dramatically from the last quarter of the nineteenth century through the first quarter of the twentieth. This was the era of the spiritualist movement, as it was called. Séances became quite popular beginning in the 1870s and continued to be popular well into the twentieth century.

Even before the Civil War was over, Mary Lincoln had spiritual mediums attempting to contact her deceased boy, Willie, in the White House. President Lincoln himself was in attendance for one such effort. In 1890, Charles Kennard of Baltimore, Maryland, began marketing what he called the "Ouija board" as a product that can be used to help anyone contact the dead. The board was patented after a demonstration for the chief patent officer in which he demanded the applicant and his lawyer spell out his name, but it was marketed as both entertainment and as a "mystical oracle" (Rodriguez McRobbie).

Certainly many people then, as now, would dismiss all this as superstitious nonsense. This same time period was one in which the promises of the eighteenth-century Enlightenment had been, and continued to be, delivered. There was a considerable challenge to any claims of supernatural events. Science was, in many respects, advancing alongside a cultural conflict with superstition. In the 1890s, for example, Marie Curie was working on radiation and X-rays while Max Planck was beginning to open physics to quantum theory. Technologies such as the telephone, the electric light, and the airplane were being developed and incorporated into the cultural mainstream.

Be that as it may, the division between science and technology, on the one hand, and spiritualism and the supernatural, on the other, was not as clearly defined as one might suppose. Consider the case of Madame Helena Blavatsky. Blavatsky was born in Ukraine in 1831. She traveled extensively, although it is likely that she exaggerated the extent of the travel she undertook in her youth. Blavatsky developed the reputation of a mystic, and she was highly respected among many for her views on spirituality and religion of an unorthodox sort. She had an affection, albeit of an unconventional sort, for Eastern religions associated with Tibet and India. Although a following grew around her because of her spirituality, this following was self-consciously respectful of what appeared to be an objective, empirical, even scientific approach that she had for spiritual things. Could scientific methods validate supernatural and spiritual claims? Blavatsky was one of those who thought that question could be answered in the affirmative. Her name is strongly associated with a movement called Theosophy.

Blavatsky started the Theosophical Society in 1875 in New York City along with a reporter named Henry Steel Olcott, who wrote about supposedly verifiable supernatural phenomenon such as séances and levitations. Eventually, there were branches of the Theosophical Society spread across Europe, North America, and Asia. The organization, like the movement itself, became bigger than its founder (in the sense that others drew from it and added to it in a variety of ways that Blavatsky did not control). She had a few important writings such as *Isis Unveiled* and *The Secret Doctrine*, which showed an intelligent mind working on a variety of esoteric topics all of which she placed under the umbrella of Theosophy. Her society produced various "lodges," or communities, in Europe, the United States, and India. Despite the elements of Eastern mysticism with which Blavatsky was enamored, Theosophy and the Theosophical Society are both offshoots of the Western Esotericism that mistakenly traced its origins back to the fictional Hermes Trismegistus and ancient Egypt—the same location, in time and place, that Court de Gebelin had mistakenly identified as the origin of Tarot.

It should be understood that the emergence of science in the modern world was, to a surprisingly high degree, predicated on the study of magic in the Early Modern and medieval world. The contributions to physics made by the likes of Curie, Planck, or Einstein depended on the work of Isaac Newton in the seventeenth century. Newton, it is now well known, was an avid student of that central field of sorcery known as alchemy. The same can be said of Newton's peer in the British Royal Academy of the Sciences, Robert Boyle. They saw themselves as following the philosophy of Hermes Trismegistus, the greatest of all sorcerers—the same figure associated with that philosophy of magic, Hermeticism, that underlaid the various societies which supposedly held the secrets of all manner of sorcery besides alchemy and astrology. It can be pointed out here that the study of astrology and astronomy are linked, not only by the fact that both involve studying the stars and planets but by the lives of some of the greatest astronomers in scientific history. Copernicus, Brahe, and Kepler all were involved in astrological prognostications of various sorts and, of course, played critical roles in astronomy by establishing scientific knowledge of the heliocentric solar system in the sixteenth century.

Science, as we know it, emerged from magic in the sense that the pursuit of occult knowledge in the esoteric tradition known as Hermeticism led to methods and information that are now regarded as scientific. Of course, science and magic are distinct. We associate science with facts, empiricism, verification, and objectivity. Yet, among those of a different time who studied the occult powers hidden in nature, searching out their secrets, there was a belief that the rational and the supernatural were not mutually exclusive. Only much later did the distinction between science and magic gradually become vivid. As late as the end of the nineteenth century and beginning of the twentieth, many people sought to link the rational and the supernatural to a scientific worldview, in which there was a place for spiritual mediums, extrasensory perception, Tarot, and so on. Indeed, this endeavor to maintain a worldview that accommodates both science and the supernatural continues today in quite a few cultural corners.

The Golden Dawn

Tarot cards had been associated with Hermetic magic by Court de Gebelin. Hermetic magic had been associated with science in the Renaissance and Early Modern periods. The interest in secret societies, along with the belief that such societies had (untraceable) origins back to Medieval or even Ancient times, is also one of the cultural ingredients that resulted in Tarot becoming a topic of great interest to those later in the nineteenth century who were creating secret societies based on esotericism and the occult. Madame Blavatsky's Theosophical Society represented this cultural trend. Another was the Society for Psychical Research founded in England in 1882, which is still scientifically studying the paranormal today. Although Blavatsky was viewed as a charlatan by many, her reputation among others was so high as to attract a significant following and a great deal of attention.

In her 1888 book *The Secret Doctrine*, Blavatsky claimed that the Tarot was originally derived from ancient Babylonian sources dating back even further than Egypt, to the antediluvian period (Decker and Dummett, 34). One of the people with whom Blavatsky had consulted while writing *The Secret Doctrine* was a man named MacGregor Mathers, who, with a colleague named Dr. William Wynn Westcott, were members of the London-based lodge of the Theosophical Society. Westcott provided translations of Kabbalistic writings to the Theosophical Society. Both men delivered a number of public lectures related to Hermeticism. They were also member of the Rosicrucian Society of England. In 1877 and 1878, the London lodge was experiencing a degree of internal conflict between members who prioritized Western Hermetic traditions and those who, like Blavatsky and Olcott, were increasingly interested in variations of Eastern spiritual traditions. Mathers and Westcott would part ways with the Theosophical Society and form a new organization (although they presented it as if it was actually ancient), the Hermetic Order of the Golden Dawn.

In *A History of the Occult Tarot*, Ronald Decker and Michael Dummett write, "It is with the Hermetic Order of the Golden Dawn that the introduction of Tarot occultism into Britain is principally bound up. . . . The order lasted only a little more than a decade before disintegrating into hostile factions; but while it lasted, it was by far the most successful occult society ever created" (91). Decker and Dummett go on to credit Mathers and Westcott with the order's success.

Dr. Westcott was a more fascinating man than most people could have been aware. He was a coroner in London from 1880 to 1918. Those who knew him as a medical professional would likely have been quite surprised that, in his off time, he was also heavily involved with ritual magic and the extensive study of occult literature. He did not keep this life so secret as to deny it. Indeed, he published under his own name in both professions. However, it appears that he kept these two worlds quite apart from each other. Mathers was a different sort of character. He seems to have loved developing a public persona as a ritual-performing magus, although he would be quick to distance himself from anything associated with public entertainment, such as stage magic or fortune-telling. Mathers was also so intensely proud of his Celtic background that he added "MacGregor" to his name, rendering his full name as Samuel Lidell MacGregor Mathers.

The Golden Dawn would eventually include well over 200 members. Unlike many other earlier nineteenth-century esoteric societies, the Golden Dawn included women as full members. Their main emphasis and interests were in the realm of ritual magic, rather than fortune-telling or other more "practical" forms of magic (which is not to say that they rejected or disbelieved such things).

The group's founding document, so to speak, is known as the Cipher Manuscript. It purported to date back to late medieval times and, indeed, it was written in a coded text from 1499 created by an abbot named Johan Trithemius. Although the coded language was in fact nearly three centuries old, the actual words and information were not. Dr. Westcott seems to have fabricated a story about obtaining the manuscript, and a number of stories and theories have been advanced to explain its origins. However, all of the material in the Cipher Manuscript is comparable to that associated with previous nineteenth-century secret societies with a predilection for claiming medieval origins. The work of Eliphas Levi and Papus seems to have been a major influence on whoever actually wrote the Cipher Manuscript. The same can be said about the importance of Kabbalah, which informs much of the document's structure and concepts.

The Cipher Manuscript provided a strong sense of identity and direction for the Golden Dawn as an organization. Several of its members were already familiar with occult secret societies and intrigued with esoteric forms of magic. Accordingly, the Golden Dawn developed a hierarchical structure for their society. There were three "orders" within the Golden Dawn, with each order having certain levels of membership and status. Technically speaking, the Golden Dawn was the first order (although that name came to denote the entire society). After rising through the first order, members could join an inner order known as the Order of the Ruby Red and Golden Cross. The Rosicrucian aspects of the secret society are clearly evident in this title. A very small number of individuals might be able to rise to the third order of "Secret Chiefs" and become masters of the society. Advancement through the order, and the various ranks within, required demonstrating knowledge of occult studies in theoretical and practical terms.

According to Helen Farley's *Cultural History of Tarot*, only about one third of the membership advanced to the second order. Doing so required a significant amount of studying Tarot. Along with the Cipher Manuscript and its information on Tarot, members of the Golden Dawn also had access to a secret document known as *Book T* which went into great detail about esoteric occultism in Tarot. Much of *Book T* was derivative from the work of those, like Eliphas Levi and Papus, who were discussed in the previous chapter. That is, there were numerous connections and associations, usually referred to as correspondences, with esoteric subjects. For example, the Kabbalistic Tree of Life and its *sephiroth* had correspondences with the cards.

The Tetragrammaton, the name of God (YHVH), corresponded to the suit signs and the court cards. However, the court cards were modified in a surprising way. The knights were elevated to kings, and the kings demoted to princes while the pages were recast as princesses. Levi's association of the trumps with the Hebrew alphabet was retained in an altered form as some of the numbering was changed. For example, "the Fool" was put in the first position by the Golden Dawn instead of the twenty-first. The pathways between the *sephiroth* on the Tree of Life were given correspondences to the trumps. This linked the Major Arcana to the Tree of Life of the Kabbalah. Where Papus had created linkages between the planets or astrological signs and the Major Arcana, so, too, did the Golden Dawn. Again, they made some modifications.

MacGregor Mathers made a tarot deck that was copied by many members of the Golden Dawn and eventually, if indirectly, became quite influential on tarot decks throughout the twentieth century. He and the Golden Dawn had done more than simply make slight modifications to preexisting tarot decks. While the Golden Dawn certainly did not actually create the material with which they conducted their rituals and practiced their theories of esoteric magic, they did firmly connect esoteric concepts to the cards and, then, strongly incorporated those cards into the rituals and practices of their society. In other words, they fully developed a place for Tarot in the actual performance and experience of Hermetic magic. Whereas Court de Gebelin had, many years before, put forward the notion that the cards were actually a book with a partially understood mysterious connection to that ancient form of magical philosophy known as Hermeticism, the Golden Dawn had taken the steps to fully articulate that linkage. The cards were no longer a game, which is what they certainly were originally created to be. Now, they were thoroughly and elaborately designed to fit the purposes and traditions of an esoteric secret society with a wide-ranging base of knowledge on Hermetic magic. In a sense, the Golden Dawn completed the process of turning the Tarot into the book of magic that Court de Gebelin had mistakenly imagined them to be. Now they really were associated with Hermetic magic. Further, they served as an actual document for the instruction of astrological, alchemical, and Kabbalistic knowledge. The cards were also now incorporated into actual rituals performed by members of the Golden Dawn.

The deck that Mathers designed was executed by his wife, Moina. Other members made their own copies and some modifications followed. Over time, these decks became the most respected and imitated tarot cards to be found. Consequently, the Golden Dawn has had an influence in the world of Tarot that would be hard to exaggerate. It is interesting that a secret and exclusive group would also be responsible for popularizing the Tarot. The fact remains, however, that as the Golden Dawn began to dissolve due to intractable differences between some of its members, their cards and their fascination with the world of magic would emanate into popular culture in Great Britain and the United States.

Arthur Edward Waite and Pamela Colman Smith

Arthur Edward Waite and Pamela Colman Smith were both born with connections to the United States. Waite was born in New York in 1857 to an English mother and an American father. His father, a captain, died at sea when Waite was just a baby, prompting his mother to return to England, where Arthur would live for the rest of his life. Pamela Colman Smith was born in London in 1878 to American parents. The name Colman was her mother's last name; Smith was her father's. Both Waite and Colman Smith, it might be noted, had strong attachments to the Catholic Church. Waite was very devoted to his faith as a young man, and Colman Smith became a Catholic as an adult in 1911.

In 1886, Waite began to work on translating Eliphas Levi's work into English. In 1889, he used the *nom de plume* "Grand Orient" to anonymously write *A Handbook of Cartomancy, Fortune-Telling, and Occult Divination*, which went through several editions. He joined the Golden Dawn in 1891, and continued to translate Levi's *Dogma and Ritual of High Magic* which he finished in 1896. By that time, he had also written a preface for an English translation of Papus's *Tarot of the Bohemians*. The book he is known best for is *The Pictorial Key to the Tarot*, which was published by Rider in 1911 after being expanded from a smaller version published the year before as *The Key to the Tarot*.

Waite was among those who contributed to the rising interest in magic and secret societies such as the Golden Dawn, but he is also partly responsible for the dissolution of the Golden Dawn. Waite had never been on particularly good terms with either Westcott or Mathers, and in 1903, working with two other men (Palmer Thomas and Marcus Blackden), Waite made an attempt to take control of the Golden Dawn and a handful of other esoteric organizations. The effect was, at best, a partial success. Waite had gained some influence and administrative authority, but only by splitting up the groups which reassembled under new organizational names under familiar leadership. In fairness, Waite was not the only member attempting to assert personal control, nor was the Golden Dawn the only esoteric society experiencing internal challenges.

Throughout 1909 and 1910, Aleister Crowley, the most infamous member of the Golden Dawn, revealed secrets of the organization's rites and doctrines in print and in public demonstrations. The secrecy of the Golden Dawn's teachings and practices had thus been broken. That fact created a reason, or justification, for Waite to go about revealing more secrets. It was in this context that Waite's *Pictorial Key to the Tarot* was published. What was being revealed, though, was not only the teachings about the Tarot, but much of the imagery, iconography, and symbolism of the cards themselves as developed within the Golden Dawn by Mathers and others.

Waite went beyond simply revealing the Golden Dawn's system of Tarot (which was, of course, built on the foundation created by Ettiella, Levi, and Papus). Waite developed modifications and elaborations that would have great impact on the future of Tarot. Further, by collaborating with Pamela Colman Smith, the artistic strength of the cards' images resulted in what might reasonably be considered the most important tarot deck ever produced. Ronald Decker and Michael Dummett wrote that "many of the later occultist packs have borrowed from Pamela Colman Smith's design; it could almost be said to have established a standard pattern for occultist Tarot packs. But the designer never benefited from its success; conventional nomenclature was not even to attach her name to it" (*A History of the Occult Tarot*, 131). The deck was known for many decades as the Rider-Waite deck, Rider being the name of the publisher. In modern texts and conversation, this injustice has been addressed by commonly referring to the deck as the Rider-Waite-Colman Smith deck or the Waite-Colman Smith deck.

Pamela Colman Smith had studied art at the Pratt Institute in Brooklyn, New York. She moved to Jamaica in 1898, but after her father died, she relocated to England in 1900 and eventually got a studio in London. She had a number of friends who were writers, as well as others who were involved in theater. She was friends with a prominent actress named Ellen Terry, and she was acquainted with the famous Irish writers Bram Stoker and William Butler Yeats. Yeats was a member of the Golden Dawn. It was Yeats who encouraged her to join the Golden Dawn in 1901. However, as the order began to disintegrate, Yeats and Waite parted ways and Colman Smith went with Waite (although she remained on good terms with Yeats).

Pamela Colman Smith was paid a flat sum, probably a rather small one at that, for her work on the illustrations for the cards. Had she been paid royalties, the financial troubles in her life would have been greatly mitigated, perhaps even eliminated. The deck became a commercial success. The collaboration between Waite and Colman Smith is the most important in the history of Tarot. It relates to bridging the distance between the "elite" culture associated with practitioners and students of esoteric and Hermetic magic, on the one hand, and the popular culture within the United Kingdom and the United States, on the other. Put differently, the Waite-Colman Smith deck has played a critical role in the popularization of Tarot.

Historians of magic, such as Frances Yates and Carlo Ginzburg, have noted that the history of magic can be followed along two separate tracks. One of those tracks is that of the elite culture. Certain information and resources associated with the study of magic have always been limited to a select few, wealthy, or more highly educated people with the social status to indulge the exploration of magical texts, rituals, and experiments. Consider, for example, the Renaissance-era magus in need of an ability to learn Greek or Arabic in order to obtain rare texts on astrology, or consider seventeenth-century alchemists such as Isaac Newton or Robert Boyle. These brilliant men of science were continuously exploring alchemy in their quest to create gold or extend the duration of life. Indeed, it is the elite cultural form of the study of Hermetic magic that ultimately leads to what we now think of as science.

Contrast this with the history of magic in popular culture. Here, one will encounter the "wise women" of the later Middle Ages who were knowledgeable, for instance, about herbal magic that could help heal the problems of everyday folks, from toothaches to pregnancies. Popular magic might also encompass various forms of "counter-magic" intended to break suspected curses. An example of this from the seventeenth century might be found amidst the Salem witch trials when John Indian, the husband of Tituba (one of the earliest victims of the witch scare) suggested making a witch cake. A witch cake was a form of counter-magic that involved mixing some form of grain with the urine of a person thought to be afflicted by a witch. The cake was fed to a dog. It was believed that, while the dog was eating the cake, the witch would experience pain and could therefore be identified.

The point here is that magic in the popular culture and magic amongst society's elites was often on two different tracks. Indeed, historians of magic often study their subject in these two separate categorical distinctions. Tarot cards, however, have developed strong connections to the history of elite magic as well as the popular culture. The work of Arthur Edward Waite reflects an association of the elite tradition of the past, yet the deck he created with Colman Smith has had a profound appeal within popular culture. The result has been a bridging of the distinction between popular and elite magic in the context of Tarot. This bridging would take time to develop over the twentieth century and would even spread to other forms of magic. Astrology, for example, was once the province of an elite culture that had the ability to study the astronomical phenomenon associated with the art (although common people would certainly have some rudimentary understanding of some aspects of astrology). Over time, ordinary people (that is, the popular culture) have been able to develop a knowledge of astrology and incorporate it into their daily lives, whether as simple entertainment and amusement or as a serious interest. This bridge from elite to popular culture in Tarot was not necessarily the intended purpose of Waite and Colman Smith, but it is one result of their work that is often overlooked or unrealized.

Waite, like Eliphas Levi, had a sense that the various forms of Hermetic magic contained a larger philosophical picture. Tarot, was the tool that brought all of these elements together. Tarot included astrological, alchemical, spiritual, Kabbalistic, Masonic, and Rosicrucian varieties of magic. It provided an organizational *schema*, or paradigm, through which all forms of magic could be understood and experienced. In the eighteenth century, Court de Gebelin looked at that small group of women playing a card game as being too ignorant to understand what they held in their hands—pages to a secret book on the philosophy of Hermetic magic. Court de Gebelin had let his imagination run away with him. It was, really, just a game. But, his idea sparked the imaginations of everyone from Allietta to Waite. In 1910, it was Waite's turn to write the next page in the history of magic. His book, *The Pictorial Key to the Tarot*, began to distill what Levi understood to be forms of High Magic and used tarot cards as the pages with which this information could be conveyed to the masses. All of the major elements from the history of Hermetic magic and Kabbalah that had become associated with Tarot over the previous centuries reached a state of cohesive maturity in the Waite-Colman Smith deck.

One element in particular went all the way back to the Renaissance era. A deck of cards from Ferrara, Italy, known as the Sola-Busca deck, inspired the most special feature unique to the Waite-Colman Smith Tarot. This fifteenth-century deck includes what came to be known as the Minor and Major Arcana—that is, the *tarocchi* trumps along with the numbered suit and court cards. This author believes that the deck could very well be a set of two decks produced by the same artist using overlapping elements but nonetheless functioning as two separate decks for play—in other words, two distinct decks produced in the same style to be kept together until the owner wished to play either *tarocchi* (in which case they would use the appropriate cards) or another game using the other cards. Others have made the case that the cards were intended to be a single deck with occult meaning embedded throughout, forming a master narrative with an alchemical, historical, and spiritual theme (www.wopc.co.uk/italy/sola-busca). No matter how one interprets or theorizes on the hidden meanings of the cards, they have a great significance because of the fact that they are the earliest extant example (indeed, the only extant early example) of both types of decks being combined. Also of great significance is the fact that the "standard" deck portion, the numbered suit cards, have images of people and landscapes on them rather than simply a picture of the suit emblem, as in showing merely four cups for the "Four of Cups."

The Sola-Busca family of Milan owned the metal plates that were created (by an unknown artist) to print the original cards. Photographs of all seventy-eight individual images were donated to the British Museum in 1907. It is there that Arthur Edward Waite and Pamela Colman Smith were able to see and study the images. They were inspired by these images to illustrate their deck in a comparable manner. In some instances, such as the "Three of Swords" or the "Eight of Pentacles," they copied the Sola-Busca deck quite closely. Others, such as the "Two of Pentacles" or the "Six of Cups," are quite different. Previous decks, such as the Tarot de Marseilles or the Grand Etteilla, used little or none of this sort of imagery on the numbered suit cards. Waite used the iconography to illustrate meaning in each individual card. To the extent that this could be done following the imagery of the Sola-Busca deck, he did so. Elsewhere, he designed the cards differently. Thus, the Waite-Colman Smith deck was filled with meaningful symbolic imagery that had previously been limited only to the Major Arcana (that is, the original *tarocchi* or trump) cards.

The meanings with which all of the cards were symbolically illustrated had much to do with the historical evolution of esoteric Tarot and the teachings of the Golden Dawn. Yet, whereas members of the Golden Dawn had kept their teachings, and their cards, secret, Arthur Edward Waite was destined to deliver all that into the public domain along with a beautifully illustrated set of cards and with a book that provided details on each individual card (albeit in a somewhat quasi-cryptic description).

One area in which Waite diverged from the Golden Dawn's teaching on Tarot is seen with the court cards. Waite returned to the traditional structure of a Page, Knight, Queen, and King. The influence of the Grand Etteilla deck is evident in the Aces, where a human hand is shown holding the emblem of the suit. Another deviation from the Golden Dawn can be found in rejecting Mathers's naming of card XXI as "the Universe" rather than the traditional title of "the World." In most respects, however, Waite and Colman Smith use the iconography to represent themes embraced by the Golden Dawn's penchant for incorporating Hermetic, Rosicrucian, Masonic, Kabbalistic, and astrological themes.

In astrological terms, Waite did things such as incorporating the sigil of Venus into "the Empress" card and the astrological sign of Aries (a ram) into "the Emperor" card. "The Fool" and "Death" both were designed to include roses (indicating Rosicrucianism). Freemasonry was represented in the "High Priestess" card with the pillars of Jachin and Boaz, as well as in the "Chariot" card with the use of sphinxes. This is also representative of the Egyptian theme associated with Hermeticism. The "Wheel of Fortune" also incorporated Egyptian imagery by using a sphinx and the god Anubis. The "Wheel of Fortune" used a Kabbalistic element as well by using the letters to spell out "TARO" or "ROTA." The letters were interspersed with the Hebrew letters of the Tetragrammaton. "The Magician" card was illustrated with one of each of the four symbols—wands, cups, swords, and pentacles—on a table. The card is recognizably similar to the Tarot de Marseilles version which has a table laden with miscellaneous objects. Referred to as *Le Bateleur* by the French, and *Il Bagatello* by the Italians, previous cards presented something more akin to an entertainer or sleight-of-hand artist. Waite presented his Magician as a more sophisticated magus. It should be noted, though, that the Waite-Colman Smith deck was not actually the first one to show "the Magician" with the four suits on his table. A man named Jean-Baptiste Pitois, aka Paul Christian, was the first to illustrate the table with the suit symbols. At that time, in the second half of the nineteenth century, the card was not yet being referred to as "the Magician."

Waite's Christian influences also appear throughout the deck. The four evangelists of the Christian gospels appear on "the World" and "Wheel of Fortune" cards, although they are referred to as the "four living creatures of Ezekiel." In fact, the symbols do originate in Ezekiel, but they were adopted by, and adapted to, Christian tradition representing the gospel writers Matthew, Mark, Luke, and John. It is for this reason that one sees each of them with a book as indicated in the "Wheel of Fortune" card. Other Christian symbols used by Waite and Colman Smith include the "Temperance" and "Judgment" cards, both of which depict an angel. "Judgment," of course, is an explicitly Christian reference, painted in such a way as to evoke the belief in a physical resurrection as described in the New Testament (see Matthew 27). "The Hierophant" card is also a Christian reference, based on what was originally called "the Pope" in older decks. So, too, was "the High Priestess" originally known as "the Popess" (as discussed in the previous chapter). Of course, in these last two instances, we are not actually looking at Waite's and Colman Smith's representations. They were, for the most part, following established conventions. "The Devil," too, is an obvious Christian (or Judeo-Christian) figure represented in the cards. Waite and Colman Smith, however, chose to incorporate Adam and Eve into their picture of the Devil. They used Adam and Eve in "the Lovers" card, as well, and here, again, is another card depicting an angel.

Waite's *Pictorial Key to the Tarot* made a major contribution to tarot card users in providing one of the best known and most used card layouts: the Celtic Cross. Waite referred to it as "an ancient Celtic method of divination." However, no indication about what makes the layout Celtic is given. Like William Butler Yeats, Waite associated the Arthurian legend of the Holy Grail with the Tarot. Both men saw a correspondence between the suits and Celtic myths, the most obvious connection being the suit of cups with the grail. The spiritual quest of the Arthurian knights could easily be compared metaphorically to the personal spiritual journey of the tarotist.

In some respects, Waite seems to be offering a scholarly critique of other writers on the subject going back to Court de Gebelin and Etteilla, whom he criticized for having no evidence to support a supposed ancient Egyptian origin for the cards. Waite also questioned the validity of associating the trumps of the Tarot with Hebrew letters. Despite criticisms such as these, Waite evinced the view that there is a long history of secret societies that possess esoteric knowledge of the true meaning of the Tarot. He did, however, also make the occasional assertion that some people who have been associated with such organizations have, themselves, failed to properly understand the Tarot. He writes suggestively that he intends to clarify the facts, but he ends up simply asserting that he is in possession of greater knowledge without ever actually revealing that knowledge. He wants to impress the reader by saying he can reveal hidden mysteries. Yet, he fails to do so. Decker and Dummett's *A History of the Occult Tarot* captures this tendency of Waite very well noting a "tone of supercilious superiority common in Waite's writing" (137).

While Waite expresses an interest in what might be referred to as higher, or philosophical, forms of magic, and criticizes fortune-telling as something simple, yet not near as impressive or important, in the end, *The Pictorial Key* actually offers its readers little else. Even in terms of fortune-telling, the book is nowhere close to being as instructive as a novice would hope. As Decker and Dummett write, "He derided techniques for revealing the future; but in the end he had no other use for his Tarot pack to propose to those purchasers among whom the qualifications of special research could not be expected" (*A History of the Occult Tarot*, 141).

Aleister Crowley

Aleister Crowley was born in Great Britain in 1875. He traveled the world as much as, or more than, Madame Blavatsky claimed to have done. He once said that "ordinary morality is only for ordinary people." Crowley was, of course, neither an ordinary person nor a moral person. William Butler Yeats famously described Crowley as "an unspeakably mad person." The British press called him "the wickedest man in the world," and Crowley described himself as "the Great Beast 666" and "Baphomet" (the satanic deity that the opponents of the Knights Templar once accused them of worshipping). He was an interesting, though disturbing, person whose connections to the history of Tarot add to the interest people have had with him. The British rock stars the Beatles and Ozzy Osbourne both made significant references to Crowley—the former on the cover of their *Sergeant Pepper* album, and the latter in the eponymously titled song "Mr. Crowley."

Crowley briefly attended Cambridge University before leaving in 1898, when he began to rapidly squander his rather significant inheritance. He went to Switzerland, where he developed his skills as a mountain climber. He was good at it. In 1902, he went on an expedition to the Himalayas to climb K2. It was in Switzerland where he met a chemist (who fancied himself an alchemist) named Julian Baker, a member of the Golden Dawn. Baker had a friend named George C. Jones, who was also a chemist and a member of the Golden Dawn. Jones introduced Crowley, who was already intrigued with magic, to the subject of theurgy. Jones also represented Crowley in his initiation to the Golden Dawn that same year.

Crowley was not well liked by many members of the Golden Dawn. Yeats clearly did not like him, while Florence Farr, an officer in the order, refused his application for advancement in rank and touched off an internal conflict. Farr had become aware of Crowley practicing ritualized sex and doing so with men as well as women. Crowley went to Mathers in Paris and was able to get Mathers, without consulting anyone back in London, to grant him admission to the Second Order. By 1907, Crowley had traveled to America and, during that time, came to feel that he could give himself advancements in rank and ignore the rules of the order as well as its official leadership. By that time, too, the Golden Dawn had begun to splinter and form separate groups. Crowley started one of his own called the Argentum Astrum (the Silver Star). He had attempted to seize property and loyalties from Dr. Westcott, of whom Crowley said that the coroner's interest in corpses was more than medical. This slander could refer to necromancy or even necrophilia.

Crowley also argued with Westcott, Mathers, and others over the publication of information associated with Golden Dawn documents, such as the Cipher Manuscript and the secret rituals done within the order. Crowley wanted to publish this information in a journal called *Equinox*. None of this would have brought a great deal of public attention had Mathers not decided to sue Crowley. Mathers won, but the case brought unwanted and embarrassing attention to all parties. The press had a field day, and secrets were made known. Crowley capitalized on the matter by doing public demonstrations of the rituals and speaking about magic and the secret society to paying audiences.

One of the people involved in Crowley's performances was Victor Neuburg (who danced during rituals). Late that year (1909), Crowley and Neuburg were in the Algerian desert of Bou Saada, attempting to commune with a demon called Charanzon, Demon of the Abyss. Supposedly, they made contact with the demon and were severely traumatized by it. Crowley considered himself to be the reincarnation of Edward Kelly, a scrier (or spiritual medium) from Elizabethan times who was associated with the famous mathematician and sorcerer John Dee. Crowley also considered himself the reincarnation of Eliphas Levi, who had died the same year Crowley was born. Like Dee and Kelly, Crowley and Neuberg attempted to channel ancient spirits. Neuburg and Crowley also conducted sexualized magical rituals. In 1913, they spent several weeks doing so in Paris hoping to invoke planetary gods for some purpose. Yet, by the end of this period, their friendship had come to an end. Among other reasons, the fact that Neuburg had decided not to share some unexpectedly gained money with Crowley resulted in their decision to part ways.

Crowley had actually been married for several years before he got involved with Neuberg. His wife was Rose Kelly Skerrett. The two quickly had a daughter who Crowley named Nuit Ma Athanoor Hecate Sappho Jezebel Lilith, and in less than a year, they all went on a global tour climbing mountains in Nepal, Calcutta, and Indo-China. Rose and the baby were sent home two months before Crowley himself arrived back in England. The trip would certainly have been too grueling, and in fact, the baby died of typhoid before Crowley returned home but he blamed his wife for the death. Crowley was involved with other women. Several of them held the title of "the Scarlet Woman," which was supposedly in fulfilment of a prophecy. The first of the Scarlet Women was Leah Hirsig, a schoolteacher who had a child with Crowley.

When the First World War began in 1914, the public interest in Crowley and the Golden Dawn dwindled. Crowley left England at the beginning of the war and went to America. There, he began writing anti-British articles in New York, falsely claiming to be an Irishman. In the years after the war, Crowley came up with the defense that he was actually trying to prod Germans to speak out ever more aggressively against the British so as to reveal the true extent of their hostility. The British public did not buy the ploy. It was during his time in America, away from the war, that Crowley met Leah Hirsig. Crowley also promoted himself as a magus with the title of the Great Beast. The ceremony, in New Hampshire, involved baptizing a frog that had been named Jesus Christ, crucifying the amphibian, and eating it (Decker and Dummett, 149).

After the war, Crowley bought some land on the island of Sicily where, in 1920, he set up what has come to be called the Abbey of Thelema. It must have been a horrible place. It was notoriously unclean; diseases (among them typhus and hepatitis) spread among the residents. It was also a disturbingly bad environment for the children who were neglected there. Leah Hirsig had a daughter who died there. Hirsig also had a miscarriage during that period of her life. For Crowley, it may have seemed like the Garden of Eden . . . for a little while. He had women fighting over him and satisfying his desires. He indulged his lust for heroin as well. A young man named Charles Loveday died from hepatitis there as well. His widow, Betty May, would later report to the media in London on what happened at the Abbey of Thelema. Word got out that there was a great deal of drug abuse, physical violence, satanic worship, and even bestiality. Loveday, for example, was said to have consumed cat's blood in one of Crowley's satanic rituals. The magazine *John Bull* referred to Crowley as "the wickedest man in the world" at this time, and the moniker has endured. The Italian government (this was during the reign of Mussolini) investigated the matter but found no evidence to show that Loveday was ritualistically murdered. Crowley fled to Tunis with Hirsig while the others went their own ways.

By the late 1920s, Crowley was back in London where he published the first parts of an autobiography that he referred to as an autohagiography (telling the reader about his degree of modesty). In 1929, Crowley married one of his Scarlet Women. She was a Nicaraguan woman named Maria Teresa Sanchez. He nonetheless continued relationships with other Scarlet Women in the years that followed. Crowley was bankrupt by the 1930s, thereafter living off of the women that he had relationships with. He also had a son around this time. He had been approached by a young woman who had become interested in Crowley and had paid attention to a legal trial Crowley had just lost to a writer named Nina Hammett. The young woman offered to have a child with Crowley, who accepted the arrangement. The child was named Aleister Ataturk Crowley.

Crowley not only had the attributes of a cult leader and self-promoting showman, he was also a true believer (in himself and in the spirit-filled world of the supernatural). He was also a somewhat prolific writer. In 1909, he wrote *Liber 777*, revealing material from the Golden Dawn's secret texts and rituals. He wrote a novel called *Diary of a Drug Fiend*, which was based partly on his own experiences. Crowley wrote a number of other essays, articles, and miscellanea on magic and the occult. In the context of Tarot, his most significant writing by far was the *Book of Thoth*, from 1944, just a few years before he died. It was accompanied by the illustrations of Lady Frieda Harris. The book and the associated deck will be discussed in the chapter on Tarot and art.

Tarot Comes to America

Aleister Crowley was never representative of the esoteric occultists of his day (or of any other time period). Nor was Crowley generally representative of the tarot community. He was a controversial and licentious figure. Crowley was well-known mainly because he was so different. Besides that, he was a notorious self-promoter. For that reason, he did contribute to the further popularization of Tarot in Europe and America. Crowley's writings, and the deck he and Frieda Harris made, had (and continue to have) an impact in the United States. However, Tarot had begun to gain a greater place in American culture despite Crowley. Arthur Edward Waite's *Pictorial Key to the Tarot* was published in the United States, and, along with the deck he made with Pamela Colman Smith, he began to have a greater influence than Crowley.

While Americans had organized branches of European Hermetic societies before the early 1900s, in the 1920s and 1930s they also began to develop their own, uniquely American organizations and leaders in the tarot community. These developments are, of course, related. Tarot was incorporated into Hermetic or Rosicrucian societies in America, as in Europe. However, by 1970 (at the latest) Tarot would stand alone, in sociocultural terms, separated from the occult and mystical societies that had introduced Tarot to many Americans. Tarot captured an audience quite independent from those who had earlier viewed the Tarot in the context of the tradition of Hermetic esotericism. Indeed, by the 1970s many of those who developed an interest in tarot cards would do so without any reference or regard to the esoteric history of the cards. Perhaps they saw the cards on television, in a film, or at a small shop in a city while on vacation. From there, they became intrigued enough to purchase a deck and a manual on how to use them. In such ways as this, Tarot increasingly worked its way into American popular culture somewhat independently of the esoteric tradition in which it had developed, yet fully capable of reconnecting with that tradition should any neophyte wish to pursue their interest in the cards further down the path of tarot history.

In 1858, Paschal Beverly Randolph established a Rosicrucian society in New York City. Randolph was a fascinating man who grew up in New York City, traveled the world extensively (he was a sailor in his youth), and developed a reputation as a great clairvoyant, medium, and esotericist. His mixed ethnic background seems to have allowed him the desire to seek mystical knowledge from many parts of the globe as well as allowing him to be seen as a person connected to a diverse range of concepts. For these reasons alone, Randolph is worth consideration. However, Randolph's association with Tarot is miniscule. He was best known for being an advocate of sexual magic. He is mentioned here simply to point out that Rosicrucian societies and the Hermetic tradition in American culture can be traced to much earlier than the twentieth century. Randolph may have been the first person to establish an esoteric society in the United States.

For its part, the Order of the Golden Dawn established temple locations in New York City and Chicago in 1897, and by 1920, in Philadelphia and Los Angeles. As the Golden Dawn became internally divided in England, so, too, did the organizational structure in American chapters. The successor of the Golden Dawn became known as the order of *Alpha et Omega*. One of their Chicago members was Paul Foster Case.

Case was born in 1884 in the state of New York. He developed an interest in stage magic as a teenager and liked to use playing cards. His interest in playing cards led to an interest in tarot cards in 1900. In 1916, Case published a series of articles on Tarot in an occult magazine, *The Word*. While a member of *Alpha et Omega*, Case developed an interest in sexual magic (in ritualistic and spiritual terms) as well as an interest in a woman named Lilli Geise, who was also a member of the order. The two were married. Their relationship and the topic of sexual magic caused some division within the order and drew a rebuke from Moina Mathers, the widow of the Golden Dawn founder. Case resigned and began to write a series of documents that, collectively, were used to create a correspondence course on Hermetic knowledge. These correspondence course materials became the basis of a new esoteric order that Case established in Los Angeles in 1923. Much of the material to be taught was derived from the Golden Dawn and focused on the three areas of Hermeticism: alchemy, astrology, and theurgy.

The organization that Case started took its name from the sacred area of the ancient Oracle of Delphi in Greece known as the Adytum. The term "Adytum" is used by the group to more generally refer to holy areas and is, most important, intended to include the biblical sanctuary of the Temple of Solomon known as the Holy of Holies. The organization is called the Builders of the Adytum (B.O.T.A). It remains active today and has a large membership, having expanded through North America and Europe.

Case wrote quite a lot on Tarot. He produced the articles mentioned above in the periodical, *The Word*. He also wrote articles elsewhere. His correspondence course materials include documents on the Tarot. In 1919, Case wrote *An Introduction to the Study of Tarot*. In the preface, he wrote, "I have said nothing of the divinatory uses of the Tarot, not because I agree with those who deprecate its application to the art of divination; but rather because it is my belief that the best results in foretelling the future with the Tarot can be obtained by none who are not thoroughly grounded in the philosophy of the cards. Familiarity with their astrological meanings is particularly indispensable for accurate divination."

So, much like A. E. Waite, whose *Pictorial Key to the Tarot* appeared in print in America a few years previous, Paul Foster Case was publishing a book that piqued curiosity about divination. They both simultaneously assert the power of divination associated with the cards while downplaying what they will deliver on that topic in terms of instructions to the reader. In an earlier writing, found under the title, *Wisdom of the Tarot*, Case made his instructional approach to Tarot clear. He teaches occult meanings about numbers, astrology, color symbolism, the Hebrew alphabet, the "Tree of Life," and so on, but always in the context of a philosophical, even spiritual vocabulary. In short, Case offers the reader lessons on what they need to know *before* they can begin to use the cards for divination. In doing so, however, he suggests an intellectually and spiritually gratifying, even enlightening, experience for the reader.

He also offers the reader the opportunity to purchase cards which can be colored by the purchaser. Instructions for how to color them are included. The cards have an evolutionary link to the Golden Dawn teachings and in several respects are similar to the ones made by Arthur Edward Waite and Pamela Colman Smith, but they are limited to the Major Arcana. This program of personal fulfilment and enlightenment is presented using the tarot cards as the means to an esoteric and Hermetic philosophical end. It is, in other words, not a set of instructions on divination, although there is the claim that the cards can certainly serve that purpose. Rather, Case has actually built an instructional program on Hermeticism in the very manner that, back in the eighteenth century, Court de Gebelin (mistakenly) imagined the cards were secretly intended to provide.

For Case, Tarot was part of the larger context of spiritual enlightenment associated with a variety of traditions, ranging from Rosicrucianism to Kabbalah. Tarot could not only be made to fit neatly into such a broad range of topics, but it could also serve as a text through which to introduce all of those subjects—exactly as Court de Gebelin imagined. In American popular culture, however, many people would want to learn primarily about the tarot cards themselves (as opposed to the esoteric traditions associated with them). Such people would be drawn to Case's writings, but would likely be somewhat disappointed in not finding a "how to" manual for divination. The same could be said of Arthur Edward Waite's *Pictorial Key to the Tarot*.

Paul Foster Case was not the only person to start up an organization in America that promised spiritual satisfaction and personal enlightenment in the 1920s and 1930s. Elbert Benjamine, better known as C. C. Zain, followed a similar path. He came to Los Angeles in 1915, soon thereafter starting the Church of Light. He believed himself to have had a series of divine revelations from certain "Masters" who communicated with him on "the inner plane." These revelations formed the basis of a twenty-two-volume correspondence course which he developed for Hermetic magic that focused largely on astrology supported by Kabbalah. It took years to produce before he finished it in 1934.

One of the volumes in this course was on the Tarot. Zain emphasized and elaborated upon (one might say, embellished) the supposed Egyptian origins of the Tarot. He produced his own deck, which began to go on sale in 1936. The artwork was a mixture of Egyptian and Greco-Roman styles. One interesting quality of the cards was that he placed astrological symbols on each of the cards in his pack. Cynthia Giles's book *The Tarot; History, Mystery and Lore* says that "Case and Zaine . . . strengthened the connections between the Tarot and . . . numerology and astrology" (58).

The fact that both Case and Zaine developed temples (religious organizations, if you will) along with correspondence courses on Hermeticism, as well as tarot manuals and decks, suggests that Tarot in America was taking root in a small segment of the popular culture. More than that, it suggests that Americans, themselves, were playing a role in the evolution of Tarot prior to the Second World War. In this same time period, Tarot was also working its way into the popular culture of America through more mainstream channels. A great example of this can be found in a popular women's magazine called *My Weekly*, which, in 1935, distributed a deck of cards known as the

Thomson-Leng Tarot (Katz, 276). As significant as all that may be, influences from Great Britain, and from the Golden Dawn, continued to reach America and shape public perceptions about Tarot.

Israel Regardie is another important figure from the period before the Second World War. However, after several years away from the subject, he continued to write on the topics of occultism and Tarot into the 1970s. He was born in London in 1907 and his family emigrated to the United States in 1921. He developed an interest in the esoteric and the occult after reading Madame Blavatsky and Aleister Crowley. He wrote to Crowley and was later asked to come to Paris to be Crowley's secretary. The first time the two had dinner together was at a formal event followed by drinking cognac. Regardie witnessed Crowley initiate sex with his current Scarlet Woman, a Pole named Miroslava. It wasn't long before Miroslava left Crowley. Regardie was the one who had to inform Crowley, who not only replaced her with the next Scarlet Woman, but also ordered Regardie to visit prostitutes to lose his virginity (Decker and Dummett, 167).

Regardie returned to the United States in 1937 to find that Crowley had written about Regardie as a betrayer who had robbed and insulted his bene-factor. Insulted, Regardie ceased having any involvement with Crowley at that point and, in fact, halted any involvement with occultists for several years. That did not stop Regardie, however, from beginning a career writing about Crowley, the Golden Dawn, and occult magic. By 1940, he had published the four-volume set *The Golden Dawn*, which was about the organization, its rituals, and its teachings. The sources included numerous manuals from the Golden Dawn that Regardie had obtained through Crowley. Regardie became a psychotherapist in New York. In 1947, the same year Crowley died, he moved to Los Angeles.

The 1960s saw some significant growth in the presence of Tarot in American culture and Regardie was riding that wave as well as contribut-ing to it. In 1960, for example, a new printing of Waite's *Pictorial Key to the Tarot*, along with the accompanying deck, was released. In 1966, Gertrude Moakley's research on the artist, Bonifacio Bembo, and his artwork on one of the first tarot decks to emerge in Renaissance Italy was also being published. (This particular topic is examined elsewhere in this book.) And, in 1968, a young entrepreneur named Stuart Kaplan brought back a tarot deck (the *Swiss 1JJ*) from the Nuremberg Toy Fair, selling 200,000 units. Tarot cards suddenly became available in department stores across the United States. In 1970, Stuart Kaplan, through his company, US Games, Inc., started publish-ing his own decks. He later became the most successful publisher of cards in the United States.

In the 1970s, Regardie wrote a book on Crowley's early career (which was not as hostile to Crowley as one might have imagined). He also edited and published several of Crowley's own writings. By the end of that decade, Regardie had also produced the "Golden Dawn Tarot" deck. He continued to write on Crowley and occultism, contributing to the founding of new temples in Los Angeles, California, and Columbus, Georgia. The popularity of Tarot was growing in those years, and Regardie, with his background and his literary output, helped contribute to the rising popularity of Tarot and the occult.

The New Age Movement and Eden Gray

It may be said in fairness that tarot cards were never designed to be fortune-telling devices. Indeed, the deck, as we now know it, is composed of two decks that were not originally intended to even be combined, much less combined for any particular purpose. The trumps of the Renaissance-era *tarocchi* were also not designed for purposes of meditation or philosophical inquiry. Yet, it is also fair to say, at a minimum, that the imagery originally selected for the *tarocchi* did reflect some philosophical thought. They were certainly not randomly collected images. They were meaningful. Thus, the cards were amenable to a further degree of thought and philosophical speculation. From the very outset, the game of trumps, played with what we now call the Major Arcana of Tarot, while not originally built for the purpose to which it was eventually employed, was nonetheless perfectly suited to it. Its development may be surprising, but it is understandable. Helen Farley, in *A Cultural History of Tarot*, concluded, "Tarot has evolved and been accommodated within the cultural currents of different times; its purpose altered to suit the prevailing attitudes and beliefs. The symbolism on the cards likewise reflects the fickle results of this human reflection" (173). By the 1960s and 1970s, Tarot had long been associated with divination and hermetic philosophy. It was also firmly linked to Kabbalah and an artistic tradition of its own. Yet, Tarot still would continue to evolve and grow as it found a new place in the cultural transformations of the New Age movement in America.

We tend to associate New Age with the late 1960s and the early 1970s, an association I myself make below. But, it should be understood that the term predates the 1960s. One of the first to popularize the term in America was a theosophist named Alice Bailey in the 1930s. The term is an astrological one, referring to the transition from the "Age of Pisces" to the "Age of Aquarius" (which is difficult to say or read without one's mind hearing the song of that name from the 1967 musical *Hair* and recorded by the Fifth Dimension).

The time period of the late 1960s and early 1970s was certainly one of strife and frequently radical change. This was the era of the Cuban Missile Crisis, Vietnam War and accompanying protests, as well as the assassinations of John F. Kennedy, Martin Luther King, and Bobby Kennedy. In many ways, it was the height of the Cold War. Popular music was undergoing a great change with bands such as the Beatles, Rolling Stones, and the Who leading the British Invasion. American musicians such as Bob Dylan and Jimi Hendrix were challenging society to defy tradition and convention. The use of marijuana and, to a lesser extent, psychedelic drugs such as LSD entered the mainstream of popular culture in a way that epitomized the rejection of the establishment which, while having embraced alcohol, criminalized other recreational drugs. Attitudes about sexuality also broke with convention and tradition in what has been referred to as a sexual revolution. However, while there is overlap between the two, it would not be entirely accurate to equate the radical and revolutionary aspects of popular culture in the 1960s and 1970s with the New Age movement.

The rebellion of young people against their parents was part of the 1960s counterculture but not inherently part of the New Age movement. In fact, parents as well as children were involved in the New Age (although, it was not a mainstream movement). And, whereas the call to action in the form of protests and public defiance was integral to the call for social justice and reform associated with the counterculture, the New Age was often more inwardly directed. The distinction between the counterculture and the New Age movement is important even though one finds obvious examples of overlap in instances such as the "hippie" communes that developed at the time.

When one looks more specifically at the New Age, a number of characteristics that will relate to the evolution of Tarot in the 1960s and 1970s emerge. As Helen Farley wrote, "eclecticism and syncretism were integral to the movement" (152). Concepts such as the Gaia hypothesis of NASA scientist James Lovelock, which saw the planet as a living organism, could be blended with currents in feminism, interest in Eastern religions, "primitive" societies, Jungian psychology, and even neo-paganism. Farley then explains that "New Age practitioners will experiment with several techniques in sequence or at the same time. Contemporary Tarot echoed this eclectic approach, frequently combining the symbolism from two or more traditions within the same deck" (157). While I agree with Farley's assessment, I would add that, long before the New Age movement of the 1960s and 1970s, Tarot had already come to represent a construction of an eclectic collection of symbols and concepts. In this sense, Tarot was ahead of the curve; ready to offer the popular culture both a device (the cards) and a philosophical concept (and Tarot may rightly be referred to as a philosophical concept) fully capable of, not only incorporating other ideas and symbols, but channeling inchoate concepts into a more fully realized form, capable of being expressed and understood by those who might not otherwise grasp or articulate such ideas.

Despite the fact that tarot cards could be viewed as an eclectic collection of concepts with several different uses, such as a device for ritualized magic or a manual for Hermetic philosophy, the popular culture of America was much more interested in its use as a divinatory device. Fortune-telling had always been the most attractive aspect of the cards in popular culture. Yet, writers such as Arthur Edward Waite and Paul Foster Case tended to only hint at this most intriguing function. By the time of the New Age movement of the 1960s, the public had been waiting a long time for a "how to" manual on tarot cards and fortune-telling. In 1970, they got it.

Eden Gray's *A Complete Guide to the Tarot*, published in 1970, is perhaps the best-known book in America on the subject of Tarot. Gray had published some other material on Tarot in the 1960s, increasingly infusing mystical elements (Kabbalah, numerology, astrology) into her writing. *A Complete Guide to the Tarot* was much more conducive to the tarot novice seeking initial instruction. It was, in effect, a very good instruction manual for beginners. Whereas previous books actually provided merely the sense that the authors knew more than they were willing to reveal, offering the reader a rather vague familiarity with the cards, Gray was offering the means to learn how to read effectively. And, whereas most previous writers asserted that divination was possible with the cards but that a philosophy of magic and an association with ritual were not just the truly significant traits of the cards but prerequisites to their use in divination, Gray offered a clear focus on divination directed to a readership that was not likely to be familiar with the esoteric background associated with the cards.

These two elements of Gray's writing—clear introductory instructions on how to read the cards, and a focus on divination—resulted in her achieving a prominent position in American Tarot culture. A third factor associated with her books is also important: she used the Waite-Colman Smith deck. The illustrations in *A Complete Guide to the Tarot* are from that deck, and her explorations of the symbolism and imagery of the deck as they relate to using Tarot strengthened the link between her popular book and the increasingly popular deck. She also relied on Waite's *Pictorial Key to the Tarot*, but as I've indicated, Gray's book is a much more effective manual for the beginner than Waite's book. Of course, other books and decks had been published in America as a culture of Tarot had developed throughout the first half of the twentieth century.

We might say that Gray was like Case, Zain, and others, who published on and popularized the use of tarot cards throughout twentieth-century America. Yet, Gray took things to the next level in linking Tarot with popular culture. Her book struck a chord with a segment of American popular culture, introducing many to the Waite-Colman Smith deck. While the deck she used was already established among tarot enthusiasts, it became quite a bit more popular through its association with Gray's book. The fact that much of Gray's reading audience were novices introduced the deck to a large number of people who would see that deck as both their first tarot deck and, in a sense, the quasi-official deck of Tarot. The fact that the deck had been in print for sixty years gave it the credibility of age. Its original context being England and the Golden Dawn added to its credibility. And, the fact that it was more readily available than many alternatives further cemented the commercial and popular success of the Waite-Colman Smith deck. Both the deck and the book, which are still often paired together, gained a popularity that blossomed in the last quarter of the twentieth century.

Eden Gray's life spanned the entirety of the twentieth century. She was born as Priscilla Partridge in the summer of 1901 and died in January 1999. She was an actor on stage and in film in the 1920s. Although not terribly successful as an actress, it is interesting that she was in a film with Ronald Reagan. Her role in *Kings Row* (1942), however, was uncredited. Gray and her husband traveled extensively, living in a variety of cities in America as well as in London and Paris. By the 1950s she had already developed an interest in metaphysical subjects. She was operating Inspiration House, a bookstore and publisher in New York City that, among other things, sold products associated with Tarot. In 1960, Gray self-published a book titled *Tarot Revealed* which would later be revised, published, and reprinted. Although not Gray's most famous work, it is still found on the personal bookshelves of many tarotists today.

Mary Greer, an eminent name in the tarot community in the first two decades of the twenty-first century, and someone who was acquainted with Eden Gray, wrote on her blog that it was probably at Inspiration House that Gray began to encounter people who were looking for and not finding an appropriate level of instruction for novices with an interest in using the cards for divination. Greer has this to say of Gray: "Eden Gray's tarot books formed the main impetus to the hippie adoption of the Tarot as spiritual guide for navigating a world-turned-on-its-head, leading directly to the booming Tarot Renaissance that began in 1969 and continues to this day" (Greer, "Eden Gray's Fool's Journey").

Indeed, there was a "Tarot Renaissance" that began around this time. Greer gives 1969 as the pivotal year, noting that at least five tarot decks and twelve books on the subject were published that year (Greer, "1969: The Tarot Renaissance"). Of course, this has to be seen as part of a long-term trend, rather than a single year with several relevant events. Eden Gray certainly had as much to do with this "Renaissance" as anyone else. Gray seems to have sensed that Tarot could be a welcome element in the cultural conglomeration of exotic influences permeating American popular culture in the period.

Tarot has some of the key traits that interested people who were part of the New Age movement and the counterculture, as well as those who are intrigued by the metaphysical and those who are simply amused with the concept of divination. Its Renaissance origins, or its supposed ancient Egyptian origins, would be part of this. Its association with free-spirited gypsies would also have given it special attention at the time (despite the inaccuracy of that particular legend). The symbols associated with the cards had always been fascinating, but found a particularly receptive audience in the 1970s. Tarot's association with astrology, too, had an obvious resonance with American popular culture at the dawning of the Age of Aquarius.

Mary Greer and other prominent tarotists since the 1990s, reflect back on those years when Gray's books and the Waite-Colman Smith deck were finding their way from New Age bookstore shelves into American homes and American popular culture, with a bit of nostalgia. At least, one could say that important memories for important people in Tarot are connected to the emergence of Eden Gray's writings and the association those writings had with the Waite-Colman Smith deck. Mary Greer, in an interview with this author, said that her interest in Tarot was first sparked when she was a tenth grader and a friend of hers obtained one of Gray's earlier writings on Tarot, *Tarot Revealed*. Greer went out and got a copy for herself, along with the deck. She continued reading Gray's books, becoming particularly fond of the 1971 book, *Mastering the Tarot* (author's interview with Mary Greer, August 13, 2017).

The desire for greater self-awareness and the sense of the world as increasingly chaotic also made Gray's work resonate through the culture, particularly her exploration of "the Fool's Journey" in which she discussed the meanings of each card of the Major Arcana, beginning with "the Fool," in the context of a journey through life with its trials and tribulations. She seemed to be offering her readers meaning in both the personal and philosophical senses. The conceptual development of "the Fool's Journey" has become a widely practiced way of learning about the Major Arcana cards. It has also served as a way of opening a window into a meditative process for any individual pondering life's ups and downs, the process of maturing, or significant moments—all in the context of the philosophical meanings associated with the cards' iconography and how they may relate to the individual's personal life experiences.

A Complete Guide to the Tarot has been reprinted in numerous editions over the years. The year 2020 was its fiftieth anniversary, and it continues to be popular with beginners and established tarotists. Eden Gray's book represents a watershed moment in the history of Tarot because, on its own, it provides one of the best introductions to the topic for those with an interest in learning to use the cards, while in the cultural context, it drew upon a major movement (the New Age) of the 1960s in ways that benefited from popular, even trendy phenomenon while simultaneously drawing on (and contributing to) more enduring qualities.

By the late 1970s, Tarot had become popular enough to merit its own encyclopedia. In 1978, Stuart Kaplan published the first of four volumes of an *Encyclopedia of Tarot*, and that same year he sold 200,000 tarot decks (Liebenson). Every scholarly researcher of Tarot that I have read includes it in their bibliography. Kaplan is a major figure in the Tarot community. He founded US Games Systems, the largest publisher of tarot cards. Kaplan claims to "have the largest collection in the world of tarot cards and books on tarot cards and the history of playing cards" (Liebenson).

In the New Age movement of the 1960s and 1970s, Tarot showed an ability to continue absorbing important aspects of contemporary culture. For example, the interests in shamanism, crystal-healing, and Eastern and Native-American traditions all found their way into association with the Tarot. As Helen Farley wrote, "The New Age is an intoxicating mix of East and West, where Buddhist Tantra bumps up against Native-American shamanism, crystal healing and past-life regressions. Auras are examined, angels are consulted and groups gather to meditate for peace and environmental healing. Tarot is an integral part of this worldview, its symbolism confidently projecting each of these apparently divergent streams, to emerge as the New Age tool *par excellence*" (Farley, 151).

Along with this clearly established ability to mean many different things to many different people under the umbrella of a tarot community came a significant change. The earlier advocates of Tarot, from Court de Gebelin all the way to Aleister Crowley, had presupposed that there was a singular, truly proper, and genuine form of Tarot. But, in modern American popular culture, Tarot could be all things to everyone. In my view, this versatility, which allows people to share involvement in a community despite their variety of interpretations of that community, while simultaneously sharing a sense of togetherness with one another and separateness from others, gives Tarot a characteristic usually associated with successful religious organizations or fans of the National Football League. Returning to Helen Farley's analysis: "With the Advent of the New Age, tarot designers felt able to 're-imagine' the deck, no longer afraid to experiment, comfortable with creating links to other cultures or to create decks that fulfilled roles other than divination" (Farley, 151).

An excellent illustration of this new direction in Tarot is the Noble *Motherpeace* round deck which was introduced in 1983. It reflects a stream of feminism as it has developed in the Goddess movement. In fact, that same year also saw the introduction of a *Tarot of Wicca*. Two feminists, Vicki Noble (a student of history and women's studies) and Karen Vogel (who has degrees in anthropology and biology), in Berkeley, California, had developed a deck that incorporated images and concepts associated with goddess worship and feminine spirituality from around the globe and throughout time. The round cards are a significant departure from convention yet, the traditional structure of Tarot, modified to the feminist theme, remains clear.

The *Motherpeace* round deck also represents another major change to Tarot that has become increasingly significant since the 1980s: Tarot as more of a meditation tool rather than a tool of divination. Emily Auger, in *Tarot and Other Meditation Decks*, noted that this is not a movement rejecting the use of Tarot as a supernatural tool for divining the future or some other hidden aspect of life (48). The occult esotericism remains, but increasing attention and interest has been given to meditation rather than revelation. However, one might argue that meditation and inner personal reflection are, in fact, a type of revelation. It seems to me that the cards are now a little less magical and a little more mystical than they seemed to previous generations, but these have always been two sides of the same coin. As Cynthia Giles and others have noted, a distinction is made between magic (which seeks to achieve something) and mysticism (which seeks to experience something) (73).

The use of the cards for meditative purposes began to develop in a significant way partly as a product of the Tarot Renaissance of the 1980s. Mary K. Greer's *Tarot for Your Self* epitomizes the trend. Published in 1984, the book has been revised and printed in a recent new edition. While *Tarot for Your Self* used some traditional conventions, it is driven by an effort to personalize the experience of reading the cards by connecting their meanings to various aspects of the reader's own life. For example, the author discusses the personality types associated with each of the court cards in the deck and then the reader is asked to consider people in their lives who share those attributes. Having done that, the reader is on the way to interpreting the cards in various layouts through a much more personal lens. Foretelling the future becomes somewhat irrelevant. It is now about considering a variety of possibilities in one's own behavior or relationships while drawing upon the meanings suggested in the cards. Exercises and using a journal are encouraged, making the cards something of a means toward an end—namely, personal growth from a meditative and mystical experience.

It would be an exaggeration to suggest that the use of Tarot has completely shifted from fortune-telling to meditation. Tarot is too complex. The Hermetic tradition that has long been attached to Tarot incorporates philosophical elements and the influences of magical societies such as the Golden Dawn further advanced the philosophical aspects of Tarot even while insisting upon their divinatory magic properties. We may consider meditation and self-reflection as akin to philosophical exercises. Further, a psychological component to the cards is drawn in to both contexts: magic and meditative.

The *Motherpeace* round deck is far from the only themed deck to emerge from the New Age movement. Neopaganism, Shamanism, nature, and antinuclear themes were used to develop a variety of tarot decks from the 1970s through the end of the twentieth century. So, too, were topics such as Arthuriana, Celtic traditions, voodoo, and Native-American traditions. While many decks focused on topics just outside of the mainstream, even traditional Judeo-Christian themes found a place in this Tarot Renaissance.

At a time when conservative Christians in America were often deriding the New Age movement, the New Age movement itself was embracing Christianity. In 1969, Corine Heline wrote a book called *The Bible and the Tarot*, published by New Age Press. The author's approach is primarily through the Kabbalah, as one might guess. She uses this to move closer to the linkages between tarot traditions and biblical content. Others would follow in her footsteps by developing tarot decks. For example, in 1983 Kathleen Binger built off of the association of Hebrew letters with the cards by writing about the meanings of the letters on the cards and adding a scriptural passage to each card in her *Bible Tarot* deck. Her "Magician" card, for example, has Moses before the Pharaoh defeating the Pharaoh's magicians who had turned their staffs into snakes. Moses's staff turns into a bigger snake and eats the others. In 1995, Leslie Lewis created the *Christian Bible Tarot*, which, again, incorporated a biblical quotation on each card and built off of the tradition of Hebrew letters on the cards of the Major Arcana.

By the late 1990s, Tarot had developed a niche in American popular culture. Tarot was certainly connected to other facets of popular culture, among them the New Age movement. It is equally true that Tarot itself is an eclectic and syncretistic amalgam of other cultural phenomenon such as astrology and Kabbalah. That being said, Tarot also stands alone in several important ways. For instance, people with an interest in Tarot might not involve themselves directly in any specifically New Age activities. They might not hold any deep interest in Kabbalah or astrology. Put simply, they might be interested in Tarot independent of its connections to these other things. Perhaps they have fun doing readings, or they might like the imagery and wish to collect cards. They may enjoy Tarot as little more than a parlor game. On the other hand, some people may see Tarot as a focal point that brings together a number of related interests that do include astrology, art, Kabbalah, and so on. For them, Tarot is at the center of a collection of interests rather than at the periphery of other interests. The point is that Tarot carved out a significant place in the culture of America in its own right rather than as an offshoot or peripheral topic.

Tarot Goes into the Twenty-First Century

Interest in Tarot accelerated in the 1990s and gained an increasing number of fans and critics. It is little surprise, then, to see that there were many more decks to choose from and many more books to read. This also meant that certain people with a background in Tarot would move to the fore. Stuart Kaplan of US Games Systems, for example, saw his tarot cards business, which had developed in the 1960s, expand impressively, stocking bookstores and small novelty shops across the country. On the literary side, Rachel Pollack became an important spokesperson for, and popularizer of, Tarot.

In 1980, Rachel Pollack began to write a two-volume book, *Seventy-Eight Degrees of Wisdom: A Book of Tarot.* It became one of the most widely read books on Tarot in the last quarter of the twentieth century. She describes her first experience with Tarot when she was teaching English in upstate New York. At the time, she knew the cards only from their mention in T. S. Eliot's, *The Waste Land.* A colleague gave her a reading, and a couple weeks later, Pollack bought Eden Gray's book and a pack of Waite-Colman Smith cards in Montreal. She notes that this occurred just around the beginning of a new cultural interest in Tarot. In fact, Pollack, herself, would eventually contribute greatly to that cultural interest. By 1997, Tarot had reached a new level of popularity. *Seventy-Eight Degrees of Wisdom* has gone through multiple editions and into a combined volume.

Pollack was having an impact that not only rode the crest of the movement as it came out of the previous generation, she guided the growing movement into a new cultural identity—changing with the times, but also changing the times. Looking back at the early 1970s, when she first got involved with Tarot, she wrote in her preface to the 1997 edition of *Seventy-Eight Degrees of Wisdom,*

> In those days a long-time split still existed in the Tarot world. On one side stood the grand tradition of the occultists, from Antoine Court de Gebelin

down through the Hermetic Order of the Golden Dawn and its descendants. On the other we found the tradition of readings, almost despised by the occultists. To some extent, this reflected a gender split as well. The great esoteric writers were almost all men. . . . Tarot readers were mostly women. It is not an accident that when most people visualize a Tarot reader, they see a woman in a headscarf.

Over the years since, women have continued to develop a prominent place in the tarot community and have gained greater respect within it as well as in the wider culture. Gray and Pollack, along with Mary Greer and a few others, have elevated the status of women in the tarot community while simultaneously extending its popularity within American culture. More than that, they have reached into a variety of subcultures where environments that welcomed Tarot have shared in the growth.

The book cemented Pollack's status as an icon in the tarot community. Its title indicates the book's structure in examining each of the seventy-eight cards in the deck and viewing the Tarot as a source of wisdom. The author takes a philosophical approach to her discussion of the cards and the meanings they display or unveil. Like Eden Gray before her, Pollack provides her readers with information on how to use the cards. It would be an ideal first book for a novice. However, there is something about Pollack's book that makes it both functional and relatable to more experienced tarot enthusiasts as well. It is, in the end, simply one of the better examples of the category of guidebooks. Even so, its popularity and effectiveness, along with its obvious connections to the history and traditions of the craft, have resulted in the book having a special place in the literary tradition of Tarot, alongside Waite and Gray.

In 2014, Emily Auger edited a two-volume anthology, *Tarot in Culture*. The books' forward was written by Pollack. Pollack gives a brief but illustrative review of the history of tarot literature. She writes, "The written literature about Tarot has an odd history, one of different camps that were either contemptuous of each other or simply ignored each other altogether. Roughly, there have been three such groups. The oldest, the people who got there first really, are the esotericists. Related to the esoteric works but distinct from them are the guidebooks. The third group is that of the historians." Auger then says that cultural criticism, an approach that allows examination of traditions and attitudes, has become yet another layer in the literature on Tarot.

The years between Pollack's *78 Degrees of Wisdom* and Auger's *Tarot in Culture* included an important anthology of essays on Tarot edited by James Wanless and Angeles Arrien, two PhDs who put together an anthology called

Wheel of Tarot: A New Revolution, with about twenty other scholars, several of whom hold doctorates representing various disciplines. The book, published in 1992, was an important milestone in that it demonstrated interest in Tarot had reached a level beyond or, at least, outside of that traditional association with magic.

One of the contributors, Jane English, has a background in subatomic particle physics. Her work appears alongside an essay by Mary Greer on the Celtic Cross tarot spread. Greer writes about the desire all people have for "oracular knowledge" but doesn't present Tarot as oracular. Instead, she writes, "The Tarot encourages you to look at life symbolically—not so much by means of omens, but as simultaneous levels of meaning" ("Permutations," 51).

The fact that people with a background in science can be found among the members of the tarot community might give some people a false sense of objective validation to those who wish to elevate Tarot on the basis of some supposedly scientific foundation. Such attempts can easily be taken too far and are deservedly dismissed by critics. Even so, science and Tarot are no more incompatible than religion and Tarot. Just as one can find tarot cards based on the Bible, so, too, can one find tarot cards based on physics.

The *Tarot of Physics* deck, self-published by Dan Horn and Corrine Kenner substitutes the four traditional suits with suits of "Energy," "Space," "Time," and "Matter." The aces represent the most basic concept associated with the suit and the tens represent a more complex concept associated with the suit. The Major Arcana cards bare the same titles as traditional decks, but they reference a concept in physics that can be logically associated with the traditional meaning of the card. For example, the "Strength" card illustrates the concept of "Leverage," using a simple drawing of a fulcrum, lever, and a weight.

Returning to the book *Wheel of Tarot*: it served, on the one hand, to demonstrate that Tarot had broadened its cultural scope sufficiently to allow categories such as psychology, art, literature, and anthropology to be used alongside Tarot in ways that created a greater depth of meaning for those with an established interest in Tarot. On the other hand, the scholarly contributors to this anthology were demonstrating to their reading audience, and to the wider society, that it would be erroneous and rather narrow-minded to imagine Tarot as appropriate only for carnivals or Renaissance fair entertainment. The conventional view of critics of Tarot that it is a superstitious plaything, lacking in substance, unable to withstand the objective scrutiny of a rational skeptic was now actually too weak of a case to maintain unless, that is, critics of Tarot ignored such books as *Wheel of Tarot* and, inaccurately, assumed that the tarotists of the 1990s were all the sorts of charlatans and ignoramuses that populated the landscapes of preconceived stereotypes rather than the community of authors and practitioners that could be found throughout the growing and diverse society of America's intellectual tarot community.

Having said all that, let us still continue to acknowledge that there remained, as always, a presence of gullible people and con artists in the world of Tarot, just as one finds such figures in the world of business, politics, and religion. Yet, by the 1990s, if one wished to read, for example, about "The Psychodynamic Effects of Tarot Symbolism," or "An Experimental Test on the Basis of Probability Theory," such topics could be found in the essays of *Wheel of Tarot*. By the 1990s, Tarot was demonstrably incorporated into the intellectual interests of more highly educated people and had an increasing potential to be associated with a number of arcane subjects. Simultaneously, its association with American popular culture was, as we have seen in this chapter, expanding to a significant degree.

While Tarot has developed along lines that would have been unanticipated by previous generations, the foundations and traditions established in the nineteenth and early twentieth centuries remained, for the most part, largely intact and secure. An excellent illustration of this is seen in the work of Benebell Wen, author of the 2015 book *The Holistic Tarot: An Integrative Approach to Using Tarot for Personal Growth*. Wen reflects the modern paradigm of seeing Tarot in terms of meditation and personal reflection, a therapeutic tool of self-care, so to speak. Simultaneously, she also draws deeply from the well of traditional tarot concepts as presented in the seminal literature from the field going from Levi and Papus to Waite, Crowley, and Gray. She encourages her readers to develop a knowledge of astrology, symbolism, hermeticism, and the other esoteric and occult elements of Tarot.

Wen is a corporate lawyer by profession for whom Tarot is a passion, but not one that produces her primary income. Even so, her book won two significant awards in 2015: the Tarot Professionals Tarotsophy Book Award and the American Tarot Association's Readers' Choice Award. She has an extensive website with blogs, instructional videos, and online courses in addition to information about her book and a deck she designed and illustrated called the Spirit-Keeper's Tarot.

She does not care to view Tarot as a system of fortune-telling. Rather, she sees the cards as a "gadget" for developing a lens through which the reader can contemplate a variety of ways to consider their circumstances and objectives in life. Once such perspectives are developed, the ability to make better decisions or to maintain a more positive and constructive outlook can be achieved. Put differently, she is not interested in using Tarot for fortune-telling as much as for fortune-creating. The *Hoilistic Tarot* approach is disinterested in psychic readings that are improvisational, or "intuitive," in the sense that a background knowledge is unnecessary. Such an approach, she argues, might just as well use rocks, tealeaves, or the shape of clouds, instead of tarot cards. Rather, Wen argues for the need to have an interdisciplinary approach to the cards that is informed by their historical connections to the esoteric and occult. She refers to this approach as "tarot analytics."

Wen represents one of the best examples of twenty-first century tarotists who have built off of the oldest traditions associated with the cards, as well as the qualities that have accrued to Tarot since the New Age through to the end of the twentieth century. If one can consider Benebell Wen as representative of the best of the current generation of tarotists, the culture of Tarot seems to be self-aware of a solid foundation capable of projecting growth well into the foreseeable future.

Conclusion

Tarot was not unknown in America at the beginning of the twentieth century. Nor were secret societies anything new to America at that point. Yet, one such secret society, the Hermetic Order of the Golden Dawn, as we have seen, began to have a profound impact on the place of Tarot in American culture from the 1910s onward. Golden Dawn alumni, Arthur Edward Waite and Aleister Crowley, contributed significantly to the popularization of Tarot in America. Yet, the importation of Tarot from Great Britain did not enter American culture without being altered and modified.

One of the more significant evolutionary changes to Tarot as a result of its "Americanization" is that its place in the popular culture has become much more relevant. We have seen how people such as Paul Foster Case and C. C. Zain presented Tarot to a much broader audience than one limited to the salons and parlors of aristocratic London. True, Waite aimed for a wider readership, but he seemed to present himself as an elitist in both his social circle and his possession of esoteric wisdom. Magic remained, for him and his social milieu, an environment that was entered by a privileged few. Case and Zain seemed to have a desire to throw the doors wide open. Perhaps this is a bit of an overstatement, but over the century, the trend lines are clear.

Tarot became the province of the popular culture by the 1970s (if not earlier). Despite its association with a history of hidden knowledge protected by a small group of enlightened individuals (indeed, partly because of that history) common Americans from a variety of social backgrounds began to take an interest in Tarot while, simultaneously, access to things Tarot became increasingly easier by the 1990s. Books, by then, could be found everywhere. And, everywhere, books on Tarot had become more easily digestible, even entertaining, to those seeking to know. The Waite-Colman Smith deck had reached the status of an industry standard as well as a respectable, eminent, elderly prototype upon which new innovative forms could be modeled, respectfully or mischievously.

Part of this was simply a matter of commercialization. The mass-production associated with the aftermath of the industrial revolution allowed the large-scale manufacturing, distribution, and advertising of tarot cards (just like it has done with candy, toys, pens, clothing, and other things). These socioeconomic developments alone account, in a limited way, for the growth of Tarot in the twentieth century. Tarot has permeated into American popular culture while, simultaneously, cultural phenomena have increasingly embraced Tarot and significantly widened its presence and influence.

The cultural position of Tarot has demonstrably been established on an enduring foundation which is both esoteric and popular—a seemingly contradictory combination. At the same time, one might add that Tarot has also evolved in ways that, at first glance, seem inconsistent. Early tarotists insisted that the cards gave them the ability to see into the future even though they publicly offered very little in terms of exactly how that was done. By the 1970s and 1980s, tarotists were publishing relatively detailed information on how to use the cards for fortune-telling. Yet, they were also elaborating upon the philosophical dimension of the cards. This began the trend toward self-improvement, meditation, and introspection. Nonetheless, the association between Tarot and fortune-telling has not waned. Tarot can be seen and used in a variety of ways and its cultural history supports and justifies these different views and uses, making Tarot culturally adaptable as well as stable.

Tarot had always had characteristics that allowed for syncretistic growth. As we saw in the previous chapter, beliefs about ancient magical philosophy could be grafted onto the cards just as surely as their imagery resonated with important themes in religion, ambition, history, and so on. In this chapter, we saw how social movements could be identified with Tarot and how Tarot could be modified to further strengthen such linkages. Although I used the example of the New Age movement to illustrate the point in this chapter, we shall see in later chapters on television and movies how other aspects of popular culture draw upon and build off of Tarot.

CHAPTER 3

Who Are These People?
The Tarot Community in American Culture

People are strange. You don't have to be a fan of the Doors music to know that. So, it would surprise no one to say that there are some strange people associated with Tarot. In this chapter, we will discuss some of these people in the hopes of getting a sense, broadly speaking, of what kinds of people are drawn to Tarot and what sorts of people make up what can loosely be called the tarot community in contemporary society. I take it as a given that, since people are strange, tarot people are also strange. Conversely, if one does not consider "normal" people to be strange, then neither should we think that the people associated with Tarot are strange. And, while they might embrace such a categorization, I doubt that they are actually any stranger than anyone else.

Having said all that, the general public does tend to view Tarot as something strange and, therefore, one would expect that a whole community of people associated with Tarot would be deemed as a strange community. What we are really talking about, here, has more to do with reputations or stereotypes that are applied by the mainstream culture to many distinct subgroups of that culture. In this chapter, I will focus more on the actual people that make up the tarot community (an admittedly debatable term) rather than examining the attitudes and suppositions of the wider society when viewing that smaller community.

We shall begin the chapter by considering the negative light in which Tarot has often been placed, but we will quickly move toward how tarotists respond to being viewed negatively and how they try to present themselves to the wider world. Going beyond image and reputation, this chapter will demonstrate that there is a wide social and economic diversity within the tarot community. I also wish to suggest to the reader that scholars, particularly in social and behavioral categories such as anthropology, sociology, and psychology, can be rather comfortable in the world of Tarot.

While there may be scam artists, con men, crackpots, and idiots found playing with tarot decks or reading books on the subject, the fact is that the same could be said about business people, religious leaders, teachers, young people, old people, wealthy people, and those with a low income. It would create an inaccurate representation to focus on the eccentric or the negative. What follows is my attempt at showing the modern tarot community in a way that provides both a general picture of the people that make up that community and a bit of nuance that includes some of the more unique or successful figures that are widely recognized and influential among the community's members.

Criminals and Sinners

In 1975, Rosalie Kimberlin went to get a tarot reading in Venice Beach, California. The reader was a feminist and a Wiccan who, four years earlier, started a group known as the Susan B. Anthony Coven. She had a shop that sold candles and miscellany items associated with magic. Upon completion of the reading, Kimberlin arrested the tarotist, who went by the name Zsuzsanna Budapest. Fortune-telling was a crime. Kimberlin was an undercover police officer. The case went to court where Budapest argued that she was the first witch to be prosecuted in America since the Salem trials.

Zsuzsanna Budapest took that last name in recognition of the main city in her country of origin. She had come to America as a child during the Cold War as a political refugee. Her mother, it was claimed, was a witch. In fact, Budapest claimed that she came from an 800-year line of witches. Her religious views and theology, though, were strongly feminist. Wicca, as a religion, has strong feminist elements. Budapest is most widely known for her activism as a feminist Wiccan and her role as a tarotist is, in some respects, quite secondary.

Fortune-telling was against the law in California in 1975, and the fact is, Zsuzsanna was guilty. After an appeal to the California Supreme Court and a significant amount of public attention, however, Budapest prevailed. The reading of tarot cards was deemed to be associated with her religious beliefs, and therefore, a ban on reading the cards was tantamount to religious discrimination.

In the summer of 2014, a similar sting operation occurred in Minden, Nevada, when an undercover officer paid Helena Welch $25 for a tarot card reading at a place called the Psychic Spa. During the reading, Welch informed the woman that her husband was cheating on her and that the problem could be fixed for $700. The officer appeared willing to pay. Welch gave her three roses and a plastic bag labeled, "Spiritual Karma Cleanser." Instructions were given to the woman to bathe with the "cleanser" and to return the following day with the rose petals. At that point, Welch was arrested (*Record Courier*, July 23, 2014).

One significant difference between these stories is that the first one involves an arrest simply for being paid to tell a fortune (with tarot cards) while, in the second story, there is an additional element involving an assertion of marital infidelity along with a large expense to remove a supposed problem using supernatural means. Reading tarot cards could be viewed not only in the context of religious expression but, more significantly here, in terms of entertainment or advice. The offer to remove a curse or to fix an imagined problem with supernatural powers pushes the matter into the category of a fraud. Certainly, some have argued that the reading of tarot cards, prima facie, is a fraud. As the California Supreme Court determined in the case mentioned above, it is hard to legally define "fortune-telling." Not only would coming up with a definition of fortune-telling result in debates about individual categories such as astrology, palm reading, and tarot cards, it could also easily require an examination of things like political pollsters or stock market advisers. Even without the freedom of speech issues that offer protections to tarot readers, a blanket ban on fortune-telling would be extremely problematic in legal terms. Fraud, however, is easier to define and to demonstrate in a courtroom. Thus, the use of fortune-telling as a tool with which to commit fraud is something worth inquiring about, but the legal focus should be on the fraud. Even so, several states still have laws against fortune-telling. These laws are basically archaic and have been left largely untested since the case of Zsuzsanna Budapest in 1975.

In Oklahoma, fortune-telling for a fee was outlawed in 1915. Yet, the law is left almost entirely unenforced . . . almost. In March of 2017, Sonia Lisa Marks was charged with fortune-telling for a fee (*NewsOK*, February 17, 2017). The fifty-two-year-old woman operated a business which presented her as a "psychic reader." She was also charged with "obtaining money under false pretenses." The first charge, fortune-telling, is only a misdemeanor, but the second charge is a felony. Marks had come to Oklahoma City from Ohio, where she had a record of conning several clients out of a great deal of money in fortune-telling scams. She had earlier been extradited from Oklahoma back to Ohio where she pleaded guilty, was placed on probation, and given a hefty fine. She went back to Oklahoma City, but got in trouble with the law again after an undercover detective paid for a card reading and gave Marks a story about trying to find a man to marry. After the tarot reading, Marks told her that for another $125 she could cleanse the woman's aura and that would enable her to find the right man.

A local news article (*NewsOK*, February 17, 2017) covering the story interviewed Oklahoma City tarot readers. One such tarot reader said "it is absolutely unethical" to upsell clients and tell them you can fix bad fortunes for more money. Sadly, it is not an unusual type of scam to convince a person that they have a bad fortune and to then follow up with increasingly expensive promises to undo a curse (or something comparable) for more money.

Such stories tend to feed a narrative of tarot readers and psychics as con artists. Some are, although, in fairness, one could also argue that anyone who is committing such crimes is not, in fact, a tarotist or a psychic. Rather, they are con artists falsely using that identity. It would be similar to pointing out that a con artist who poses as a police officer, minister, or life insurance salesman is not, in fact, a police officer, minister, or life insurance salesman. Therefore, the reputation of those professions should not be sullied by the con artists who pose as such.

Sometimes, tarot readers are involved in rather positive outcomes after horrible crimes are committed. Jayne Braiden, a tarot reader in England, did a reading for a man named Star Randel-Hanson in 2015 (*Telegraph*, May 27, 2016). During the reading, which involved the "Judgment" and "the Devil" cards, Randel-Hanson confessed to a murder. At that point, Braiden called the police. When she explained where she was (at her tarot parlor), the dispatcher treated the call as a lower priority. Instead of taking a few minutes to arrive, the police took close to an hour to get there. By then, Randel-Hanson had divulged the location of the body of the man he had murdered.

In Westminster, Colorado, a young woman named Lea Porter disappeared in 2014. At first, the police suspected her ex-boyfriend, but suspicion eventually settled upon a man named Christopher Waide who had been a high school friend of Porter's. Her brother was able to get a confession out of Waide, who had been feigning concern and a desire to help find Lea. The men met at a park where Waide was using tarot cards. Porter recorded the entire conversation on his phone. Later, while in prison, Waide said that he confessed to the murder because, "the cards were saying to me that my guilt over that would destroy me unless I let it out" (*ABC News*, October 21, 2016, online).

Stories linking Tarot to crime can be presented in any number of ways. Such stories might present Tarot as good, bad, or irrelevant. Something similar can be said about Tarot and religion (I will limit this discussion on Tarot and religion to Christianity). Reference to the Bible will almost certainly be made in the context of any debate about what Christians ought to believe. I would remind the reader that tarot cards did not exist until the fifteenth century. This is many centuries after even the last part of the Bible was written (scholars estimate that the book of Revelation was written around the year 100). Therefore, tarot cards are not mentioned in the Bible. Yet, divination is. So, too, is sorcery, magic, and so on. If one wishes to categorize Tarot under one of these headings, the Bible's comments on those subjects might be applicable.

There is another problem. As a historian of magic and early Christian history, I would point out that when people living in the time period of early Christianity spoke negatively about supernatural things, they used words with a negative connotation—of course. However, the same beliefs and behaviors might be thought of positively in different contexts, and therefore, different word choices were used. Put differently, what Christians referred to as miracles, their critics referred to as evil or fraudulent forms of magic. For example, the story of Jesus turning water into wine would likely be viewed as a trick or, perhaps, sorcery. A more relevant example to Tarot can be found by comparing the story of Jesus' birth, as told in the gospel of Matthew, with the text that many fundamentalist Christians would point to in explaining their opposition to Tarot in the Old Testament book, Deuteronomy.

The story of Jesus's birth involves people called "magi" who used their knowledge of the stars in order to find Jesus. In Deuteronomy 18, one reads that divination is forbidden and evil. The magi (singular, "magus") are, by definition, people who do magic. In fact, the English word "magic" is etymologically derived from this root word. The magi in the story of Jesus's birth are practicing a specific form of magic, astrology, that is explicitly forbidden. Yet, they are presented to the reader of Matthew as though they are good people ("wise men") who are among the very first to revere Jesus. The "wise men" knew ahead of time that Jesus would be born and where that would happen. They also knew what and who he was to become. These are examples of divination, which, elsewhere in the Bible, is described as sinful, but in this context, is described in quite positive terms. It reflects well upon the magi, but more than that, it validates Jesus's identity to the reader. The use of the star (which, by the way, is the name of a tarot card) is a clear indication of astrology. Even in the unlikely event that the magi were to be understood as physically following a star (or some other object), the story depends upon astrological magic (or, if one prefers, astrological miracle). Much more likely, early Christians (as well as anyone else hearing the story) would have understood the notion of "following a star" as a way of describing the use of astrological knowledge; despite the fact that astrological knowledge is strongly associated with magic. Nonetheless, this story was intended to be understood in a positive connotation even by people who considered astrology to have a (sometimes) evil connotation. Note, too, that the story contains absolutely no suggestion that the magi should stop using their magic, or that their use of magic was morally excused only because of the positive purpose of finding Jesus.

My point here is simple. The use of the Bible in determining whether Tarot is "good" or "bad" will depend on highly subjective criteria. One first has to choose which biblical passages will be used for "proof texts." That choice will shape the answer in either positive or negative terms. Next, one must decide what is meant by words such as "magic" or "divination." One can interpret these terms positively or negatively and, furthermore, use biblical supports for either interpretation. My supposition on this matter would be that delving into this question will lead to an answer that is a greater reflection on a person's attitude *before* examining the Bible than *after* such an examination. Somewhat separately, I would also suppose that if an honest inquiry is made by an open-minded individual as to what the Bible has to say about such things, the predispositions of the people being asked to explain the Bible will carry more weight (in a hidden way) than the Bible itself. Again, differing interpretations can be substantiated using different biblical passages. Having said all that, somewhat customary responses to such questions have been formulated and passed on as conventional wisdom within the context of American Christian fundamentalism.

Let us consider some prominent Protestant Christian leaders who are well-known to American audiences. Billy Graham was, perhaps, the most eminent speaker in American Protestant circles throughout the second half of the twentieth century. Although a Southern Baptist, he had the respect of a very large number of Christians outside of that denomination (which, by itself, is a very large group). Like many preachers, Graham spent time answering the questions of the faithful or of those with an interest in the faith. It was not hard to find Graham's thoughts on Tarot. In a question and answer format, Graham responded to the following question which was posted to his website:

> For Christmas, my aunt gave our 12-year-old son a game that's supposed to be able to answer questions about the future. I asked her about it because I've never wanted anything to do with things like this, but she laughed and said it was just for fun. What would you say? (Graham, "Occult Games")

His answer:

> No doubt your aunt thought this is only an innocent game, but you're right to
> be concerned about it, because it could open the door to something that would
> be spiritually harmful to your son. Why is this? For one thing, playing this
> game could make your son think that things like astrology, tarot cards, palm
> readings, Ouija boards and similar activities are simply harmless pastimes. But
> they're not because they may bring a person into contact with occult spiritual
> forces that are absolutely opposed to God. This is why the Bible warns us not
> to have anything to do with them. (Graham, "Occult Games")

Although Graham explicitly states that "the Bible warns us not to have anything to do with them," the fact is, as I stated above, the Bible does not mention tarot cards (nor does it mention palm readings or Ouija boards). Note,
too, that Graham included astrology, which, as I said, was the means through
which the magi achieved their special status in the Bible as "wise men" and
the heralds of the advent of Christ.

Another prominent evangelical figure, associated with television minis-
tries, is Pat Robertson. His views are comparable to Graham's (and others),
and he references the same passage in Deuteronomy when talking about
magic. Robertson also expresses concerns about the demonic. He is in line
with that segment of the population that fears tarot cards are a portal by
which (actual) demons attack people (Robertson, "Tarot Cards"). In a segment called "Bring it On" for one of the shows on Robertson's television network, Robertson answers a question from one of his viewers who identifies
herself as a "believer in Christ." She notes that she had used tarot cards in
the past and they accurately told her she would be pregnant. She also says
that she never uses them for evil purposes.

Robertson's response is that the cards are definitely evil, and that the Bible
is clear on this topic. He then connects the cards to astrology (again, ignoring the magi and their praiseworthy use of astrology in this context) and
other forms of magic. Robertson insists that these forms of divination have
real power and that the power is connected to what he calls "spirits," which
are, in fact, "devils," he says. He speaks of the ability of astrologers and tarotists to accurately predict future events but insists that this is done through
demonic agency. He then tells his questioner that God will provide answers
to questions about the future. Robertson concludes by relating a story from
his life in which God revealed the sex of his child while his wife was pregnant.

Just as Christians can disagree on any other issue, so, too, will Christians be
found on different sides of the question regarding the religious and spiritual

propriety of Tarot. In an earlier chapter, I mentioned a couple of examples of Christian themes that were incorporated into Tarot with a clearly positive intention favorable to Christianity. Corine Heline's 1969 book *The Bible and the Tarot* was one such example. Another example from that chapter was Kathleen Binger's 1983 *Bible Tarot* deck which, like Leslie Lewis's 1995 *Christian Bible Tarot*, quoted scriptural passages and relied on illustrations from biblical stories to convey concepts associated with Tarot. Let us consider another example of the use of Tarot by those who see it, not only as consistent with Christianity, but as a spiritual benefit to their faith.

Wynn Wagner, an archbishop of the Old Catholic Church, wrote a book in 2012 called *Tarot for Christians: Lessons from Christ's Fool*, which begins with a scriptural reference from I Corinthians 4:10: "We are fools for Christ's sake." After a brief discussion of the history of Tarot and a bit of focus on Arthur Edward Waite, Pamela Colman Smith, and their tarot deck, the author goes through each card in the Major Arcana consecutively. Each card is introduced along with a scriptural passage.

The book's structure is based, to a significant degree, on "the Fool's Journey" associated with Eden Gray's book on Tarot. Archbishop Wagner is also familiar with various Kabbalistic concepts, symbolic elements, and philosophical constructs incorporated into Tarot. The meanings of each card are explored in a philosophical context as they would relate to the spiritual development of a Christian spiritual seeker. Along the way, the reader also gets a strong sense of the meanings embedded in individual cards, as well as the Tarot itself in the broad sense.

Wagner is not really interested in fortune-telling or divination in his exploration of the Tarot. His use of the cards is more meditative and prayerful with an eye toward personal spiritual growth. Each of the cards is clearly and comfortably situated in a broad religious context that the author, and the inclined reader, can embrace more strongly as they meditate upon these meanings. As discussed elsewhere in this book, the cards are loaded with specifically Christian symbolism. Consider the "Judgment" card, for example. Other cards, "the Hierophant" and "the High Priestess" started their histories off with more explicitly Christian names, "the Pope" and "Popess," respectively. Of course, the tongue-in-cheek reference to a female pope can fairly be dismissed as non-Christian. Still, the origin of tarot cards is in the clearly Christian cultural context of Renaissance-era Italy.

It is interesting to consider one card in particular to get a sense of how the Christian motifs, symbols, and meanings of Tarot have been reconsidered in a way that seems to lead people to reject, rather than embrace, the Christian identity of the cards. I'm thinking of "the Devil" card. A tarot card with a picture of the devil on it can be a bit off-putting to some people's religious sensibilities. It might understandably trigger a sense of foreboding or, perhaps, might be perceived as a declaration of evil—a sign that the whole context of Tarot is, for lack of a better word, devilish. In a way, such a person would be "judging a book by its cover." Put differently, one might see the cards as evil because one of the cards is "the Devil" and the devil is evil. Yet, consider something as obvious as it is overlooked: the devil also appears in the Bible, and Christians do not judge the Bible to be evil—just the opposite. So, in simple point of fact, the notion that a card called "the Devil" should cause some sort of trepidation in the mind of a Christian looking at tarot cards is both an inadequate explanation and rather inconsistent thinking. If such thinking was to be taken seriously, then the cards that show angels, gospel writers, the symbols of the Holy Spirit, and so on, should actually inspire the opposite reaction, should they not? I would posit that the cards themselves do not elicit any negative reaction from religiously minded Christians, or anyone else for that matter. Rather, there is a culturally constructed image associated with the cards that define them as dangerous or bad. Religion is just one cultural tool used in creating this reputation.

From the Fringe to the (not Quite) Mainstream

The reputation that Tarot has among religious people, then, is complicated by a couple of factors. First, defining "religious people" is problematic. There is quite a wide spectrum of attitudes that fit into possible definitions even if one were to limit their effort to Christians (broadly defined). Second, if one does arrive at a working definition for "religious people" in American culture, another problem would emerge in terms of establishing just what attitude that category of people have with regard to Tarot. Indeed, I have seen a spectrum of attitudes toward Tarot among the many people in my life that I, perhaps loosely, would define as "religious." We have just seen above that some religious leaders preach strongly against tarot cards while others find them quite useful for what might be called "spiritual exercises" (if I may steal a phrase from St. Ignatius of Loyola).

There is yet another matter to consider within the context of spirituality and Tarot, which is the place of the supernatural. Some people consider the tarot cards to have a "magical" quality in the sense that something supernatural is active and controlled by the reader. This is why they are viewed so negatively by some leaders of religious institutions. Not all who believe something magical happens with Tarot see the cards as bad. There are those who like the cards because of their "magical" qualities. So, we have an interesting point of agreement among both detractors and defenders: something magical is thought to be happening. It should also be pointed out, however, that there are defenders and detractors who would say that nothing supernatural is happening in a tarot card reading.

When asked if she thought there was anything supernatural associated with the cards, Rachel Pollack (a quite prominent tarotist) replied, "Supernatural? Don't know. Maybe" (Pollack, personal interview). This is hardly the response of someone taking a hard stand on the issue of supernatural powers and Tarot. For her, perhaps, it doesn't matter. I asked another prominent tarotist, Mary Greer, how do religion and spirituality relate to Tarot? She said that one can offer a range of experiences to people in teaching Tarot. Greer said she tends to respect and reflect the attitude of the student when she is teaching a person how to read Tarot. When working with the general public, Greer says she likes to keep things very secular in tone (Greer, personal interview). It might be pointed out here that Greer is also a priestess in the Fellowship of Isis, a group of people from a variety of religious backgrounds. They share a dedication to honoring the feminine elements in all the world's religious cultural traditions. For those who can properly be labeled as expert readers and teachers within the tarot community, there is room for a range of interpretations when it comes to understanding the place of religion and spirituality. There is also no such thing as an official position on how Tarot fits in with magic or the supernatural.

It does seem clear, however, that when a negative reputation is attached to the cards, it is very often explained in terms of religious belief or supernatural power. Yet, many people who would not describe themselves as particularly religious, even many people who are somewhat indifferent to religion, may also view tarot cards as suspicious or scary. They may associate Tarot with con artists. They might associate Tarot with dangerous supernatural forces. While these associations might lead some people away from ever interacting with tarot cards, other people are actually attracted to the cards for the very same reasons. A tarot reader who I interviewed in Oklahoma City in 2015 told me that many of her customers come to her for a reading partly because it makes them feel like they are doing "something naughty." A tarot scholar named Marcus Katz has written on this topic, from a broad cultural perspective rather than from the perspective of religious studies (Katz, "Tarot on the Threshold"). Katz is interested in more than the way outsiders view Tarot and the tarot community. He is also interested in how Tarot serves as a subject area or focal point of cultural interaction between tarot enthusiasts and others.

In other words, an ironic situation has occurred with Tarot at the level of popular culture. The mainstream of culture tends to appropriate Tarot as a symbol of the fringe or threshold. Yet, practitioners seek to promote a recognition of the subject within the mainstream while simultaneously preserving Tarot's esoteric mysteriousness, which helps to market Tarot (Katz, "Tarot on the Threshold," 290–91). Tarot has a certain popularity, or garners a certain amount of interest, because of the fact that it is a bit weird, perhaps even dangerous and, certainly, is perceived as outside of the mainstream. The success of tarotists in attracting an audience to themselves in particular, or to Tarot in general, would, theoretically, reduce the "exotic" or esoteric reputation upon which its interest is built. Yet, as Katz argues, the opposite happened and continues to happen in the first two decades of the twenty first century.

The increasing number of venues (psychic fairs, bookstores, video-conferencing, online environments, and so on) indicate that Tarot has a growing mass market. However, Tarot continues to be perceived as fringe or liminal. "[F]rom the year 2000," Katz writes, "we see a rapid growth of initiatives to elevate Tarot studies and increase its appeal across a broad audience, both in the United States and in Europe" (Katz, 282). He then discusses the American Tarot Association (ATA) and the Tarot Certification Board (TCB). These organizations reflect significant popular interest in Tarot. Yet, as Katz makes clear, these are also organizations that have a small core of leaders who invest a significant amount of time and energy while the majority of participants are active at a rather peripheral level, investing only small amounts of time and effort.

Katz himself is a member of the Tarot Association of the British Isles (TABI) which "seeks to promote high levels of academic rigor, professional practice, and collaborative Tarot projects in the arts, history, and religious studies in addition to professional training for Tarot newcomers" (285). Important groups in the United States include San Francisco, California's Bay Area Tarot Symposium and the Los Angeles Tarot Symposium. At the other end of the country, in New York City, there is an annual Tarot Readers Studio which began when the Tarot School was founded in that city in 1995. The Tarot Readers Studio attracts an audience from around the world. Those who speak and present at the Tarot Readers Studio are among the leading lights of the American tarot community and have included, among others, Mary Greer and Rachel Pollack.

Katz says, "Although these conferences appeal to 'serious' students, for most of the population, Tarot remains an ephemeral, borderline subject" (288). This brings us back to the matter of what people think of Tarot. What is it in the minds of "regular" Americans? For Katz, "a Tarot deck is widely recognized yet spuriously associated, without its audiences having any apparent awareness of the sources by which they have learned of it" (272). I would argue that, for many, those sources come from the religious communities with which they are associated.

At the beginning of the twenty-first century, the tarot community began to establish an online presence. Yahoo started a discussion forum in 2000. The tarot website aeclectic.com started in 2001. In 2009, *Touchstone Tarot* was developed as an iPhone application. There are numerous examples from all sorts of electronic media that demonstrate the ubiquitous availability of Tarot. In these examples, as with "brick-and-mortar" locations, there remains the tendency that Katz identified in which a small group of very active individuals take leading roles in popularizing Tarot by, in part, building upon its mysterious reputation with the general public. Even as that interest grows within the popular culture, the reputation of Tarot seems to persist despite the fact that "insiders" see Tarot in quite different terms.

For many others, their understanding of Tarot is shaped by how it is presented in the popular culture. Television and movies, of course, are quite important sources of influence. Other sources can involve the marketing of any variety of products. We have already discussed this in other chapters. So, here, let us briefly consider an example of how this phenomenon of Tarot as a marketing device has developed even outside America and Europe.

The 1990s saw a proliferation of Tarot into Asian markets which is still expanding. Japan has used Tarot in manga, comic book art, as well as anime. Tarot cards have been used as free gifts (*furoku*) for viewers and readers of these media. The Morinaga Chocolate Company even ran a campaign that gave tokens with its candy, offering a deck of tarot cards for customers that collected enough tokens. In order for such campaigns to succeed there must already be an interest in the culture, but that interest (in Japan or anywhere else) is certainly not founded on a widespread knowledge and appreciation of the Western esoteric tradition that developed Tarot. Rather, people seem to become intrigued with the cards because they heard of them in a story, saw them in a scary movie, had a reading one time, or were told by somebody that they are evil.

Put differently, people often have a strong but very superficial understanding of Tarot, even though the cards are quite capable of eliciting a strong mental or emotional response when encountered. Katz sums it up accurately: "Tarot remains a threshold activity with both liminal and illegitimate associations in popular culture. Tarot as a cultural phenomenon demonstrates the manner in which a body of knowledge can be widely disseminated whilst lacking substantial depth of information. It also evinces an area of interest where a small majority of active parties can constellate larger groups of generally inactive individuals" (290).

Some Sociology Grad Student Learns to Read the Cards and Joins the Tarot Community

Emily Auger's two-volume collection of writings, *Tarot in Culture* (2014), has a great chapter entitled "Becoming a Tarot Diviner." It is actually an excerpt from a doctoral dissertation by a sociologist named Danny Jorgenson (yes, doctoral dissertations can examine some pretty odd subjects). His work was later published as *The Esoteric Scene, Cultic Milieu, and Occult Tarot.* Jorgenson is a professor of Religious Studies in Tampa, Florida, but did his graduate research in Phoenix, Arizona—which is where he developed an interest in Tarot and in the esoteric community. Jorgenson spent significant time learning how to read the cards and learning about the beliefs and practices of people who are members of the tarot community. The people he encountered during the course of his research in the mid-to late 1970s included practitioners, enthusiasts, and individuals who sought out readings but were not, themselves, tarot practitioners of any sort. One might say that, over the time he was doing this research, Jorgenson "went native" in the sense that he became accepted into the community and took up the lifestyle (for lack of a better word) while fully developing a base of knowledge about Tarot and the community. Although he remained fully wedded to the scholarly approach and maintained his role as a scholar throughout the period, his appreciation for Tarot grew. His inclinations to reject the occultist worldview, or *weltanschauung*, of his subjects became quite tempered by a sense that he developed of the group and its members as being reasonable, yet different, people. Personally, I suppose most groups who can be defined as different from the mainstream have positive, as well as negative, characteristics simply because they are outside the mainstream.

Although he had begun to learn how to read tarot cards before, Jorgenson and his girlfriend became students of a couple that were experienced readers with a clientele. This allowed him to develop his skills and to develop personal connections to members of the community. Jorgenson describes tarot card readings as comparable to a performance, but at the same time he notes that there is a need to become familiar with an esoteric history and philosophy. He describes it this way: "[R]eading the Tarot was like telling a story. There always seemed to be a story in the cards, and my job was to find it in the symbolic images, bring it alive, weave these meanings together, and relate them to someone's life, hopefully, in a way they found meaningful" (Jorgenson, 754).

He became involved with other readers in a variety of venues. He attended workshops, conferences, psychic fairs, and a number of more informal social settings that allowed him to view and experience the life of people in (and connected to) the tarot community in the Phoenix area and beyond. He also became friends with many of the people he interviewed. He revealed the fact that he was a researcher to many of the tarotists whom he became better acquainted with, noting that they tended to approve of being research subjects as they expected to find validation in an objective, scientific examination of their lives and experiences as tarot readers. I think that says a lot about the kinds of people one should expect to encounter in the tarot community. Jorgenson acknowledged that his relationship with Ham, a man he met at a bookstore for occult topics, developed a relationship not unlike that between an adept and a master in an occult education.

Tarot readings for Jorgenson were time consuming and demanded a significant amount of effort and energy. Because of this, he eventually limited the amount of readings he did for free. As part of his research, Jorgenson attended psychic fairs in which he and his girlfriend would rent a booth and offer to do tarot readings for the public. He contrasts these readings to the more personal ones that he would do for friends and acquaintances. Reading for strangers was a different kind of "performance" in that they expected some sort of insight or dramatic moment and they expected it somewhat quickly. He also describes a difference between what are called "straight readings," based primarily on the cards, and what are called "cold readings," which involve the reader studying the querant for potential cues from their dress, appearance, voice, affect, and so on, that can be used in performing a reading.

The strongest contrast between doing a "straight reading" and a "cold reading" could be found in the comparison of settings. The setting of one's home or a friend's home, like the setting of a familiar casual environment, allows for a certain pace and style of reading that is unlikely to be available in a setting such as a psychic fair. The setting of a psychic fair, as per Jorgenson's experiences in Arizona, involves paying for a booth which would be in close proximity to the booths of other readers while any number of potential customers enters the area. Tarot readers are mixed in with palm readers and others. In fact, the operator of any particular booth may present themselves as sellers of more than one psychic skill. Customers choose, in whatever way they wish, whoever they wish to get a reading from.

In the setting of a psychic fair, Jorgenson notes, there may be quite a bit of ill will between readers who feel they did not get a good location for their booth or that they were not treated with the appropriate level of respect and dignity given to another reader. The same tendencies would be expected in a craft fair or any environment at which people are selling similar goods and services within an area that they share with peers while competing for customers. Jorgenson also notes that many of the readers are, of necessity, primarily concerned with the need to meet their expenses and obtain a profit over the course of the day. The readers are, it is important to consider, competing for customers in the setting of an open business competition. Doing so, one supposes, could bring out something ugly in people, regardless of their occupation.

From the perspective of the (potential or actual) customers at the psychic fair, there is a desire and expectation to be impressed, and to be impressed immediately, with a reading. If the narrative that begins to unfold organically from the layout of the cards does not resonate with the client, the reader will quickly intuit a sense that they are getting a customer who is dissatisfied and will likely have a negative impact on other potential clients. Thus, the pressure to perform is raised and accelerated. In such circumstances, Jorgenson says, many tarotists will resort to "cold readings" as a way of effectively engaging the client. This can certainly be understood as revealing something unseemly about the environment and about tarot readers, particularly for those who prioritize the cards and their conventional meanings over the readers. However, one could also argue that what Jorgenson calls "cold readings" overlap with the intuitive role of the psychic. That is, if one accepts the view that the purpose of the cards is to assist in an intuitively psychic process, the reader would be performing in an appropriate manner and one consistent with the expectations of the clients.

One tarot author prefers to describe the basic process of a reading in terms that are both accurate and idealized, simple and honest, without pushing salesmanship or claims of the supernatural:

> Each reading is essentially a story. . . . One card represents you and tells you who you are as a protagonist; others say what's happening to you, what did happen to you, what will happen. Other cards show up as people wandering into your story; others create plot and action. You lay out the cards, and there on the table you have the outline. You have the who, what, where, and when. You then flesh out that skeleton with your own circumstances, you populate it with the people in your life, and, using the intuitive cues provided by the cards' images, you fit your story on to the story in the cards. It's not necessarily about telling the future. It is about retelling the present. (Crispin, xii)

For many tarotists, though, there is a sense that the psychic fairs are a form of professional prostitution. Like an artist who paints according to the whims and expectations of their patron, the tarotist needs to earn a living with a skill set that they would wish to use differently. Jorgenson refers to certain tarotists as "gypsies," and he does so in a rather negative way. He says that the tarot community uses the "gypsy" label to describe the illegitimate practitioner who does not adhere to the moral order of the community. Such figures are not accepted as representative of most people in the tarot community. They are con artists. Still, a con artist can purchase a booth at a psychic fair just as easily as any legitimate or honest reader.

Yet, the psychic fair is only one setting. Things could be quite different for a tarot reader who has their own parlor and can afford to maintain an environment conducive to the style and manner in which they wish to read tarot cards. That, however, may be a luxury unavailable to some readers. There are, of course, a number of environments that would be conducive to happier, more respectable, behavior. In addition to psychic fairs, there are conferences, public lectures, book stores, and so on. These are places where, in addition to private settings, members of the tarot community can interact in more friendly forums or, as with other professions, gather to vigorously debate their differences.

The topic of how members behave is different than the topic of how members think or what they believe. Tarot, at a certain level, is part of the occult—the subject matter of things hidden and associated with the supernatural. That is to say, a tarotist may be a type of occultist or, at least, one having some familiarity with the subject. Jorgenson, a social scientist by training and profession, certainly has the inclinations of a skeptic on these matters. Yet, having placed a chunk of his life experience into this world of thought and the community of its practitioners, he concludes,

> Occult thought, in this regard, is similar to scientific ideas about objects like the id, superego, atoms, germs, black holes, anomie, and deprivation, most of which are also unavailable through ordinary experience. Like scientific knowledge, occult realities require more or less extensive training and socialization whereby the adept learns to see what is otherwise unavailable. . . . The process of becoming an occultist is a gradual experience. It generally is not marked by a single dramatic moment after which the world is suddenly different. This process may be described as interpretive drift. (761)

Making Money with Tarot Cards

Having looked at Danny Jorgenson's work as a sociologist studying the tarot community, it is evident that the people he shared space with in the psychic fairs of the 1970s in the American southwest were not getting rich.

The fact that a primary concern for many of them was to cover the expense of renting a booth and meals suggests that they could not always be sure to accomplish that minimal level of business. Something similar could be said of many tarot readers today. One might compare them to a variety of small business entrepreneurs who have modest successes or unfortunate failures. The peculiar nature of their profession does not entirely differentiate the tarot reader from, say, a restaurateur, a street vender, a used bookstore owner, a musician, or any other number of people trying to make a living. Anyone entering one of those professions knows that they might not succeed just as they know that some people have been very successful. Of course, they hope to be in the latter category, but there are no guarantees. Perhaps the most that can really be said is that, while there is certainly a market niche in America for tarot card readers (who often perform other services such as reading palms), few strike it rich. A few more, however, do well enough to stay in the business for years; maybe they are even somewhat comfortable in financial terms.

James Wanless, for example, designed a deck called the Voyager Tarot. In some respects, Wanless can be viewed as quite representative of the tarot community from the 1980s to the present. That is, his view of Tarot is to replace the cards traditional association with fortune-telling with a sense of the cards as inspiration for what he calls "fortune-creating." He considers the cards to be a tool to facilitate the user's self-directed creation of a desired future. The cards are presented as inspirational and meditative, filled with symbolic meaning that can be used to self-direct one's life by focusing on goals and character traits.

Wanless has a successful business in which he describes himself as a "life navigator and mentor." Wanless began his professional career with a doctorate in political science. In the 1970s, he was teaching at Columbia University. Now he sells a number of products and services related to making people more motivated and productive by focusing on creativity. Among other things, he holds seminars designed for businesspeople to use Tarot as a means to the end of being more materially and professionally successful.

Personally, I was brought up believing that having a job that you love is a form of wealth that everyone should strive to achieve. It seems to me that the business of tarot attracts primarily those who wish to be employed doing something they love. Indeed, as is the case with my own job as a history professor, there is so much satisfaction that comes from enjoying your vocation that it offsets low (a relative term, anyhow) pay. For others, making a living in Tarot is impossible, but this does not preclude using tarot readings as a supplementary source of income (a "side gig," in the contemporary vernacular).

This author's daughter, for example, is a graduate student in a physics program. Yet, she also has an online business in which she sells tarot readings and astrological charts (www.etsy.com/shop/SeafoamReadings). For her, as for many others, there is something gratifying in the experience of reading a stranger's cards and getting feedback in their reactions. It is also gratifying that a base of customers wishes to patronize your particular brand of tarot reading, just as it would be gratifying to a person who sells food to know that there is a base of customers that wish to buy their burgers or burritos from you instead of "the other guy" or anyone else.

As someone who studies astronomy, her use of astrology in reading tarot can be expected to have a significant depth of meaning. Of course, astronomy and astrology are extremely different things. Still, the former evolved from the later as the scientific revolution took place in the sixteenth and seventeenth centuries. Copernicus, Brahe, Kepler, and other great astronomers in history used their art (it was not yet called a science) to make horoscopes. They are connected, although, admittedly, the distinctions between astronomy and astrology are enormous and significant. Nonetheless, a person who is knowledgeable in both areas can find a number of interesting ways to use a background in astronomy to better develop the astrological facets that are part of Tarot. Having done so, imagine the possibilities in terms of making tarot readings more elaborate, interesting, and personalized. To be clear, she sees only a very small overlap between physics and metaphysics and she finds the common tendency to link the two to be inappropriate. While some of her card spreads and interpretations have an astrological leaning, for the most part, she follows conventional and traditional form and interpretations in her tarot readings and the meanings she assigns to cards.

Although my daughter makes a small amount of money in this endeavor and does not invest as much of her time in Tarot and astrology as she does in physics, she enjoys the experience and is able to make use of the income as anyone who has struggled through the costs of graduate school can appreciate. Yet, in interviewing my daughter about her online tarot business, I learned even more about her clientele than about her as a proprietor.

Her prices are intended to be as low as possible for her customers while also making it worthwhile for herself. The prices she offers are comparable to what some others in the business charge. However, there are some readers who charge significantly more for their services. She allows customers to pick a particular layout of cards and a topic to be explored. She sends a picture of the layout and a written narrative of her reading of those cards all on a PDF file. For her, it is more fun than business in that "it doesn't feel like a chore." She calls it a hobby.

While online identities can be tricky, even deliberately deceitful, it seems clear that many of her clients are women fifty years of age or older. Another large segment of her clientele are young men and women under age twenty-five. The gap in the age groups of her customer base has raised the question in her mind of a possible decline in the interest of Tarot in American culture between the late 1980s and around the year 2000. She wonders if Tarot has, since then, entered a new cultural phase with increasing interest and new directions. Although most of her clients are from the United States and Canada, she has had a number from South Africa, Malaysia, and the United Kingdom. It seems to her that the male customers are a bit more interested in financial topics while the women tend to ask more relationship-oriented questions, even though they will seek readings on a broad range of questions and topics.

Quite a few inquiries are about life advice. Her clients usually do not ask for help with major decisions, but the more serious the matter, the less likely she is to advise. She makes it clear that she is not a counselor nor would she want to be asked for medical or legal advice, although people will occasionally ask for such things. The customers sometimes believe that she is a psychic or is presenting herself as such. They may also assume a connection between Tarot and astrology. This is one of the reasons why she added astrological readings (she started the online shop doing only Tarot). Some of what she offers is purely astrological, separated from Tarot. Her tarot readings, however, do include astrological elements.

Some people already know what they want to hear and are, in all honesty, simply seeking validation. Others are looking for an answer in a rather random manner and find it fun to allow that answer to come in the form of a tarot reading. This makes the reading a bit like a sophisticated coin toss. At other times, however, her clients approach her with more significant issues and seem to be seeking an answer with quite weighty implications. She is developing a document for her website that lists her ethical boundaries. She makes it clear that she is not a counselor and that medical or legal advice should be sought elsewhere from professionals in those fields. She does Tarot as entertainment and, at other times, to spur meditation.

I asked her about being part of a wider community and to what extent did her experiences make her feel connected to a tarot community. She reported modest connections with like-minded people being developed but not friendships or business partnerships. If one was inclined, she says, the possibility of interacting more deeply in the online world is open to those seeking such a thing. The fact that she has the shop and the skill set associated with reading Tarot has resulted in inquiries and reactions from people that she goes to school with or encounters in other social settings.

Some people find it strange that a grad student in physics would have an interest in Tarot. Others find it amusing. They might react by asking for a reading. But, they might also find it off-putting, spooky, or even religiously offensive in some cases.

Another interview I conducted to get a sense of members of the tarot community who are in the business of Tarot, so to speak, involved a small shop in Norman, Oklahoma, called Sandalwood and Sage. Sandalwood and Sage is owned by Deborah Clark and Natasha Rice. I interviewed Natasha in her shop, which I had visited as a customer several times before asking her to answer questions and give comments on the Tarot part of her business. Deborah and Natasha have been in business for over twenty-five years. They left Norman for a few years and lived in Columbus, Ohio, where they continued to operate, but then they moved back to Norman in 2007.

Tarot cards and books are a relatively small, but not insignificant portion of their inventory and sales. The cards are kept in a glass display box with a couple of shelves. This space does not hold all their stock, so there is some outside the case. They sell a lot of different decks. They don't stock many decks in quantity. Four copies of any particular deck would be about the most that they would have on hand at any given time. Decks are kept sealed in original packaging, and Natasha or Deborah will use a computer to show what individual cards look like if a potential customer wants to see (in order to avoid opening the package before making the sale).

According to Natasha, some customers buy cards as an impulse purchase. Others take the purchase of a deck more seriously. The latter group would often have a preference for Sandalwood and Sage as a setting because the proprietors would be viewed as able to provide better customer service than a large chain bookstore such as Barnes and Noble. The customer experience would include a higher level of professional confidence in the sales staff as well as a higher comfort level. Going into a store where tarot cards are a small part of an inventory that includes many items that are quite unrelated or designed to appeal to a very different category of customer would make a tarot customer at Sandalwood and Sage feel more at ease than, for example, at a Barnes and Noble. The entire shop has a certain "vibe" that would, in the case of a large bookstore, be limited to a section of a single shelf, if it could be created at all.

The decline of brick-and-mortar bookstores has modestly increased traffic in customers browsing for tarot cards. As with other products that the store sells, people sometimes browse in their store but proceed to buy online—the same issue that affects many different types of brick-and-mortar locations, from office supplies to home appliances.

While browsing the book section of Sandalwood and Sage, I noticed a copy of Eliphas Levi's *History of Magic*, translated by Arthur Edward Waite, an interesting document to anyone with an interest in the Western esoteric tradition. But, the shop caters to a primarily progressive customer base. Bumper stickers, T-shirts, and other items frequently push a political or social message. There is also a strong New Age and neopagan component to the shop's inventory.

Tarot cards and crystals, however, appeal to people across the political spectrum. Natasha knows that many of her customers are politically conservative. She has had conversations with some of her regular customers, hearing comments from other customers that indicate they are conservative voters. If one considers the voting data of the city of Norman, the surrounding area, and the state as a whole, they will find that the area is quite conservative despite the fact that there is a major university campus (the University of Oklahoma, better known as OU) in Norman. The success of their business would require appealing to conservative customers despite having some inventory that is clearly geared toward progressives. Their customers from outside of Norman would likely be from distinctly conservative communities. The statistical probability that they would have, and need, conservative customers is high. Unlike many of the T-shirts and bumper stickers sold in the store, tarot cards do not assert a political message and, therefore, are among the products that might grab the attention of conservative customers.

There are occasional tarot readings done in the store. A tarot reader might be at the store for a weekend and receive clients while attracting potential customers to Sandalwood and Sage. For Natasha and Deborah, Tarot is a small, if distinctly important, part of their business. It contributes to sales because it contributes to the unique character of their shop. Those looking for something outside the mainstream that can be both fun and a little bit deviant or weird but, also thoughtful or provocative, find this shop delightful. Tarot fits well into the creation of such an environment. This is what seems to make their business work, and it is, at the same time, characteristic of what many people in the tarot community find attractive.

Stuart Kaplan, a graduate of the University of Pennsylvania's Wharton School with a degree in marketing and finance, may be the most important name to know when considering Tarot as a business. He began getting involved with Tarot while on a business trip in Germany in the 1960s. He encountered his first deck at a toy fair (the *Swiss 1JJ* deck), and immediately placed an order for a huge amount and bought the rights to the product. Back in the United States, he began to sell tarot cards through mainstream bookstores. By providing mass-produced and affordable decks to the American consumer, Kaplan eventually became the epitome of the successful tarot card business.

Because of his entrepreneurship, Kaplan deserves to be considered a leader in the Tarot Renaissance that began in the late 1960s. He has written pamphlets and developed numerous concepts for a variety of decks over the years. In addition to marketing new tarot card decks, Kaplan's company, US Games Systems, also sells versions of many old European decks, including the Tarot de Marseilles. He has also written and edited one of the most significant publications in Tarot: the multi-volume *Encyclopedia of Tarot*. In fact, Kaplan has written several other pieces on Tarot. When he first began in the tarot business in the 1960s he wrote *Tarot Cards for Fun and Fortune Telling*. In 2018, he co-wrote (with Mary Greer, Elizabeth Foley O'Connor, and Melinda Boyd Parsons) a biography on Pamela Colman Smith, the artist who illustrated the most famous tarot deck, the Waite-Colman Smith deck. Kaplan owns the rights to that deck as well.

While Kaplan is clearly an astute businessperson, one gets the sense that the accumulation of wealth is a means to an end. He loves the artwork associated with Tarot, and perhaps more important, Kaplan is a collector of all things Tarot. It seems that his life's work has as much to do with his accumulation of cards and the paraphernalia of the history and culture of Tarot as it does with succeeding in business. This is not to say that Kaplan is dispassionate about his financial endeavors. Yet, over the course of his long life, he has amassed a collection of incredibly interesting items. For example, he obtained a deck that was made by Abner Doubleday, the Civil War Union general who became famous for inventing baseball. Kaplan has also acquired a large number of personal items and writings of famous figures in the history of Tarot. He even had a card from the Visconti-Sforza deck—the oldest of decks, dating to the fifteenth century. It was one of several items that went to auction at Christie's in New York City in 2006, where it sold for $20,000 to the Peterhof museum in Russia (Winick).

In between the local or online tarot readers and the vastly successful Stuart Kaplan, there are many successful figures in the tarot community who are able to travel around the world lecturing, attending conferences, and teaching seminars. They have a significant personal following and, at times, are able to extend their reach to realms outside the world of Tarot. They are authors of books and articles. One good example of this is Rachel Pollack. She is the author of *78 Degrees of Wisdom*, one of the best books on reading tarot cards, and a designer of tarot decks. Interestingly, she is also a comic book author who wrote a series of issues in the DC Vertigo imprint,

Doom Patrol. She has also worked with bestselling writer, Neil Gaiman as a consultant for his writing.

Like many businesses, then, Tarot attracts people who seek to make a living doing what they love. Not many succeed. Yet, as a point of comparison, consider music. The few rock stars out there inspire countless others to dare to live out a dream, and although they may not get far, they often enjoy the experience of their ("fool's") journey. As a niche market, Tarot is on a solid foundation in the sense that there are so many readers, decks, books, and stores that indicate the existence of a large base of customers and the possibility of a significant volume of financial transactions. There is clearly a sizable community of people spending their time and money on Tarot. I take that to mean that Tarot has a secure place in the economic culture of the country.

What Are These People Thinking? Tarot and Psychology

An interesting psychological experiment was done in 1948 by Bertram Forer. Forer gave his students a test that claimed to be using data given by the students to assess their personality characteristics. The results of the test were not actually collected or considered in the context of the individual student taking the test. Instead, each student was given what appeared to be their individual test results but, in fact, were identical descriptions listing character/personality traits. Although every student got the exact same feedback from the faux test, each student thought that the description was a very accurate representation of their individual personality. The feeling that the description is individualized and accurate, even though it is generalized and applied to anyone, is called the "Forer Effect."

This experiment has been repeated in a number of ways over the years and certain commonalities have been determined to be associated with the testing procedures and the results. The descriptions supplied to the individual subjects of the experiment are made up of vague generalizations, including:

> You are more capable than you appear, but you do not use your potential
> You are too much of an independent thinker to easily accept the statements
> of others at face value
> You have a tendency to be self-critical

Most of the traits described in the supposedly objectively developed profiles are positive traits. A few are negative and a few more can be interpreted as somewhat positive/somewhat negative. This is a critical component of the

Forer Effect. The experiment also requires that the subject have some confidence in the person conducting the experiment or in the process of the experiment. This is not to say that a skeptical person would be unsusceptible to the typical result.

Another critical element in the Forer Effect is confirmation bias (or self-serving bias). If the false feedback from the experiment is perceived as consistent with the subject's preconceived sense of self, they are more inclined to believe it. This is linked to the fact that most of the supposed results of the personality test are positive while only a few of the traits listed are negative—and even those may be interpreted as a mix of positive and negative attributes. Consequently, the subject finds the results easy to believe and not at all uncomfortable. The intentional vagueness of the feedback statements further strengthens the tendency toward confirmation bias by allowing the individual to interpret the information as they wish.

One can imagine how the Forer Effect would be used (intentionally or not) by tarotists or psychics. The impact on the subject is that they feel accurately described in apparently unique terms. There is a sense of awe and amazement, as if a deeply personal revelation has been given despite the fact that such is not truly the case. What appears to be specific, unique, and personal turns out to be, in fact, rather generic. Despite this, a certain "wow factor" is achieved. Perhaps what Forer was really tapping into relates, at some level, to a tendency of people to be more aware of personality traits, particularly positive and intimate ones, when they see them in themselves as opposed to when they see them generalized in most people. Our personalities, like our minds and bodies, have unique attributes. But, in so many ways, we are much like everyone else. We can be forgiven if we sometimes forget about that.

Forer was able to shed light on a psychological process in a way that is comparable to explaining a magic trick or exposing a con artist. For critics of Tarot, astrology, and the like, the Forer Effect is a useful psychological tool for explaining away some of the misplaced sense of wonder associated with magic and the supernatural. It is certainly an example of how psychology can help us to understand, at least in some ways, how Tarot works. There are other, perhaps better, ways to understand Tarot by referring to psychological concepts.

Most people have a passing familiarity with the concept developed in the 1910s by the Swiss psychologist Hermann Rorschach. Looking at inkblots, like looking at clouds, makes us think of other things besides the image in front of us. Whatever our minds project (in a metaphorical sense) onto the inkblots might suggest something about the way we think or what we think about, and Rorschach understood that this might be helpful in terms of psychological diagnostics.

In some senses, one might usefully compare the images on a tarot card to a Rorschach test. For those who "intuitively" read the Tarot, this is particularly true. That is, one can view the cards and allow their mind to make a connection that inspires some sort of meaning that can then be projected onto the reader or the querant. There are some obvious (and major) limitations to the notion that a tarot card is comparable to an inkblot. For starters, the cards are usually assigned certain meanings independent of the reader or the querant. And, whereas the inkblot test is used to help understand what a person may be thinking about or how they think, the tarot cards are usually used in a way that suggests to the person what (or how) they might think about something. That is, the former is intended to reveal something of the thought process while the latter is intended to influence the thought process. This comparison is predicated upon a gross oversimplification of both tarot cards and Rorschach inkblots. We should not delve too deeply into such a superficial comparison. Instead, let us consider another psychological test that has some interesting points of comparison with Tarot.

The Thematic Apperception Test, like the Rorschach test, is a "projective" test. Such tests are designed to use ambiguous imagery as a means for revealing subconscious concerns which, once exposed, can indicate conditions that could be improved with psychological therapy. The Thematic Apperception Test (TAT) was developed at Harvard University in the 1930s by Henry Murray and Christiana Morgan. The TAT makes use of a series of cards with a variety of ambiguous images on them. Some show a person or people; others show a setting. The cards suggest emotions and circumstances but not in a clear, unambiguous sense. It is the combination of ambiguity and suggestive elements of the pictures that make the TAT work by helping to reveal aspects of a person's mood, personality, or mentality.

An individual is given a set of these cards and asked to place them in whatever sequence they wish but to do so with the purpose of creating a narrative. The person then tells a story using the cards as a series of illustrations. This story, and the manner in which the person has used the images, is thought to reveal something of the mental state of the storyteller. This test has been effectively used, not only in clinical therapy but, also, in criminology, business, and military situations where there is a need to understand how a particular personality might respond to certain circumstances.

In some respects, the layout of a tarot reading and the narrative of the reader based on the cards is comparable to the TAT. Consider that there can be a degree of ambiguity in the conventional meanings associated with the specific tarot cards. Consider, further, that the tarotist must create a context in which to interpret the cards and there is a clear similarity with the TAT.

Both Tarot and the TAT have similar flaws that make them less useful or questionable in several situations. They are both subjectively interpreted. Therefore, a rigid consistency, if that is desired, is impossible to achieve. This applies not only to the interpretation of the results but to the administration of the test. Just as different tarotists may interpret the same card in somewhat different ways when it applies to a particular context, so, too, might psychologists interpret a person's narrative differently after observing their use of the cards in the Thematic Apperception Test.

One can certainly not equate the two: The Tarot and the TAT have far more differences than similarities in both form and function. Yet, the similarities are intriguing and they point us to the psychological elements associated with Tarot. I think this is particularly true of tarot cards when they are used, as they often are, for meditative purposes. It is essential to keep in mind that Tarot, like psychology, is not designed or intended to produce (or to express) rigid formulaic and mathematically precise evaluations. For example, consider the topic of employment. Many people share the experience of hoping for career advancement. Yet, even among people in the same career fields, a hoped-for opportunity is not always desired for the same reason or to the same degree. I might want a promotion for primarily financial reasons while someone else may want the prestige that comes with that promotion. Yet, both may be factors. We may be at different points in our careers or have different family considerations or, we may be affected differently by intra-office politics and the like. As Einstein (supposedly) once remarked, "Not everything that can be counted counts, and not everything that counts can be counted."

It might be a little less surprising, now, after reading the above, to know that tarot cards can be (and have been) used effectively in clinical psychological settings. Arthur Rosengarten is an example of a clinical psychologist who has found Tarot to be useful as a therapeutic device. Rosengarten, the author of *Tarot and Psychology: Spectrums of Possibility*, does not believe that the cards have "magical" healing properties. Rather than divination, Rosengarten sees the cards as involving what he calls "empowered randomness" (97). He contextualizes Tarot into forms of therapy that use games: role playing, expressive art therapy, and so on (14). The deck is a tool for self-exploration. Unlike Rorschach inkblots or the Thematic Apperception Test, tarot symbols not only stimulate unconscious projection, they have their own meaningfulness (99). Rosengarten uses that meaningfulness to engage with certain concepts, values, emotions, and behaviors in the clinical setting. Although the cards can be dealt at random, the concepts that they convey are always meaningful and often easily applied to individual circumstance in a way that is conducive to self-introspection.

Imagine a man at the end of his day randomly drawing a tarot card with the intention of pondering its meaning in the context of his own life. Let's say, hypothetically, that he randomly draws the "Ten of Pentacles." This card traditionally signifies family, home, legacy, and a few other related subjects. The man finds it meaningful to think about these topics in the context of his own life. Perhaps he decides to make an appointment with his lawyer to update his will. Maybe he starts thinking about some career advice he once received from his father. The point is that in some way the man has used the randomly drawn card to stimulate thought and action that he will use to improve his life in some meaningful way. One could argue that the cards are meaningless, but it is obvious that the person's actions have meaning. And, furthermore, it is clear that the person's actions can be in response to whatever random card stimulated the thoughts that led to those actions.

Rosengarten emphasizes meaningful coincidence throughout the book and links it to Jung's theory of synchronicity—a causal connection through meaning (Jung, *Synchronicity*). The "empowered randomness" of the cards, as Rosengarten puts it, can be put to practical use regardless of any supernatural or metaphysical claims. Rosengarten writes, "Freud's . . . proper aim of psychoanalysis [was] to make the unconscious conscious. This to a large degree is a key function of Tarot as well, that is, to make possibilities conscious. Tarot cards either clarify, interconnect, or amplify what already exists in consciousness, or else they bring unconscious possibilities into conscious awareness" (66). Readings in a psychologically therapeutic environment will not magically reveal any material. What they do is create an environment that helps people reveal what they feel, think, and even deny. Rosengarten emphasizes that the randomness of the cards underscores (rather than invalidates) their importance (39).

It is, essentially, unnecessary to explore whether something supernatural (i.e., magical) happens with tarot cards. Something *meaningful* happens, and that is the important, practical, matter upon which Rosengarten develops a therapeutic approach using the cards. Let us consider a couple of examples. The first example involves a women's support group for whom Rosengarten did a tarot reading. The reading resulted in the group engaging in a debate about their internal dynamics. Important elements about how members of the group viewed its purpose revealed an explanation as to why some level of dissatisfaction had developed among members who had split into two factions.

Without getting into the specific layout of the cards and examining individual card meanings, one can state that the reading opened up a dialogue on the topic of internal disagreement within the group regarding the purpose of the group. Some of the members valued the group because it provided an environment of people with shared experience that helped individual members to set aside the psychological challenges of living with their condition and simply enjoy one another's company. They found it to be therapeutic because they could leave certain concerns behind while they socialized. The other members, however, felt that the group was doing them a disservice because they were not focusing on the psychological challenges of their shared condition and, consequently, were not moving toward a conclusive outcome or coping strategy. This had been the state of affairs for some time before Rosengarten met with the group. Yet, none of the members had really understood what was going wrong. They simply felt that there was a dynamic in which some people in the group were not properly contributing or, even worse, were in denial or, perhaps, being disruptive.

The cards happened to facilitate an exploration of a genuine problem that could not be addressed until it was identified. Rather than get involved in an analysis of *how* the cards work (supernatural or coincidental), Rosengarten and the group simply *allowed* the cards to work by being open to discuss, in a meaningful way, the topics to which the cards are referential.

In another instance, Rosengarten did a study of domestic violence involving two separate, but related, groups. One group was composed of men who had been convicted of committing acts of domestic violence against women. The other group was composed of women who were survivors of domestic violence. To be clear, the group of survivors were not the actual victims of the group of perpetrators. They were unrelated and did not know of one another, but they were connected simply by the fact that all parties concerned had been involved with domestic violence.

The study, which was done in California in 1996, involved a group of thirteen men who had been convicted of domestic violence crimes. A separate group was composed completely of (thirteen) women who were survivors of domestic violence crimes. One purpose of the study was not to use the cards to get biographical details of the subjects but, rather, to see if the cards' meanings converged with tendencies seen in the groups (perpetrators and victims) as a whole (207). Another purpose was "to open empirical channels of possibility" (243). His hypothesis was that "as an acausal, synchronistic reflector of human experience, the Tarot will reveal certain meaningful underlying group trends that are consistent in the personalities of perpetrators and victims" (199). He acknowledges the fact that much of this study is not subject to valid and quantifiable research. However, he also points out that, despite the obvious empirical limitations, some aspects of the study are, in fact, objective and quantifiable.

Three of the thirteen men got "the Hermit" card, reversed, in the position of their tarot card layout for "present situation." For the women, a knight showed up five times in the "obstacle" position of the layout of cards done for them (199). Female archetypes were common in the male readings, while knights were common throughout various positions in the female readings. Interestingly, these are not mathematical likelihoods at all, but these are quite relevant symbols for the experiences and personalities of the test subjects which emerged in a statistically unlikely manner. A conventional reading of "the Hermit" card in a reversed position, for example, would suggest antisocial behavior associated with loneliness. Such a description is in line with a mindset typical of perpetrators of domestic violence against women. Having that card show up reversed in three out of thirteen readings is statistically unlikely and, yet, relevant in terms of its symbolic meaning. The fact that knights were common in the readings for females implies that the role of young men in their lives, and in the context of the subject of the reading, is unusually significant, and again, the cards that showed up in the reading (as well as the manner in which the cards appear in the layout) is outside the realm of statistical probability.

Rosengarten's hypotheses were somewhat validated by the (admittedly anecdotal) data taken from the experiment. In this experiment, the psychologist was "testing," as it were, the relevance of the cards' meaningfulness in a context where meaning was clearly established in terms of relationships, behavior, personality, and experience. This particular experiment was designed to examine if the archetypes associated with Tarot could be meaningfully filtered into a clinical context where the most and least relevant archetypes would be obvious and the clinician could easily evaluate which archetypes came to the fore in the readings. This smacks of an attempt to determine if something supernatural is taking place in the readings—which is not only scientifically unreasonable to do but also too subjective to elicit confidence in most people's conclusions. Perhaps it is fair to call such a test interesting but scientifically meaningless. The least we can say is that something weird happened.

However, the fact that Rosengarten could demonstrate therapeutic value in settings where he employs tarot cards is beyond dispute. In addition to the two case studies mentioned already, Rosengarten also writes about a client of his who was dying from HIV-related illnesses and was asked to use the Tarot as a meditative device toward the end of his life. Rosengarten suggested that the man browse through the Waite-Colman Smith deck and remove the cards that struck him as most intriguing. He was then asked to contemplate what topics or issues the images represent in general (at least, according to his personal impressions) and then to consider how those topics and issues apply to his life. The patient found this process to be comforting in his final weeks of life.

Let us now briefly return to something that was said a few paragraphs back about archetypes and the knight cards. Tarot certainly employs numerous archetypes in the imagery of the cards. Some of these are rather obvious: "the Hermit," "the High Priestess," "the Lovers," and "the Devil" are just a few. All of these cards are part of what is commonly called the Major Arcana. The Minor Arcana, which are the suit cards, have a (sub)section that we call the court cards. They include the pages, knights, queens, and kings. There are four court cards in each of the four suits, making a complete set of sixteen court cards. Each suit (wands, cups, swords, and pentacles) has its own basic meaning that touch upon matters of personality (although their meanings are not limited to personality traits). Further, each of the figures in the court are associated with certain personality traits. So, one might take all of the knights, for example, and develop their meanings by adding what is represented by the knight to what is represented by a particular suit (say, swords). Thus, the "Knight of Swords" would have features associated with knights in general added to the general features of swords; which allows for the creation of a particular set of attributes to be associated with that card.

If we consider the fact that there are four of each court card and multiply that by the four suits of the Tarot, we get sixteen combinations. Tarotists with an interest in psychology and a desire to develop archetypes have linked these sixteen cards to what psychologists call the Myers-Briggs personality types. The Myers-Briggs Type Indicator (MBTI) is summarily described by Dante DiMatteo here:

> In brief, the MBTI attempts to codify in shorthand the theory advanced by the Swiss psychoanalyst C. G. Jung in his landmark survey *Psychological Types*, published in 1923. Jung's theory of personality posited that the human psyche is governed by four primary cognitive functions (thinking, feeling, sensation, and intuition), each one of which manifests itself in one of two orientations, either extra- or introverted, yielding a total of eight "dominant" functions. Elaborating upon Jung's work in subsequent decades, Katharine Cook Briggs and her daughter, Isabel Myers, refined the theory by adding two secondary personality types, "judging" and "perception," which also take extra- or introverted forms. These two extra elements, in combination with the others previously mentioned, yield a possibility of 16 personality "types."

Each of the sixteen possible combinations is applied as corresponding to one of the tarot court cards. At a certain level, one can readily acknowledge that it is merely a convenient coincidence that there happen to be sixteen MBTI categories and sixteen court cards. True enough. It is also true, and relevant, that personality types are commonly associated with the character of kings, queens, knights, and (to a lesser extent) pages. Thus, the linkage between Tarot and the MBTI has a quite natural, even obvious feel, making it easy to further develop. Consider that there are aspects of personality and character associated with things such as age and gender. These may be broad generalizations or even sterotypes, but they are, nonetheless, applicable to some degree.

By combining the court cards with the MBTI, a grid of personality traits familiar to all is connected to a set of symbolic images (the court archetypes and the suits) that are easy to understand and relate to in terms of people that we know (including ourselves) and with whom we interact. So, when a court card shows up in a tarot card spread at a position that indicates, for example, a family member, the character traits assigned to that card will likely suggest a person or personality that the querant can identify. In this manner, the level of detail that can be offered in Tarot is greatly expanded and more deeply personalized. It certainly remains somewhat ambiguous and none of the randomness associated with cards is lost. Whether one wishes to be dismissive or accepting of such a psychological approach to Tarot, the fact remains that this system can be applied in an effective manner if one wishes. There is no claim to magical or supernatural power in this context, nor is there a claim to precision. That is, the tarotist will admit that he or she cannot assert that a precise thing will happen to a specifically named person in an exact location at a predetermined moment in time. Rather, what is being asserted is that insights can be gleaned from the random drawing of cards that place symbolic imagery and concepts into a layout or spread with assigned meanings in each position. Put even more simply, this method is capable of giving an open-minded person some things to think about that are as useful or profound as that person will allow. Or, maybe it's all bullshit. If so, that conclusion, too, is dependent on the perspective of the individual considering Tarot, not on Tarot itself.

In her *Cultural History of Tarot*, Helen Farley has a criticism worth quoting at length:

> Just as the New Age has tried to align itself with the "reputable" pursuit of science, it has frequently manipulated the jargon and principles of psychology to substantiate its claims. The psychotherapist most frequently used to this end is Carl Jung . . . with his theories of archetypes, the collective

unconscious and synchronicity. Jung's work is frequently used to validate the correspondences between tarot symbolism and the symbolism within mythology, art, and literature as well as esoteric ideas and motifs from other cultures. Sallie Nichols, in her book, *Jung and Tarot: An Archetypal Journey* urged us to connect with the "archetypes" present in tarot symbolism to aid us on our journey toward wholeness, called by Jung "individuation." Other tarotists saw the four suits of the minor arcana as corresponding to Jung's four functions of personality. (155)

Fair enough—and yet the fact that it "works" remains. The psychological concepts that are applied in the use of Tarot can, and do, have practical benefits for meditation and therapy, even if one reasonably posits that these concepts are artificially grafted upon a stack of pictures with no meaning other than that which is assigned to those pictures. There is a further nuance to consider in tempering Farley's criticism. It may be true, to some extent, to argue that tarot readers have latched onto Jung's name in arguing for some form of validation by way of association with psychology. It is clear that tarotists do not depend upon this association. Rachel Pollack, for example, has expressed some criticisms of Jungian influences upon tarot readers. In an interview with this author, Pollack criticized Jungian readers for sometimes imposing a view upon the cards rather than allowing a "free-flowing energy" to come from the cards and stimulate a reaction in the interpretation of the reader or the querant. The point being that tarot readers are quite comfortable criticizing or even rejecting Jungian-derived interpretations. I conclude, therefore, that an effort to claim validity by association with Jung is neither sought nor needed in the mind of at least one well-known member of the tarot community. Pollack's views are probably not entirely unique in this regard.

Tarot readers often refer to a dichotomy of card reading styles between conventional readers, who use the traditional meanings associated with the cards' symbolism, and intuitive readers, who tend to allow a fluid, even open-ended, interpretation of cards based on an immediate and instinctive response of a person to the card in front of them. Psychologists who allow for the intuitive model, allowing their clients to interpret the meaning of cards without regard to established convention, argue that doing so allows the client to speak freely and openly, even initiating discussion and dialogue. Two such psychologists, Kooch and Victor Daniels, point out that the monologue of an expert reader of the cards is not as useful as a dialogue brought about by reactions to the cards. As we saw with Rosengarten, the authors would also claim that "a subjective interpretation of an evocative image can be useful" in a psychological interaction (Daniels and Daniels, 20–46).

They tell other psychologists that "those who already use art therapy, play therapy, a sand tray, or psychodrama are likely to be able to slide seamlessly into working similarly with cards" (87). Their book, *Tarot at a Crossroads: The Unexpected Meeting of Tarot and Psychology*, offers some examples of how they use Tarot in therapeutic settings. For example, she advises people along these lines (paraphrasing): Select a card that represents one's self. Select another card that represents the *other* (an important person) in one's life. Then, select a card (or two or three) that describes the emotional or mental state perceived in the other. Similarly, select a card(s) that represents the mental/emotional state for one's self in this relationship with the other. Above each of these, select a card that would represent the ideal self/the ideal other. Then, above all these, select a card that represents a resolution to the issue(s) associated with the relationship (chapter 5).

The intent of the exercise is to stimulate dialogue and reveal important aspects about the relationship and how it is perceived. The traditional or conventional meanings of the cards are disregarded in the exercise. Instead, the images on the cards are examined and evaluated by the client, who then uses their own definitions of the cards to talk about their relationships and organize an outline of the psychological dynamics active within those relationships.

In chapter eight, the authors look at group dynamics in families, workplaces, and so on by using selected cards to represent people. The client uses projective dialogue to create interactions between the figures represented by the cards and thereby offers insights into aspects of the relationships. Client choice in positioning the cards can also be instructive in various ways. For example, closeness or distance from the client's card can be used to indicate the closeness of a relationship. An inverted card can be used to indicate some negative aspect the client perceives in the relationship. Focusing a bit on images can be beneficial in terms of creating some distance between the client and the other individuals in their lives by discussing emotions or behaviors in a more general way that can, later, be more clearly applied to their understanding of those specific relationships. As the authors put it, "discussing images can be a non-threatening way to get people to talk about ideas or suggest possibilities" (162).

In other respects, Daniels and Daniels do use the traditional conventions associated with the symbols of Tarot. One chapter, for example, looks at the numbers of the suit cards, ace through ten, and discusses so-called "divinatory meanings" associated with each card. They also discuss the traditional meanings of the suits (chapter 14). The following chapter goes into a discussion of the court cards that examines some of the ground we covered above in discussing how the Myers-Briggs Type Indicator can correspond to the court cards. Daniels and Daniels broaden the meanings a little bit in order to reduce the limitations that could be imposed on the court cards by age and gender. For example, Knights do not necessarily have to be male figures if, for instance, they could more easily be associated with a person on a quest or one fighting for a cause. Pages do not have to automatically refer to young people; they could refer to youthful traits, or someone who is a student or an apprentice (240).

One of the chapters in *Tarot at the Crossroads* is illustrated with a deck known as the *Pagan Ways Tarot* (designed by Anna Franklin). Daniels and Daniels discuss these cards in terms of what they call "psychological links" to a variety of psychologists. Of course, Freud and Jung are discussed. Other examples include Martin Seligman and Alfred Adler. Each of these "psychological links" is elaborated upon by reference to concepts associated with that psychologist in what the authors call a "reflection." Alfred Adler, famous for coining the term "inferiority complex," is discussed for his theory of "individual psychology." Seligman became infamously associated with torture after the United States government drew upon his research into "learned helplessness" in order to interrogate terrorism suspects (Seligman was not personally involved in overseeing torture). At any rate, Daniels and Daniels use the tarot deck and their backgrounds in psychology in this way to create linkages between the two that are quite interesting. In particular, I was fascinated at the connection made between the "Death" card and the famous model developed by Elisabeth Kubler-Ross positing five stages of grief associated with death (denial, anger, bargaining, depression, and acceptance). Linking the "Death" card to Kubler-Ross's five stages is obvious, even simple, but the linkage also demonstrates the ease and appropriateness of linking Tarot with psychology on a therapeutic and meditative level.

I don't wish to exaggerate or to glorify Tarot as powerful or profound. It does have its limitations. Rather, I wish to show that it has potential value in more places than a carnival booth. It should not be dismissed derisively any more than it should be presented as a panacea.

Conclusion

This chapter attempts to answer the question who are the people that make up the tarot community. The answer is difficult to arrive at because they are clearly such a diverse set. They may be viewed, stereotypically, as cons or as superstitious, and maybe some are. It is clear, though, that some of them are quite intelligent and as decent as any other group in society. Religiously, they are a group that is sometimes maligned by traditional or conservative religious leaders. And, yet, among their number, the tarot community counts many religiously minded individuals of their own as well as a number of spiritual individuals (if one prefers to make a distinction between religiosity and spirituality). They may be neopagan, New Age, irreligious, or they may maintain a sense of neutrality and respect to whatever faith may be held by those they encounter. In short, it would be a mistake to try to define a basic religious mentality for the tarot community; it is simply too diverse to support such generalizations.

With regard to defining the tarot community in some economic or monetary sense, we are, again, unable to say anything definitive because there is such an extensive range of possibilities for locating people who make a living or a few extra dollars in Tarot. There are a small number of people who have significant financial success. At the same time, there are many who try and fail to make a living with Tarot, and more to the point, there are many people who exist in between these extremes.

In this last context, consider Jane Stern. She is best known for the work she does with her husband, Michael, as writers who specialize in culinary and travel topics. They are quite successful in their professional environment and are regular guests of National Public Radio's *The Splendid Table* program. Much of their work connects culinary and travel topics to popular culture. One of Jane Stern's books is on the subject of Tarot. Her book, *Confessions of a Tarot Reader*, presents the cards as tools for a self-discovery.

Her book is structured with one chapter for each of the twenty-two cards of the Major Arcana. While she does discuss the traditional meanings of each card in an interpretive manner, she ties these meanings to circumstances and experiences that are readily identifiable to the personal experiences common to life. For example, she explores the process of looking for answers within one's own self while discussing the "Hermit" card. In discussing the "Justice" card, she opines on the importance of being honest with one's self and doing what is right. Balance and moderation are the elements associated with the "Temperance" card and, therefore, become the subject of the chapter on that card. Whether we view these topics as philosophical or psychological, there is an obvious linkage between the meanings associated with tarot cards and the issues associated with living a happy, productive life. Why, then, wouldn't there be more books such as these?

We have also seen in this chapter that psychology and psychics, astronomers and astrologers, can all find a place in the tarot community. Even among themselves, there can be a great deal of difference in how they perceive their own community. In a review of the Ronald Decker and Michael Dummett book *History of the Occult Tarot*, Lee Burston took issue with the authors' inclination to believe that tarot enthusiasts follow the trends set by various authorities in their community over the decades. Bursten rejects the very notion that there is or ever has been any actual "authority" in the tarot community. Consequently, it would be impossible to make the claim that tarotists follow such authorities. Bursten says, "Tarotists have always been an independent and free-thinking lot, who tend to rely on their own preferences rather than slavishly following particular doctrines."

One possible point of agreement that may be found between tarotists and their critics regardless of background and perspective is that they are a weird people. I think most of them would wear that as a badge of honor while their critics might see it as evidence of deviance or being misguided. In one way or another, most of the tarotists that I have encountered or read strike me as somewhat other than normal. Yet, the word "normal" is almost too broadly defined to be useful. Besides, who wants to be normal?

PART II

CHAPTER 4

The Art of Tarot

Tarot as Renaissance Art

Tarot cards were created during the Renaissance, and art was an important part of Tarot since the beginning. Long before Tarot developed a reputation for magic, it was a canvas for artists. *Tarocchi* (to use the original Italian name) decks were created by artists. The game cards were created in northern Italy, the very heart of the Renaissance. The artist Bonifacio Bembo painted one of the earliest extant decks, the Visconti-Sforza deck. As discussed in chapter one, this deck was created around 1450 when Francesco Sforza married Bianca Maria Visconti, uniting the two powerful families and making Francesco Sforza the Duke of Milan. Albrecht Durer, the northern Renaissance master, created some pieces of artwork based on images from Italian *tarocchi* after his first trip to Italy in 1494. His 1514 engraving, *Melencolia*, is an example and can be found in the Metropolitan Museum of Art in New York City.

Also discussed in the first chapter was the Sola Busca deck, which was produced by the artist Nicola di maestro Antonio in 1491. It is unknown whether Nicola composed the seventy-eight figures as his invention or if he had been commissioned. It is certain, however, that copies of the deck were reserved for a number of clients. The artist engraved copper plates so that the cards could be reproduced. The copper plates have survived. The trumps (what would later be called the Major Arcana) and the court cards (of what would later be called the Minor Arcana) depict kings and heroes of ancient Greece and Rome along with people and events from biblical history. The numeral cards have fantastic

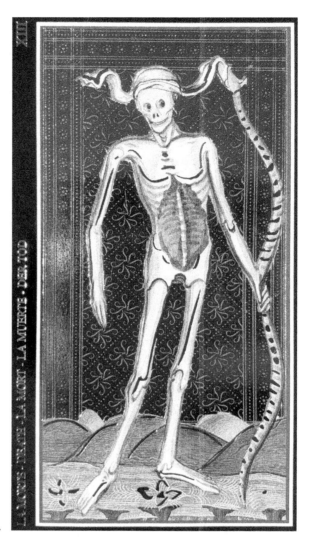

A modern version of the "Death" card based on the Visconti-Sforza Tarot.

figures and scenes mixed with alchemical allegories and representations of daily life. The cards are slightly larger than typical tarot cards. The symbols are somewhat modified versions of the contemporaneous standard. The coins are simplified as discs. Wands have been made into clubs. Cups have been modified into more sophisticated amphorae. Swords remain swords.

While all of the cards represent a set, I would contend that they are, in fact, two games. This would be something like having checkers and chess pieces in a matching set and sharing the same board. There is no decisive evidence that

I am aware of that would indicate both decks being used in a single game or for a single purpose in which the cards are all mixed. One must remember that *tarocchi* was a game played with the trumps and that other, distinctly separate games were played with the numbered (and court) cards. It is not until the nineteenth century that the two decks are combined into one and the parts referred to as Major Arcana and Minor Arcana.

In the early nineteenth century, a set of these cards was studied by Pietro Zani in Naples. Zani's interest was in engraving, but he indicated that the cards were kept as two separated decks in different collections. The cards were also studied by another Italian, Count Leopoldo Cicognara, who gives no indication that there is a single game or use that involves combining the trumps (the *tarocchi*) with the pip and court cards. Cicognara's interests were in dating the cards' origins.

In the eighteenth century, the cards were owned by the Busca family of Milan. They were obtained by the Busca-Serbolini family in the nineteenth century. Thus, the name of the cards—Sola-Busca—is derived from families that had owned them. Only one complete set of the cards is extant. Those cards were obtained by the Pinacoteca (Art Gallery) di Brera in Milan in 2009. They were purchased for 800,000 Euros (over 950,000 American dollars) by the Ministry of Italian Heritage.

William Hughes Willshire wrote about these cards in 1876 for the British Museum in *A Descriptive Catalogue of Playing and Other Cards in the British Museum*. Willshire described twenty-three cards of the Sola-Busca Tarot, which indicates that they had been distinct and separate from the other playing cards. The British Museum had acquired the set in 1845. In 1907, the Busca-Serbolini family donated a series of photographs to the British Museum. These photographs included all seventy-eight cards.

Arthur Edward Waite and Pamela Colman Smith's Deck

The Sola Busca deck became quite influential on Arthur Edward Waite and the artist Pamela Colman Smith, who after seeing images of it displayed in London, used it as a model for their 1909 deck. Since then, the Waite-Colman Smith deck has become the most recognized and imitated deck, as well as the most commonly used deck, in the English-speaking world.

By that time, of course, the linkage between Tarot and magic had been embraced and developed. Tarot had been grafted on to an esoteric tradition that included Kabbalah, alchemy, astrology, and other forms of magic each with their own iconographic traditions that allow for a collage of symbolism to be associated with each individual card. In essence, the individual cards, which held symbolic meaning from the beginning, could be modified with additional imagery in order to illustrate their characteristic traits relative to esotericism. Waite and Colman Smith represent this trend most effectively. As Helen Farley explains in her book *A Cultural History of Tarot*, when describing some of the features of the Waite-Colman Smith deck,

> The Aces featured a large hand appearing from a cloud and holding one of the suit signs. The pip cards two through ten were the most unusual feature of Waite's deck . . . [They] featured the requisite number of suit emblems but these were incorporated into a scene in which people, buildings and landscapes were also accommodated. These scenes were designed to correspond to their divinatory meanings as ascribed by Waite. These minor arcana cards, which originally corresponded to those of the ordinary playing card deck, were totally transformed to facilitate tarot's role in divination; a powerful illustration of tarot's evolution from a game to an esoteric device. (145)

In sociological and cultural terms, Tarot functions on a level that is both symbolic and allegorical. A card or its imagery may represent a particular concept. For example, the woman taking firm yet gentle control of a lion by holding its jaws represents strength. This is symbolic in that the picture represents a particular virtue. Allegory, however, is the use of a story, a narrative, that uses symbolic representations. Allegory does not need to be oral or written. It can be visual and, consequently, tarot cards can use allegory and symbolism just as much as, say, a mural, a portrait, or a fresco. This is the dynamic that Tarot taps into and that Arthur Edward Waite and Pamela Colman Smith, in particular, captured with their deck of cards. It must be said, as a reminder, that Tarot had been moving in this direction from the time that Court de Gebelin and Jean-Baptiste Alliette began to associate Tarot with magic in the eighteenth century. However, the artwork of Pamela Colman Smith and the concepts that Arthur Edward Waite wished to illustrate clearly demonstrated how powerful art could be when applied to the esoteric meanings of Tarot.

The year 1909 represents the beginning of a turning point in the history of Tarot because the artwork of the Waite-Colman Smith deck would eventually establish a widely recognized, respected, and employed set of images. In the years that preceded the creation of the Waite-Colman Smith deck, the artwork of Tarot was far from standardized even though some decks, such as that of Ettiella's and what came to be known as the Tarot de Marseilles were generally recognized.

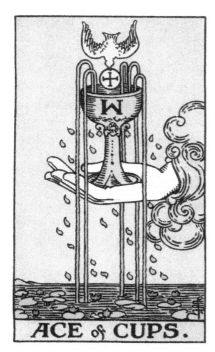

"Ace of Cups" card from the Waite-Colman Smith Tarot.

"Strength" card from the Waite-Colman Smith Tarot.

Waite and Colman Smith were members of the Golden Dawn. Members of the Golden Dawn had always been encouraged to make their own personal deck of cards. It was at the time that the organization began to dissolve that this deck was produced. It is also quite important to note that Waite published a book, *The Pictorial Key to the Tarot*. It was for that purpose, in fact, that he had paid Pamela Colman Smith to make the illustrations. The dissolution of the Golden Dawn ended the secrecy associated with the group's teachings about Tarot and allowed for greater public attention and diffusion of Tarot into popular culture. That process was gradual but it was stimulated by Waite's book and Colman Smith's art.

Pamela Colman Smith's background in art was linked to the symbolist movement that emerged in the 1880s and carried through the first decade of the twentieth century. She was not a prominent artist, nor was the symbolist movement as significant as other artistic movements of the period, such as post-impressionism in France or expressionism in Germany. Paul Gauguin and James Whistler are categorized as part of the symbolist movement although they are more strongly associated with impressionism. Edvard

Munch's *Dance of Life*, which might be the best example of the genre, shows a woman at three stages of life: virginal in white, older and carnal in red, then elderly and closer to death in black. The images are simplified and the colors are basic. Emotion and idea are emphasized over realism.

Symbolism is, in fact, more associated with writing than with the visual arts, but as in the earlier nineteenth-century case of Romanticism, there is an element of spirituality and an aspect of rejecting modernity while embracing the natural. The symbolists were less conventional and traditional in their religious expression and often open to spiritualism. An example of this can be seen with Joseph Peladin, a French writer who was a devotee of the occult and a Rosicrucian. He was influenced by the writings of Eliphas Levi and personally acquainted with Gerard Encausse, aka Papus, both of whom were major figures in nineteenth-century occultism. Peladin organized the *Salon of the Rose and Cross* in Paris. The salon was the location of both an occult society and several art exhibits.

One can see how Pamela Colman Smith is representative of this movement with links between the occult and art. The symbolist movement, however, was not entirely occultist even though it is associated with the names Peladin and Colman Smith. Symbolist art emphasizes emotion over realism. It was drawn to the world of dreams and focused on weighty topics such as death and evil. It is also characterized by imagery that is intended to be suggestive rather than explicit. I think that this last statement hints at the lasting power of Colman Smith's work on tarot cards.

Consider what was said earlier about how Tarot functions on a level that is both symbolic and allegorical. There is an ambiguity in the imagery on the cards that is partially focused through the meanings assigned to the positions in which the cards might be laid (for example, past, present, future). The esoteric meanings of the cards, and therefore, the artwork, should allow for a range of meaning to be latent until they are personalized and specified in the mind of the querant or through the interpretation of the reader. The allegorical nature of the cards allows a lot of ambiguity but it also prompts toward suggestiveness. As a person begins to take in the meanings suggested in the cards' imagery, their own experiences, attitudes, and beliefs will naturally impose more detail on to the suggested material and move from the implicit to the explicit.

While art, generally speaking, has great potential for such a process, symbolist art, in particular, is quite effective in allowing the transition from a general range of meaning and ambiguity in the cards to a specific emotional or psychological resonance for the particular person whose contact with the cards has the intent and purpose to discover some personal truth. The artwork of Pamela Colman Smith, I believe, was ideal for the form and function of Tarot. I would go even further: the value of the symbolist influences would continue to produce the same effective results for Tarot long after the symbolist movement itself faded from the scene or evolved into other forms such as fauvism.

It is interesting, too, that the time period in which the Waite-Colman Smith deck was created was one of increasing commercialization and mass-production. Such circumstances may have allowed the set of images to eventually reach a wider audience. The Waite-Colman Smith deck would eventually become the most popular and recognizable tarot deck in the world. Many other tarot decks are clearly based upon, or influenced by, it.

Emily Auger, who has a doctorate in art history and has written extensively on Tarot, studied more than one hundred twentieth-century tarot decks (mostly from the last three decades), finding that the Waite-Colman Smith deck serves "as an effective prototype or, to use the anthropological term, 'type specimen,' relative to which others might be analyzed" (*Tarot and Other Meditation Decks*, ix) The basic principles and concepts, fully expressed in the Waite-Colman Smith deck, have found numerous variations of expression in other decks that have attached additional elements without ever completely negating tradition.

At one level, then, the artwork of Pamela Colman Smith became the standard for a majority of tarot card decks. It is representative of the core elements and concepts associated with Tarot while, at the same time, it has a broadly accepted form and a nearly universally accepted style. At another level, Colman Smith's artwork reflects the esoteric tradition that had been established over the previous two centuries prior to the production of the Waite-Colman Smith deck in 1909. Of course, much of the credit for the insertion of this esoteric tradition into the artistic imagery belongs to Arthur Edward Waite. It was his effort, after all, that defined the meanings and concepts that were intended to be represented in the artwork of Colman Smith.

The significance of Pamela Colman Smith has been more fully appreciated in recent years. A 2018 book edited and published by Stuart Kaplan is the first significant biography of the most important artist in tarot history. Along with Kaplan, Mary Greer is one of the contributing writers of a book that is biographical as well as a resource for studying the sources related to Colman Smith and, therefore indirectly, her period and place in the history of Tarot.

The basic principles and concepts, fully expressed in the Waite-Colman Smith deck, have found numerous variations of expression in other decks that have attached additional elements without ever completely negating tradition. A number of decks have Arthurian themes. For example, there is a Merlin deck by R. J. Stewart and Miranda Gray in which the Major Arcana cards all represent stages of the life of Merlin based on Geoffrey of Monmouth's twelfth-century *Vita Merlini*. Auger points to this to demonstrate that the archetype (as associated with the famous psychologist Carl Jung) is frequently used to validate correspondences between Tarot and mythology, literature, and art (*Tarot and Other Meditation Decks, passim*).

Just as numerology, alchemy, and astrology were grafted on to the Tarot in the past, so, too, have modern artistic movements and literary traditions which reflect the appeal of a variety of communities. There is, for example, an herbal deck that is one of many themed tarot decks produced by Stuart Kaplan's company, US Games Systems. It grafts the lore and mystique of herbs on to the Tarot, thereby appealing to a particular community whose interests can be bridged in such a themed deck. Although herbs are obviously central to the imagery, the deck is based on the Waite-Colman Smith images. Herbal magic, of course, has a very long tradition and it serves as yet another example of Tarot incorporating other forms of magic (or vice versa).

Aleister Crowley, Lady Frieda Harris, and the Thoth Deck

The Thoth Deck, the Tarot created by the notorious occultist Aleister Crowley and the artist Lady Frieda Harris, has the status, unofficial and subjective as it may be, of being the second most important deck of the twentieth century. It was produced for the sake of illustrating Crowley's 1944 *Book of Thoth*, which can refer to the book that Crowley wrote about the Tarot, as well as to the Tarot itself and to the deck that was later created from Lady Harris's artwork.

The book included some of Crowley's earlier writings as well as material written specifically for the book. The project began when the two met in 1937. Harris gave Crowley a stipend while they were engaged with the project. So, it would be inaccurate to refer to Crowley as her patron (one could more appropriately argue the opposite in terms of the financial relationship). It is clear that Crowley dictated many of the details to appear in the pictures and, at times, required work to be redone. It is also clear that Crowley's prominent status in the occult field was well-established and well-known by the time the two started working together. For her part, Lady Harris was something of a novice in the field, and Crowley was her mentor in magic. Yet, in terms of the project, it would be inaccurate to see the development of the book and its illustrations as anything other than a collaborative effort. Lady Harris arranged for a small number of public displays of her artwork,

Skullcap

XVII The Star

"The Star" card from the
Herbal Tarot.

in and around London, in 1941 and 1942. The book was finished in 1944 as the Second World War was raging and the Allies were starting to turn the tide against Nazi Germany.

The Waite-Colman Smith deck had come out a few years before the beginning of the First World War. Thus, the period of time in which these two decks were created coincides with the most disruptive and deadly period of human history. The political and military upheaval of the period would certainly have social and cultural implications too profound to explore here, but these events would certainly have an impact on the world of art that, in this chapter, provides our context for an examination of Tarot. The art world, of course, underwent a series of profound transformations and trends during this period. So, it is no surprise that the art of Frieda Harris should be quite different than the artwork of Pamela Colman Smith, despite the fact that both of them, along with their associates who shared a background in the Golden Dawn, were determined to incorporate the iconography, archetypes, and traditional symbolism of the Tarot into both decks.

Lady Harris's artistic and stylistic influences are generally described as a combination of art deco and, most especially, Projective Synthetic Geometry. There are a lot of triangles, diamonds, spheres, and the like in these cards, and that is, as the name implies, characteristic of the artistic style known as Projective Synthetic Geometry. This is particularly emphasized in foreground images. The art deco components are distinctive, yet ornamentation in art deco is frequently geometric. This provides these two styles with a natural bridge, or link, of sorts. Indeed, one can argue that art deco, and many other art forms and styles, are a pastiche of sorts. The symbolist movement and fauvism (which were influential upon Pamela Colman Smith's art) also had some influence on the development of art deco.

In other respects, I consider the style of Frieda Harris's cards as having an element more in the vein of the earlier art nouveau style of the 1890s and early 1900s. There is often a sinewy, organic, flow that makes it more elegant than the streamlined, simple, flat shapes often associated with the art deco movement and its machine-crafted appearance. The art deco movement of the 1920s and 1930s was not only an influence upon Harris's tarot art, but everything from Tiffany jewelry to the Chrysler building. In looking at Frieda Harris's tarot art, there is, I believe, even an influence from the 1910s cubism movement (particularly, synthetic cubism) which, like tarot cards in general, uses a collage style. Synthetic cubism drew upon different textures and surfaces and might use multiple media in a single piece such as Picasso's 1912, *Still Life with Chair Caning* which used rope and oil cloth. And, as is obviously the case with the art form that Harris is primarily associated with—Projective Synthetic Geometry—cubism draws heavily on geometric shapes and patterns.

In terms of imagery and symbols (although not in terms of media), tarot cards are, in essence, collages. So, the eclectic style of Harris, drawing upon the styles that had developed from the late nineteenth century through the 1930s, is well-suited to the medium of Tarot. She uses both geometric forms and organic forms. She uses a number of visual textures, and varies her style of lines from one card to another. There is a great deal of symmetry and polish in the images, although one can also find some free-flowing forms as well. All of these differences and variations are used in a manner that gives the viewer a sense of layers and depth in each card.

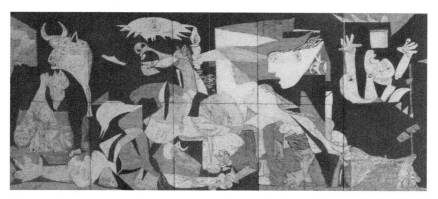

Picasso's *Guernica* (1937).

"The Tower" card, which Crowley also called "War," is a very good example of the influence of cubism in that it is a pastiche of objects which are dissected and rearranged so as to appear to be presented from more than one viewpoint at the same time. In Picasso's *Guernica*, perhaps the best-known example of cubism, there is a light that looks like an eye in the upper part of the picture. In the Crowley-Harris "Tower" card, there is a similar image in a comparable location.

Crowley renamed "the World" as "the Universe." That card, along with the "Ace of Swords," are good examples of the blending of styles into layers, each done in a different style, that creates a visual depth and provides an interesting contrast within the frame. The "Ace of Swords," is also a good example of the art nouveau influence, as are the "Two of Wands" and "Three of Cups." Although Crowley changed the name of a few of the Major Arcana cards, much of the imagery remains traditional in the sense that familiar forms are present throughout. Yet, stylistically, Harris clearly infuses the particular images with her eclectic style.

"Justice" is renamed "Adjustment," and "Strength" is renamed "Lust," but both are clearly recognizable in form, although very different than other decks in terms of style. "The Hermit" card keeps the same name and has the familiar bearded old man as a form in the picture, but again, stylistically, the card is quite distinct from previous decks. The same can be said of the "Wheel of Fortune" with the traditional elements presented in Harris's style.

Whereas the pip cards of the Waite-Colman Smith deck took a major step in the history of Tarot by using scenic images with people and interesting settings that correspond to the meanings of the cards' numbers and suits, the Crowley-Harris pip cards return to the older tradition of simply showing the object of the suit and the corresponding number of objects. That is, the "Seven

The "Tower" card from the Thoth Tarot.

of Cups," for example, is a picture of seven cups. Unlike some of the older decks, these cards are much more ornate, and there is a certain feel in the design that corresponds well with the card's meaning, but they are basically a picture of seven cups. Contrast that with the Waite-Colman Smith "Seven of Cups" and one still sees seven cups, but each one is filled with a different thing and there is a person in the foreground who, although their back is turned to the viewer, appears to look at the cups with wonder or surprise.

Although Harris publicly displayed the watercolor paintings that she did for each of the illustrations that were put in the *Book of Thoth* when it was published in 1944, an actual deck was not published until 1969. Crowley died long before, in 1947. Although Harris lived until 1962, she too did not live long enough to see the deck printed on a commercial scale. This is largely due to the fact that she was never satisfied with any proposals to produce the deck for sale in bulk. This is another significant difference between the Thoth deck and the Waite-Colman Smith deck, which was in print along with the publication of Waite's book in the teens.

Art or Craft?

During the late nineteenth and early twentieth centuries, it was not uncommon for tarotists to make their own decks or to color in the unfinished decks provided by a manufacturer. This is still occasionally done today, but most decks are mass-produced and, as such, the claim that they can accurately be called "art" may fairly be questioned on that basis alone. Even in those instances where an individual creates their own deck (partially or completely), one might reasonably be expected to use the term "craft" (no pun intended) rather than art. Emily Auger contends that Tarot is primarily a "low" form of art but emphasizes that it performs all the functions of art (*Tarot and Other Meditation Decks*, 9–10).

Salvador Dali, an artist of no small repute, created a tarot deck for his wife, Gala, in the 1970s. Movie producer Albert Broccoli asked Dali to make a deck intended to be used in the James Bond film *Live and Let Die*, which Broccoli was producing at that time ("The Tarot Card Deck Designed by Salvador Dali," *Open Culture*). However, that deal fell through. Nonetheless, Dali continued making his tarot deck as a gift for his wife. The deck was eventually published in 1984. Dali put his own image on "the Magician" card. Although Dali's style is distinct, the cards have traditional elements that make them recognizable to anyone familiar with Tarot. The numbering system and titles of the Major Arcana, as well as the suit and court cards of the Minor Arcana, follow a conventional format. Associations with famous artists, such as, in this example, can be used to assert that Tarot is, indeed, art. After all, can one claim that Dali was simply playing at crafts—drawing and coloring pictures in basic imitation of others used in the past?

So, if the person making the cards is widely recognized as a great artist, it is certainly understandable that their tarot illustrations are genuine art. There is

Salvador Dali's "Magician" card.

another consideration that might arise relative to the question of whether or not Tarot is art. That is, what if the person making the cards is not necessarily an artist but that person is employing works of art in the manufacturing of their cards? There is a good example of this involving William Blake, the English artist and poet considered to be one of the eminent figures of the Romantic period of the early nineteenth century.

The designer of the deck is Ed Buryn, who did much more than simply apply one of Blake's illustration on to a card. Blake's views on numerous topics and his writings were incorporated in his choices of pictures, but beyond that, other aspects of his deck were designed to incorporate Blake's art, poetry, and philosophy. For example, the tarot suits were replaced with Blake's "arts in eternity": painting, science, music, and poetry. The court cards of Page, Knight, Queen, and King were replaced with Child, Angel, Woman, and Man. Buryn also took issue with the now conventional terms of "Major Arcana" and "Minor Arcana," objecting to their association with secrecy because he wished to put forward a mysticism available to all and saw doing this as consistent with Blake's work. Buryn said, "Focusing on nomenclature may seem trivial, but in fact, points to the former elitist view that the tools of soul transformation and the deepest powers of mind should be reserved to a privileged group of magicians for ritualistic purposes" (Buryn, "The William Blake Tarot," in Auger 2014, 699).

Buryn viewed Blake as a philosophical man whose spiritual, psychic, and moral system had strong parallels with the metaphysical approach taken to Tarot at this point in history. Buryn argued that "Blake has exploded into our modern consciousness as a master spokesman of the soul's journey" (Buryn, "The William Blake Tarot," in Auger 2014, 705). Blake's work is filled with archetypical references incorporated into Buryn's deck. Indeed, Blake was a master symbolist, but there are a number of modifications that were made to the deck in order to better emphasize Blake's philosophy over the more medieval imagery with its overlay of Victorian influences.

Blake's *Ancient of Days*, one of his best-known illustrations, is used for "the Emperor" card. Buryn has renamed "the Emperor" card "Reason." Blake's *Albion's Angel* is used for "the Heirophant" card, renamed by Buryn as "Religion." Indeed, Buryn renamed most of the Major Arcana cards, although he certainly kept their basic meanings (even if he shifted emphasis). As one sees in other tarot decks, Buryn changed "Death" to "Transformation." "The Devil" is changed to "Error." The figure of Jesus appears in cards fourteen ("Forgiveness" is usually the "Temperance" card) and nineteen ("the Sun," which Buryn does not rename).

In spite of the name changes, Buryn kept the numbering sequence of the Major Arcana, and his deck is a complete set of all seventy-eight cards (plus one more). That extra card is called "Eternity" and is assigned the number 00. It is represented with William Blake's *Jacob's Dream*, to which Buryn added the infinity symbol (the lemniscate), which appears elsewhere in various tarot card decks. Card 0, normally called "the Fool" was renamed "Innocence," which is, of course, one of the major traits traditionally associated with "the Fool" card.

Buryn had texts and charts to supplement his deck. These go into elaborate detail about both Blake and Tarot. The symbiotic linkage of the two is

William Blake's *Ancient of Days* (1794). Blake's art has been used to
inspire a tarot deck by Ed Buryn.

impressively articulated in the texts and charts. There is a final interesting feature added to this deck. At the bottom of each of the fifty-six pip cards, Buryn
provided a "symbol window" for the user to place a symbol or bit of text that
personalizes the meaning of the card in whatever way its owner might wish.

Buryn was correct to note the importance of Blake's philosophy as it
related to one of the most important trends in the tarot culture. Tarot is
increasingly used as a meditative tool. As Buryn said, "And now it [Tarot]
is being increasingly used as an intentional tool of higher consciousness,
by psychologists and analysts, by spiritual counselors and human-potential

readers, and most importantly, by large numbers of ordinary people sincerely wanting to deepen and improve their lives through intuitive practices" (Buryn, "The William Blake Tarot," in Auger 2014, 704).

The Italian company Lo Scarabeo, working with Llewellyn (an American publishing company), sells a *Leonardo da Vinci Tarot Deck*. The Renaissance master's work is probably the most recognizable and respected artwork in history. In this deck, *The Lady with an Ermine* is used for the "Queen of Wands." Jesus, as depicted at the center of the table in Leonardo's *The Last Supper*, is used for the "Eight of Cups," commonly known as "the wish card." *The Mona Lisa* appears as the "High Priestess," wearing a papal mitre. Clearly, the creators of the deck wished to have a little fun with the images. It would be interesting to know if Leonardo had any familiarity with Tarot. I don't believe there are any references to Tarot in the sources left by Leonardo to history. However, we know that Leonardo was associated with the Sforza family, and it is not a stretch to say that it would have been possible that he saw the Visconti-Sforza deck that the miniaturist Bonifacio Bembo painted around 1450, just a couple of years before Leonardo was born.

Several issues strike me as worthwhile considerations in placing tarot cards above mere craft and elevating them to the status of artistic accomplishments. Can images so heavily correlated with symbolism and allegory fit more easily under the heading of craft than art? I would not think so. Does the mass-marketing and commercialization of the cards imply that they cannot be categorized as art, unless, perhaps we use derisive terms such as "kitsch"? I would argue that the materials and techniques employed by the artist and craftsperson are too similar (if not identical) in trying to reach a conclusion about classification as art or craft on the basis of techniques. It is, in fact, quite difficult to differentiate art from craft without developing a subjective spectrum which will allow more overlap than distinctions between the two categories.

This is an important consideration because, if we allow for a spectrum, we have the luxury of dismissing some examples of tarot card decks as unworthy of being called art while, at the same time, we may accept those examples of tarot card decks that we find difficult to dismiss or that we respect and admire so much as to insist upon referring to them as objects of art. The problem is, of course, that this is a very subjective matter. Of course, such is the nature of art.

Consider the use of collage, which can be a technique of an artist or a craftsperson. It is also a technique commonly employed in tarot decks. They routinely use numbers, astrological signs, religious symbols, and a variety of archetypal images all on one single card. The Dali deck and the William Blake deck are examples. Emily Auger points out that "the querent-reader, like the collagist, creates by selecting from a previously created inventory of elements. From the modern point of view, he aestheticizes or at least romanticizes these elements by seeing real life people and situations within their grid: he finds meaningful wholeness in the cards and the spread through their alignment with aspects of his own life" (*Tarot and Other Meditation Decks*, 52). This is just one of any number of examples that point to one of the main functions of art that differentiates it from craft: it has an intentionally or inherently provocative nature.

Here is a good illustration: in teaching a course on the history of magic several years ago, I had a student who had repeatedly asserted, in the days before the course arrived at the upcoming topic of Tarot, that the cards were utterly meaningless, nothing more than ineffectual drawings on paper. The following week, when I brought a deck into class and passed a few individual cards around the class to point out some of the specific and general characteristics of the cards, the student did not want to touch them. When I offered to do a couple readings for students to get their opinions on the experience, this student moved to the back of the room and was obviously wary.

Art is intended to engage the viewer in a provocative manner that one rarely, if ever, sees in crafts. Tarot certainly does provoke a myriad of feelings from a variety of people. Consider that many tarotists use their decks to meditate. This purpose, too, is associated with art more than crafts. Even though we know that the creative process of a craft such as knitting or leatherwork can be meditative while the object is being manufactured, in the case of art, the manufactured object is often intended to be used for meditation and contemplation. Tarot certainly serves this purpose. In fact, going all the way back to its origins as a game, the images on the cards were designed to get people contemplating universal aspects of life. Today, people who use tarot cards are often doing so for contemplative reasons rather than fortune-telling.

Craft, in contradistinction to art, is likely to be utilitarian. The tarot cards do, of course, serve a particular function. Whether deemed a device for telling fortunes or a tool for facilitating meditation, this utilitarian aspect of the deck makes them a bit more easily categorized as a craft. Yet, even if one rests their conclusion here, it should be pointed out that anything we call a craft is implicitly associated with a skill and, in the case of magic, that skill—the craft (pun intended)—is something imbued with wonder. Is this not something for which the artist strives? As Auger says, "Popular culture . . . particularly that of the twentieth century, frequently involves producers who are not named and an audience which is large and in search of entertainment or amusement, not moral or ethical edification, as is sometimes the objective of high art" (*Tarot and Other Meditation Decks*, 30).

Religious Symbolism and Tarot

Like art and religion, Tarot is syncretistic: it borrows from others and builds off what it borrows in order to develop along its own path. Tarot's history emerged not from a single moment but instead from a confluence of streams that eventually formed into a larger, meandering river. Let us now consider the use of religious symbols in Tarot, keeping in mind that these religious symbols are part of the cultural identity from which Tarot emerged and also part of the vocabulary which Tarot began to use in order to more clearly express its own uniqueness. People are often surprised to learn how much religious symbolism has been incorporated into Tarot.

Eliphas Levi, who was writing in the 1850s, wanted to emphasize distinctions in magic between cartomancy and contact with the divine. He certainly believed that Tarot could be effectively used for fortune-telling. However, he argued that Tarot was much more important as a tool for accessing greater knowledge about the universe. This mystical attitude of Levi's led him to become enamored with the Kabbalah and, in particular, with the *Sefer Yesirah* (*The Book of Formation* or, as it is often translated, *The Book of Creation*). This book of Jewish mysticism is thought by some to date back to Abraham, the patriarch of the faith. More probably, it should be attributed to a Rabbi Akiva who lived in the first and second century, CE, and was executed in 135 for being a participant in the Jewish rebellion against the Roman Empire.

Drawing on the *Sefer Yesirah*, Levi developed an understanding of correspondences between the Tree of Life and the Tarot. The Tree of Life symbolically represents spiritual realms, pathways, and stages of spiritual development. On it, there are ten key positions called *sephiroth*. Levi said that each of the ten *sephiroth* corresponded to the ten numbered cards of each suit in the Minor Arcana. Another correspondence that Levi saw in the Tarot and Kabbalah was that which linked the four letters in the name of God, YHWH (the Tetragrammaton) with the four suits in the Tarot. The letter "Yod" corresponded to the suit of wands. The first letter "He" corresponded to the suit of cups. The letter "Vav" (W) corresponded to swords, and the second letter "He" corresponded to the suit of coins. Samuel Liddell MacGregor Mathers, one of the founders of the Golden Dawn, took the association with the Tetragrammaton further by associating each letter with one of the "family" positions of the court cards: Yod-father / kings, He-mothers / queens, Vau-sons / knights, and He-daughters / pages.

Eliphas Levi also associated the twenty-two letters of the Hebrew alphabet with the twenty-two cards of the Major Arcana. He furthered that correspondence using the writings of a Jesuit mystic named Athanasius Kircher

(1602–1680), who listed correspondences between the letters of the Hebrew alphabet and various things such as planets, heavenly beings, and spiritual categories. Many modern tarot decks incorporate this symbolic scheme artistically. For example, the *Stairs of Gold* tarot by Georgio Tavaglione uses Hebrew letters prominently (along with astrological correspondences); so does the Knapp-Hall tarot pack.

While Levi adapted the *Sephiroth* on the Tree of Life into Tarot, the Golden Dawn further developed this by incorporating the pathways between the *Sephiroth*. Each of these pathways is imbued with spiritual meaning in the Kabbalah. There are twenty-two pathways that connect the *Sephiroth* just as there are twenty-two cards in the Major Arcana. The meanings traditionally associated with the pathways were then made to correspond with the meanings of the cards based on their assigned numbers. Consequently, future artists could represent these meanings in their cards.

Some of the biblical and religious symbols found on particular cards are rather obvious. For example, the Devil is on "the Devil" card, while the "Temperance" card depicts an angel. "The Hierophant" was originally called "the Pope" card. There was also, originally, a "Popess" card that was eventually changed to "the High Priestess." Both of these cards are plainly "religious" in their imagery.

Other cards, such as "Judgement," are fairly recognizable in terms of their religious connotation. This card, in the Waite-Colman Smith tarot deck, has an angel blowing a trumpet as the dead emerge from their graves. This is a reference to the book of *Revelations*, that would be recognizable to many people who have a basic familiarity with the New Testament. The Pope appears on the "Death" card. This is an intriguing image: he is shown appealing to Death, but like the other people in the picture, his fate is certain—everyone dies, regardless of their station in life.

One of the great works of art in Western civilization is a fresco in Vatican City painted by Raphael, around 1510, called *The Disputation of the Holy Sacrament*. The painting is meant, among other things, to praise the revelation of divine knowledge. It is located near another of Raphael's great frescoes, *The School at Athens*, which praises the pursuit of knowledge in the context of the humanities associated with the great ancient philosophers. At the center of *The Disputation of the Holy Sacrament*, the viewer sees the Holy Spirit, in the form of a dove, descending upon the Eucharist, the body of Christ, on the altar of communion. This imagery is clearly the inspiration for Pamela Colman Smith's artistic rendering on the "Ace of Cups." In that picture, we have a dove, with a round communion wafer in its beak, descending toward a gold chalice. The religious symbolism and composition connected to

Raphael's *Disputation of the Holy Sacrament* is obvious (which is *not* to argue that Pamela Colman Smith's art is on a par with the Renaissance master).

Another aspect of Christian symbolism found in the artwork of Tarot has to do with the four evangelists (the writers of the four New Testament gospels). Christians took the symbolism from the Old Testament book of Ezekiel 1:10, where the prophet has a vision looking into fire and seeing cherubim. These divine, four-headed beings are also referred to in Revelation 4:7, where another prophet, John, also has a vision of Heaven. These cherubim are also called *tetramorphs* (four forms). Throughout medieval history, artistic tradition has it that each of the four gospel-writing evangelists (Matthew, Mark, Luke, and John) were represented as a *tetramorph*.

If one were to travel to the famed Italian city of Venice, for instance, they would see the patron saint (Mark) of that city represented numerous times in artwork in the form of a winged lion. Matthew is represented as an angel or a winged man (it looks the same, but whether a man or an angel is usually subject to an interpretive choice). Luke is represented as a winged ox, and John is an eagle. If one were to travel to Dublin and see the *Book of Kells* at the Trinity College Library, they would find an excellent medieval example of this symbolism. This book was produced sometime between the seventh and ninth centuries and survived Viking raids after that. One of the folios (27v) contains the four evangelists in the form just described. Thus, this is an artistic tradition that existed throughout the Christian world for many centuries before the origins of tarot cards.

It shows up on tarot cards in two places. "The World" card shows the heads of a man (or angel) in the top left, an eagle in the top right corner, a bull in the bottom left, and a lion in the bottom right corner. The "Wheel of Fortune" card follows the exact same schema, although, instead of just heads, the entire bodies are portrayed; in each case, the figure is holding a book. The book, of course, is the gospel of the symbolized author. This is the style painted by Pamela Colman Smith in 1909, and it has frequently been used in the artwork of many other decks since then.

The "Wheel of Fortune" card is associated with more religious symbolism. There are eight letters on the outer level of the wheel. The letters "T-A-R-O" appear interspersed with the Hebrew letters of the Tetragrammaton (YHWH), the name of God. If one reads counterclockwise in English from the top, it says "TORA." When read clockwise, it says "TARO." What is being implied is that the Torah and the Tarot are linked. When read in English from the bottom up, the letters spell "ROTA," which means "wheel" (as in "Wheel of Fortune").

The religious elements found within the cards are examples of the iconography employed by a number of tarot artists. That religious iconography

Folio from the ninth-century Book of Kells, showing the four evangelists.

is extensive, particularly in the older decks. In modern decks, religious iconography may be said to have undergone a change toward the spiritual. It might be more accurate to characterize the change as going from traditional Christian iconography to other spiritual themes and motifs. Let us consider some examples.

There is a Gaian tarot deck by Joanna Powell Colbert which, as the name indicates, incorporates the theme of the planet as a being or living organism. Similarly, the *Green Witch Tarot* provides an emphasis on

"Wheel of Fortune" card from the Waite-Colman Smith Tarot, showing the four evangelists.

the spiritual importance of nature. The cards tend to follow established conventions, but there are some changes: "the Fool" is renamed as "the Seeker," and the suits are also renamed as Earth, Air, Fire, and Water (the four elements long associated as corresponding with the suits). There are several tarot decks that emphasize paganism, whether this involves ancient Greco-Roman, Celtic, Wiccan, or another form of iconography. There is a *Tarot of the Druids*, a *Book of Shadows Tarot*, a number of witch-themed tarot decks, and a *Robin Wood Tarot* that is quite self-consciously based on the Waite-Colman Smith deck.

Other tarot decks link the pagan and witchcraft themes with humor. For example, there is a *Tarot of Pagan Cats*, which replaces human figures with felines in settings that are plainly reminiscent of those found in the Waite-Colman Smith deck. There is a deck called the *Tarot for Hip Witches* including illustrations of beautiful young witches. The *Everyday Witch Tarot* uses amusing pictures that are also readily identifiable to people familiar with Tarot as containing conventional elements. "The Chariot" card, for example, shows a slightly confused witch on a motorcycle with a sidecar. She is at a fork in the road with one sign that says "This Way" and another sign that says "That Way."

Feminism and feminist-oriented Wicca have brought about a new channel for Tarot, especially divination, and there are several new decks as well as books. This is a subcategory of Tarot that, to those unfamiliar with the history of Tarot, might appear to be as old as the cards themselves but is more a reflection of modern communities linking themselves to Tarot in the 1970s or later. Rachel Pollack, author of one of the most important contemporary books on Tarot, *78 Degrees of Wisdom*, produced her own deck in 1993 called *Shining Woman*. People tended to treat the deck as geared more toward feminism than she expected, and in 2001, she came out with a new deck called *Shining Tribe* which put a greater emphasis on shamanism and aboriginal societies (while maintaining more traditional elements of tarot decks). Both decks are quite popular.

Just as feminist interpretations are often challenged in other aspects of social and cultural life, so, too, do feminist interpretations meet with challenges in the tarot community. Glenn Wright has written a scathing critique of what he calls "cartofeminism" wherein he criticizes the (largely successful) efforts to elevate the reputations and contributions of Pamela Colman Smith and Frieda Harris. By the later twentieth century, Colman Smith and Harris were being remembered as having made important contributions to the famous decks associated with Arthur Edward Waite and Aleister Crowley. This was a significant change in the culture of Tarot as compared to the first half of the twentieth century when the artists were viewed simply as craftswomen whose illustrations were nothing more than the product of following detailed instructions from their male "superiors."

Wright claims that the elevation in stature of these female artists is largely undeserved. He sees an effort to feminize Tarot as motivating a misleading revision in the cultural memory and historical esoteric contributions associated with the artists. Wright claims that feminists seek to appropriate authorship of the cards. When I asked a leading tarotist with a keen interest in the reputation of Pamela Colman Smith to respond to Wright's position, she simply made it clear that she considered both men, Waite and Crowley, to have made great contributions in the history of tarot (Greer, interview). She insisted that she (like others who wished to shed more light on the roles played by Pamela Colman Smith and Frieda Harris) has no wish to suppress the stature of either Waite or Crowley. Indeed, the evidence supports Greer's statement. It is not a zero-sum game where either the women or the men must win.

Wright goes on to argue that the feminist position in the tarot community was designed by Stuart Kaplan, the leading businessman in selling tarot decks, as an effort to profit by diminishing the role of men and "dumbing down" the esoteric elements of Tarot for popular consumption. There are two problems with Wright's assertions. The first is that an increase in attention for feminist interests in Tarot could have had the opposite effect. That is, an appeal to women as a customer base could reasonably have been expected to result in a loss of male customers. As it is, Tarot is a niche market. To zero in on an even smaller segment of society, seems more likely to lose potential customers, rather than to gain them. To the extent that the esoteric elements have been "dumbed down," one could easily argue that this is an element of commercialism that had begun to occur in the eighteenth century. Alternatively, one can argue that a feminist approach to the esoteric can expand, rather than diminish, an effort to explore the depths of esotericism.

The second problem with Wright's claims is that the increase in attention given to the artists of these two famous decks (who happen to be women) simply does not equate to an attack on the men who designed them. That is, a rise in their stature within the tarot community does not equate to a rejection of the men. A more reasonable argument, in my view, would be that interest in feminism translated into an increased awareness of two important tarot artists. Feminism has added something significant to Tarot. It has not taken anything away.

Returning to the topic of the syncretistic potential and nature of Tarot, we find that syncretism is reflected in the use of religious imagery. That same syncretistic nature allows for other symbolic imagery and allegorical messages to be conveyed just as easily. Let us consider, as our next example, "the Journey of the Fool."

The Journey of the Fool

In the city of Padua in northeastern Italy there is a small building known as the Scrovegni chapel. It holds an important place in the history of art because the early Renaissance master, Giotto (1276–1336), painted a large number of frescoes in the chapel. There is a set of seven frescoes known as "the Seven Virtues" and another set known as "the Seven Vices." The frescoes were painted in 1306. They are mentioned here because one of "the Seven Vices," *Stultitia*, which means "foolishness," has relevance for the Tarot.

If one looks at "the Fool" card of the Visconti-Sforza tarot deck, which was also created in northern Italy, it appears evident that the artist who made it (nearly 150 years after Giotto's masterpieces) was inspired by Giotto. In both the card and the fresco, the fool is depicted holding a club, barefooted and bare-legged, and with seven feathers in his hair (possibly representing the seven vices). The posing of the legs is also similar, although the figure on the card faces forward while the figure on the fresco is in profile.

In Tarot, "the Fool" is an important card on its own, but even more than that, it is an important card for understanding various aspects about Tarot in general and about the cards as an entire set of images. It is ironic, then, that in the early years when *tarocchi* was just a game of trumps and still a long way from evolving into its modern form, "the Fool" seems to have been a wild card, not unlike "the Joker" in modern playing card decks (which has a separate history of its own). "The Fool" card was not numbered, as were the other trump cards. Indeed, it is a point of debate if "the Fool" was actually part of the original game. According to Helen Farley's *Cultural History of Tarot*, "the Fool was found only in the Visconti-Sforza deck" and not in the remnants of the other early Italian decks (82).

The Fool leads a procession in allegorical contexts dating back to before the Renaissance. The procession itself is actually allegorical. For example, during the Black Death of the fourteenth century, artists began to portray in the visual arts, literature, and in morality plays, what they referred to as the *danse macabre* (the dance of death). Death is personified as summoning and leading people from all walks of life into the afterworld or, one might say, out of the world of the living. The procession would include kings and queens, peasants, craftsmen, priests, nuns, the elderly and the young, rich and poor, weak and strong. Each person in this parade of death symbolized a category of people while every person viewing or hearing would not only identify with one of the categories, they would also see everyone in their world as being fated to a similar experience. The Fool illustrates the futility of trying to avoid the inevitable fate that Death imposes. Alternatively, "the Fool" may be seen as illustrating the insignificance of our lives in the grand scheme of history which will go on long after we are gone just as it had been moving along before we were born.

As Tarot developed an esoteric tradition beginning in the later 1700s, the meaningfulness of the card certainly became increasingly important.

A modern version of the
"Fool" card based on the
Visconti-Sforza Tarot.

By the 1970s, Eden Gray, whose book *A Complete Guide to the Tarot* had a major impact on popularizing Tarot for fortune-telling, was writing about the card in a way that helped teach and illustrate the meaning of the Major Arcana. She wrote about "the Fool's Journey" in a manner that has had a lasting impact.

Ever since Eden Gray, people have learned about the Major Arcana and have also based personal meditations on the narrative concept of "the Fool's Journey." The basic idea is that "the Fool" represents "everyman" (or everyone) as he travels through the numbered cards of the Major Arcana. "The

Fool" must learn life lessons along this journey and develop his virtues while overcoming his vices, maturing while facing the variety of crises in life, and so on. It should be noted that some of the cards represent virtues—"Strength" and "Temperance," for example. Some of the cards represent life experiences—the "Wheel of Fortune" and "Death," for example. Several of the cards represent categories of individuals (types of people, rather than one's with the actual titles) one will encounter along life's journey, such as "the Hermit," "the Empress," or "the High Priestess." Still other cards are indicative of experiences or states of being, such as "the Tower" or "Judgement."

In chapter one, I discussed how Gertrude Moakley had argued that the original meaning of these cards was to use a parade or procession, known as a triumph, as a metaphor filled with meaning upon which the cards are based. I also noted that the sequence and symbols of part of the deck is aligned with the journey that Dante takes with Vergil in *The Divine Comedy*. Eden Gray reintroduced the idea of viewing the cards as a procession, modifying the concept to represent going through life, with its growth and experience, starting from a state of innocence and leading to a sense of satisfaction and understanding. This could be applicable as a process of youth moving toward maturity. But it could also be applied to certain aspects within life (as opposed to the entire experience of life). That is, one could look at "the Fool's Journey" not only as a metaphor for one's mortal lifespan, but, say, for one's development in a profession or one's growth in the context of a relationship. I would submit that in all instances, these approaches represent a spiritual quest (or, pilgrimage).

Joseph Campbell's *The Hero With a Thousand Faces* (1949) is a much more widely known book than Eden Gray's. So, it may be worthwhile to consider some similarities. Campbell developed the concept that "the Hero" in myth, religion, and literature tends to go through comparable processes and have comparable experiences as he grows into his (or her) destiny. These processes and experiences can be generalized (perhaps even universalized) so that we gain a transcendent sense of the meanings of stories involving heroes. Eden Gray did something comparable by focusing on the idea of "the Fool's Journey." It should be noted that Tarot allows for an incredible range of interpretation and an inexhaustible degree of narrative creativity simply by the arrangement and rearrangement of the cards' sequence. This, I believe, extends the art of Tarot to a degree not often seen in other art forms. The collection of symbolic images, archetypes, and allegorical devices that are found in Tarot might equip the tarotist with as much allegorical material as a painter or a poet has at their disposal.

The "Fool" card from the Waite-Colman Smith Tarot.

Angus Fletcher wrote of allegories, "They examine the philosophic, theological, or moral premises on which we act, and then they confront us with the perfection of certain ideals, the depravity of others" (360–61). He then goes on to say of the "strengths of the mode:" "It allows for instruction, for rationalizing, for categorizing and codifying, for casting spells and expressing unbidden compulsions" (368). Thus, while it draws upon symbolism, allegory uses symbolism as an element in the creation of a narrative which is itself representative of something. This applies to Tarot in a way that goes even beyond the imagery of the cards.

In laying out the cards and assigning meanings to the various positions in which the cards are to be laid, a narrative scaffolding is being arranged. So, if one is to say that position one represents the past, position two represents the present, and position three represents the future, an allegorical narrative is created as soon as specific cards, each charged with several symbolic elements, are set into position. The reader takes the meaning of the individual card as it is illustrated and contextualizes that meaning based on the position in which the card had been placed. When viewed on the whole and in relation to the other cards in the layout, the narrative is completed.

Imagine, then, that we add a context of occupation to our simple three-card layout of past, present, and future. We will arrive, of course, at a narrative of a person's professional life defined more specifically by the meanings associated with the cards. Note, too, that the use of past, present, and future makes the narrative sequential. Should a card representing happiness and success (for example, the "nine of cups") land in the third position, we would have a narrative that says this person's future ends with getting the job and pay that they want. In this scenario the person for whom the reading is being done (the querent) identifies as the subject of the reading. The story is about them. It can just as easily be arranged to have a different subject. One could ask about the fate of their child or their favorite football team. The cards and the positions in the layout serve as building blocks.

The sequential nature of the layouts—and there are infinite possibilities—serve to channel the narrative in a way that might easily reflect a journey of sorts. The querent is, in effect, on that journey. It is most likely a journey through time, but it can also be one of self-discovery or a quest of some sort. The querent takes a role kind of like a hero in an allegorical story. That story is told by and through the cards.

The ability for the cards to serve as pieces of a story can be told in a random (or, if you will, magical) way simply by laying out the cards as they happen to come off the deck. But, stories can be told in a deliberate, planned manner by arranging the cards of one's choosing in such a way as to imply meaning and narrative in the sequence. An artist can take the meanings associated with a sequence of cards and use those images to convey a narrative in allegorical or symbolic form.

One example of this in art can be found in a watercolor that the author's son produced for an event honoring people who were victims of human trafficking. In addition to tarot cards, he used symbolic images such as crows, a deer, and peaches to illustrate a story, in a multi-panel frame, of vulnerability, innocence, sweetness, and abuse that, over time, becomes a story of overcoming adversity. The cards are placed in a vertical sequence in the central panel of the painting and can be read and contextualized along with other images in the painting—if one knows what to look for. The top card is "the Fool," which, as stated above, is used to represent the person traveling through life's journey. In this case, she begins by being innocent and ignorant and entering an unfair world looking to take advantage in cruel ways that must be learned and, eventually, overcome. The "Ace of Pentacles" comes next, a card that represents beginnings and material concerns. Here, it reflects the need to obtain money as well as the desire of others to exploit for financial gain. After this comes "the Tower," which is generally thought of as the most ominous card in the deck and can represent chaos and catastrophe. It is followed by "the Lovers" card, which is shown inverted and can symbolize negative emotional relationships. Yet the next two cards in the sequence tell the story of overcoming adversity and moving on to a new and better life: the card of "Strength" shows an ability to endure and overcome adversity, and it is followed by the "Wheel of Fortune," representing transition. In this case, it represents a happy transition out of, and away from, a world of exploitation and into a new, happier phase of life.

A French artist living in Tuscany, Niki de Saint Phalle created a sculpture garden in the 1970s based on the Tarot. She had begun her art career doing sculptures that embedded a variety of objects (knives, the arms of dolls, tomatoes, and so forth) in plaster; she would then shoot them with a rifle while wearing a white jumpsuit. It was performance art that also involved the use of large installation pieces. After visiting Park Güell in Barcelona in the 1950s, she was inspired by the work of Antoni Gaudí to create monumental sculptures using materials that would include tilework of the sort she saw in Barcelona as well as the fantastic colors, shapes, and designs. She had gained fame for her sculptures called "Nanas," giant female forms with exaggerated curves, decorated with a variety of images on the nipples and using the vagina as a place to make a statement. For example, one of her Nanas has an actual doorway for a vagina. Saint Phalle collaborated with the kinetic artist Jean Tinguely on that project and on the tarot garden.

This sculpture rests on several acres of land donated by a wealthy family. The garden was home to several people from various backgrounds while it was being created. It cost several million dollars to build and, while some of the money was donated, much of it was earned by Saint Phalle, who could be quite a successful moneymaker when she tried. The sculptures are massive, and they are adorned with numerous features that are more about life in general than about the Tarot, in particular. Further, the iconography does not follow convention. Although some of them, like "the Hanged Man," are recognizable to anyone familiar with common tarot artforms, none of the

Tarot of the Trafficked Child, by Eric Maille.

sculptures is directly imitative of the Waite-Colman Smith deck or, for that matter, of any traditional deck.

Saint Phalle lived in the sculpture of a sphinx that was part of her "Empress" card. Her kitchen was in one of the breasts and her bedroom was in the other. All of the pieces are based on the Major Arcana. These monumental sculptures in Tuscany use a variety of media. Most are built upon welded steel frameworks and then covered with plaster or plastic to allow the surface to have bright colors applied to it. There is a great amount of mosaic tilework in the art. There is also a liberal use of mirrored tile. Ariel Levy, a writer for the *New Yorker*, gave this description of a couple of the sculptures,

> Amid peaceful olive groves and ochre fields grazed by horses and sheep sits a house-size sculpture of a sphinx, with mirrored blue hair and a bright-red crown, a flower blooming on one of her breasts and a lavender heart on the nipple of the other. The interior is covered in shards of mirror, as if a colossal disco ball had been turned inside out. . . . A sprawling, fantastical castle, with a rainbow mosaic tower, sits near a blue head some fifty feet high, sprouting a second, mirrored head crowned by a huge hand. Downhill, the Devil stands amid some shrubs, a rainbow-winged hermaphrodite with a sweet face, womanly hips, and three gold penises. It is as if a psychedelic bomb had exploded in the most picturesque part of Tuscany. (Levy)

The project, begun in the 1970s, was made open to the public in 1998. Niki Saint Phalle died in 2002. One of her goals for the garden was to create a different world into which people could escape by leaving the conventions and stresses of "the real world" behind. The artist accomplished this for herself, the close friends with whom she worked on the project, and (to some degree) for the visitors who tour the site today. The Tarot Garden represents a journey that one can take, and in traveling to the site, the tourist is on a quest—making a pilgrimage in a manner that is, in its own way, comparable to the journey of the Fool.

Tarot as "Low Art"

As noted above, Emily Auger, in her book *Tarot and Other Meditation Decks*, considers Tarot to be primarily a "low" form of art but emphasizes that it performs all the functions of art (9–10). This is true at a personal, physical, or even social level, where the functions of art may relate to politics, social commentary, religion, community, and the status of individuals or groups. Yet, when we categorize something as "low" art, we may be asserting that the quality of these characteristics is less than "high" art, or we might simply be saying that the quality of the technical skills of the artists are deficient in comparison to master artists. Thus, there is not only a subjective element involved in labeling art as "low," there is also a wide range of meaning within that categorization.

Another consideration is the sheer quantity of the decks. They are often mass-produced (although I recognize that such a term can be defined in different ways). There are many different decks available and certain decks are produced and distributed in very large numbers. The website, aeclectic.com, reviews decks for public consumption. More than a thousand decks have been reviewed on the website, so the scale of production and distribution might be taken as an indicator that this is "low" art, at least in the sense that it is not produced for an individual patron's commission; what's more, the original pieces are made for the purpose of producing copies. Tarot decks are, indeed, a business product intended to be sold to as large a consumer base as is possible. The fact that these consumers can accurately be referred to as a niche market certainly does not argue for the status of "high" art.

Of the decks reviewed at aeclectic.com, many are sold by only three different corporate entities. The largest of these is US Games Systems, which produces (the word "publishes" is often used) 131 different decks. The next largest company (as defined by the number of different decks in their catalog) is the Italian company called Lo Scarabeo, which has 115 different decks. The third is a company called Llewellyn, with forty-four different decks reviewed on aeclectic.com. Although there are many more decks than the 290 associated with these three corporations, the large majority of sales go to US Games Systems, Lo Scarabeo, and Llewellyn (Marcus Katz, "Tarot on the Threshold: Liminality and Illegitimate Knowledge," 289–90).

There are some decks that reflect somewhat silly or playful movements associated with popular culture. For example, there are Tolkien Tarot decks, Steampunk Tarot decks, and Gummy Bear Tarot decks. The aeclectic.com website mentions a deck called the Electronic Republican Tarot, featuring Ronald Reagan as "the Emperor" and Richard Nixon as "Death." This deck could use some updating. It comes with a booklet entitled *The Pictorial Key to the Republican Tarot*, an obvious imitation of Arthur Edward Waite's classic book. All of these decks show a clear inspiration and affinity with the Waite-Colman Smith deck.

Certain television shows have inspired tarot card decks. *Dark Shadows*, a very popular television soap opera from the late 1960s and early 1970s, has its own deck. The show, which will be discussed in another chapter on television and Tarot, used an actual traditional deck. The deck inspired by the show, however, uses characters, sets, and events from the series as the images and text on the cards. The deck is conventional in that it has seventy-eight cards, the standard suits, and trumps. There is also a tarot deck based on the original *Star Trek* series. The *Star Trek Tarot* follows the conventional suits, trumps, and number of cards; Scotty is used for "the Magician" card, and "the Chariot" card is, of course, the starship *Enterprise*.

The art of Tarot is ubiquitous in popular culture and it is so deeply ingrained in the public's imagination that caricatures of it can also become popular. In a 2017 episode of the comedy series *Last Man on Earth* (season 4, episode 5), the main character, Tandy Miller (played by Will Forte), appears in a Tarot-inspired T-shirt. It's produced by graphic designer Sage Aune. It appears to be a tarot card very much in the style of the Waite-Colman Smith deck, but the card's name is "the Margarita." There are other tarot card T-shirts that she has in this style. They include "the Donut," "the Pie," "the Cookie," and "the Cake." Graphic design for T-shirts can clearly be categorized more under the heading of craft than art. T-shirts with tarot imagery also have appeared in drama series. A 2014 episode (season 2, episode 5) of the show *Orphan Black* featured a tarot T-shirt. The character of Felix Dawkins (Jordan Gavaris) wore the image of the "Temperance" card from the Waite-Colman Smith deck.

Whether we consider the work of such artists as Pamela Colman Smith and Frieda Harris to be "high art" or "low art," the indisputable fact is that their work provokes thought, stirs emotions, inspires others, all while drawing upon symbolic language and archetypal imagery. It seems clear, then, that Tarot deserves to be viewed within the category of art. The art of Tarot is so intriguing because it serves both as a medium for art and as an art form. Certainly, Dali thought so. Further, those who love both art and Tarot have found, as we have seen with examples such as the William Blake tarot deck, a way to blend art with Tarot in intriguing and sophisticated ways.

Conclusion

It is reasonable to debate the place of Tarot in the history of art, but it does have a place in art history. Its origins in the Renaissance are apropos. True, none of the great masters of that era painted tarot cards. It would be great to have a Raphael, Titian, or Michelangelo tarot deck. Yet, the cards have been an attractive project to an artist as prominent as Salvador Dali. The most famous tarot decks have artwork that was produced by respectable artists, perhaps made respectable by their work on tarot cards. Pamela Colman Smith and Frieda Harris earned recognition as artists because of their work in Tarot. Even after acknowledging the subjectivity of assessing artists and their work as "respectable" or "great," one also finds that artwork generally acknowledged to be great, such as that of William Blake, can be well suited to tarot illustration. The fact that Blake was a philosopher strengthens the point that tarot offers a meaningful canvas to those with an interest in art.

We have also considered, in this chapter, that there are significant differences between "mere" craft and quality artistic work. No doubt Tarot normally occupies the more modest of these spaces, but it is not without respectable elements that merit categorization as quality art. Having said that, it remains true that pop, or low, art serves an important role in the culture. Within that space, too, Tarot deserves some attention (both good and bad).

The symbolism and conceptual meaning that can be embedded within the images of a deck of tarot cards, as we have seen, is wide-ranging. Whether we are talking about "low" or "high" art, that range of meaning is culturally significant. When considering symbolism in art, we have found that tarot cards can be, themselves, powerful symbols. An excellent example of this is found in the work of Audrey Flack, who is known for, among other things, photorealistic *vanitas*, still life paintings with moral and religious imagery. One of these, *Wheel of Fortune*, has that eponymous tarot card along with a human skull, a mirror, and a menagerie of ephemera that speak to the transience of life. The tarot card she incorporates is a perfect example of a symbol that facilitates the artist's intention to provoke the thought of the viewer. Clearly, much of the powerful symbolism permeating the culture of Western civilization has been incorporated into quite a few tarot decks. Indeed, Tarot is by no means limited to the culture of Western civilization.

I have no wish to overstate the place of Tarot in art. While pointing to some of the more impressive or respectable examples of tarot art, I remain mindful of some of the silly, simple, and unimpressive work as well. A version of *The Last Supper* on black velvet, painted with glowing colors, mass-produced in the early 1970s, could fairly expect a negative critique (or an outright dismissal) but would not diminish the respect we have for da Vinci's masterpiece. Similarly, an artistically unimportant or unimpressive tarot deck cannot, on the whole, represent the art of Tarot. Then again, the worst of the art associated with Tarot cannot be ignored or denied when one is evaluating Tarot as an art form. The point is that Tarot does offer a great deal to look at in terms of art. Some of what one sees is unimpressive; some is remarkable. These facts speak to the significance of Tarot's space in the world of art.

CHAPTER 5

Tarot Cards and Television
Inspiring Fear, Wrestling with Fate, Forming the Narrative

A Little Bit of Television History; Tarot Comes out of the (Dark) Shadows

In this chapter we will explore the place of Tarot in television. It should be noted at the start that Tarot has been on television for a very long time and continues to be used with increasing frequency and sophistication. Tarot cards are also quite conducive to being used for humor or to criticize the attitudes and behavior of those who may be termed tarot enthusiasts. Certain television series have had a natural or logical potential connection to Tarot that writers have found obvious reasons to exploit. Shows with witches, for example, are obvious candidates for the use of tarot cards. A significant number of television shows that have no evident reason to incorporate tarot cards have also used them in interesting and effective ways. This chapter will provide a few examples of those types of programs that have made use of the cards despite the fact that viewers would likely have had no expectations to see the cards used as a prop.

There are no television series main characters who make their livings as tarotists or who are primarily identified as such. A tarot reader is usually a background character or a temporary character, whether in dramas or comedies. In the long-running television series *Bones*, Cyndi Lauper played a psychic named Avalon Harmonia who appears in a handful of episodes scattered throughout the twelve-season run of the forensic mystery series. She is a bit of an exception in that she is a recurring character. In other ways, though, she is about what we would expect to see in a character designed to sympathetically portray a tarot reader while also wishing to make use of Tarot in conventional television storytelling methodology.

In the opening scene of the fifth season of *Bones*, Lauper's character reads the tarot cards of the main character, Temperance Brennan, and flips over the "Temperance" card, literally naming the querant, before proceeding to reveal an in-depth knowledge of past and future events. The cards shown are conventional, the Waite-Colman Smith deck, but the character's reading of the cards is well beyond what should realistically be expected in terms of supernatural revelation. The last card she turns over is "Death." It is interpreted in a literal way (unlike all the other cards). The next scene shifts to the other main character, Seeley Booth, who is shown in a psychologist's office where he is concluding a therapy session to get back his job. It is an interesting contrast—the psychic and the psychologist, both with their supposed insights into the human condition.

The psychic character reveals the existence of several murdered bodies and, soon, becomes a suspect herself. In the end, she is cleared of the crime after playing a role in solving it. Her psychic abilities seem to be established. Yet, just enough doubt remains to entertain the viewer with the possibility of further purposes and future appearances.

Of course, we will also consider television programming that made use of tarot cards in ways that viewers would certainly have anticipated. I would argue that, whether the subject matter and cast of characters of a series has some obvious connection to Tarot, the benefits and uses of tarot cards as a prop can be quite similar even though there is actually a wide range of these potential benefits. Before discussing those topics, let us begin with a brief historical summary of the appearances that tarot cards have made on television programs.

One of the earliest television programs to use tarot cards was the 1960s daytime soap opera *Dark Shadows*. The cards were frequently used to create an ominous sense of danger lurking in the future. They also helped provide the shows edgy vibe that made it a hit with teenagers and young adults whose interest in the supernatural was being spurred along in the 1960s. One expects to see tarot cards in a program like *Dark Shadows* just as more modern audiences expect to see them in shows such as *Buffy the Vampire Slayer* or *Charmed*. Such viewers would be interested in the shows' use of tarot cards because it reflects an already established personal interest in the supernatural or in vampires, witchcraft, and the like.

But, consider that tarot cards made their first appearance (as far as I know) on a television program in 1961 in a western called *Lawman*. The title of the episode was "Tarot." A death is foretold with "the Hanged Man" card. The use of the cards as a device or a prop to create a feeling of anxiety and foreboding is clear. It may seem strange to have the cards make an appearance in a western. Yet, one might further consider that tarot cards were also used in a 1964 episode of *The Andy Griffith Show*, in which the character of Opie gets three wishes that come true. In contrast to *Dark Shadows, Lawman* and *Andy Griffith* were shows that one might reasonably assume appealed to an audience who held negative views about tarot.

Dark Shadows plays an important part in the history of television and Tarot. The show was filmed in Manhattan, beginning in 1966 as a Dan Curtis production for ABC. The show was comparable in many ways to other daytime soap operas on the major television networks. However, that changed when the show began to abandon its typical soap opera style and take on more supernatural themes involving vampires and ghosts. This turned the ratings around and launched Jonathan Frid into stardom as the new main character, Barnabas Collins. The radical change in the show, hinging upon a transition to horror and the supernatural, resulted in popular success, as well as a much larger audience composed of teenagers freshly arrived back home after their day at school.

As *Dark Shadows* began to take off as a popular daytime daily television show, Stuart Kaplan was in Germany. Like Jonathan Frid, Kaplan was on the verge of launching a very successful career (albeit in the tarot card business rather than in acting). Kaplan had graduated from the prestigious Wharton School in Pennsylvania with a background in marketing and finance. He was looking at toy distributors in Germany and came across a small exhibition booth belonging to A. G. Müller & Cie of Neuhausen, Switzerland. That company produced tarot cards as part of their product line.

Kaplan decided to buy 5,000 decks of cards (more than A. G. Müller & Cie of Neuhausen sold per year), and more significantly, Kaplan bought the rights to publish the deck in America. The deck was called the Swiss 1JJ Tarot. The "JJ" stands for "Jupiter and Juno." These two Roman deities had been used to replace the traditional cards of the Pope and Papess because the original designer, A. G. Müller, did not want to offend the religious sensibilities of his Catholic customers. When Kaplan got back to America, he was able to sell a shipment of 100 decks to Brentano's bookstore in New York City. It is at this point that I believe Kaplan may have begun to influence television's relationship with tarot cards.

Brentano's bookstore was located in the area where *Dark Shadows* was being produced. The use of tarot cards on the television show began right around the time that Kaplan had sold his cards to Brentano's. The type

Tarot reading on *The Andy Griffith Show*, 1964.

of cards used on *Dark Shadows* are the Swiss 1JJ card decks. It, therefore, seems reasonable to suppose that Kaplan's cards were picked up at Brentano's for use as a prop for the popular television show that was capitalizing on supernatural imagery. One could easily make an argument that the two cultural phenomena had a synergistic relationship. *Dark Shadows* would use the Swiss 1JJ tarot deck in many episodes. It would have been seen by large numbers of Americans who could then go out and buy a deck of their own, contributing to the sales profits of Stuart Kaplan's new company, US Games Systems.

The business of Tarot was a subject for an earlier chapter. So, let us continue discussing the relationship between Tarot and television while building off our examination of *Dark Shadows*. *Dark Shadows* is, of course, not the only television program to make considerable use of tarot cards as a prop. Almost fifty years after *Dark Shadows* went on the air, the Showtime network began airing the series *Penny Dreadful*. An unusual tarot card deck appears in the opening credits sequence and is associated with a main character, Vanessa Ives. Among other things, the deck, as a prop, carries a certain cachet that signifies a connection to the supernatural and is associated with an ability to divine the future. This function of Tarot and television is, of course, persistent (even ubiquitous). So, this is just one link between *Dark Shadows* and *Penny Dreadful*.

Tarot readings were a common occurrence on *Dark Shadows*.

Another point of comparison to be made between these two programs from two different eras in television is that both of them relied heavily on classic literature in the horror genre. Both programs used Robert Louis Stevenson's, *The Strange Case of Dr. Jekyll and Mr. Hyde*, Bram Stoker's *Dracula*, Mary Shelley's *Frankenstein*, and Oscar Wilde's *The Picture of Dorian Gray*. The character of the werewolf is prominent in both programs, as are a number of classical horror short stories from the likes of Edgar Allan Poe and H. P. Lovecraft. The point here is that Tarot exists within a cultural milieu alongside such literature, making the cards an important prop for programs that have traded on classical horror literature as material for storylines, characters, and plot devices.

Penny Dreadful and Popular Conventions in Presenting Tarot

Stock characters such as witches can be reified by adorning them with a deck of tarot cards just as much as with a pointy hat and a black cat. The *Penny Dreadful* episode "The Nightcomers" (season 2, episode 3) is a great example. The episode is an excellent collection of witchy conventions, among them an old woman who lives alone on the moors in rural England and a rundown home with talismans and amulets decorating every room. The

Still from *Penny Dreadful*, 2015.

old woman, despised by the neighbors who rely on her to perform a variety of potentially controversial acts (including abortions), is shown gathering plants for her potions when she is not peering into people's memories and futures. There is a reference to the woman's former coven, incantations, and a past of sexual deviance. She even cooks using a cauldron. She is portrayed in a manner that reflects centuries old stereotypes and occasionally blends those with humor. At one point, the witch's protégé, Vanessa, is cooking in the cauldron and becoming frustrated with the witch's demanding attitude. The witch tells Vanessa that she used too much salt, and as soon as the witch looks away, Vanessa throws in another fistful of salt.

The episode began by setting up a flashback in which Vanessa Ives says that this woman, known as the Cut-Wife, was "the first witch I ever met." When the two meet, the witch wants to know what Vanessa wants and begins to list services she could do such as aborting a pregnancy or making a love potion. Then the witch assesses Vanessa more closely and sees a strong will and an agile mind. She has soon determined that Vanessa has a natural-born ability to wield supernatural power. The witch, who we later learn is named Joan Clayton, shows Vanessa how to look into her (Clayton's) mind and past. She says that Vanessa is a little scorpion, an image that the viewer already knows is associated with Vanessa like a totem. Vanessa had drawn an image of a scorpion with her own blood in the previous episode and does so again in later episodes. A scorpion is also shown in the opening sequence.

Entering the home of the witch represents a transformative moment in Vanessa's life. The moment that Joan Clayton consents to become Vanessa's mentor, she takes out a deck of tarot cards from a box and gives them to Vanessa. That deck is the deck shown in the opening sequence of each episode. It is also used in numerous other episodes. Clayton then challenges her new protégé to "see something." Vanessa says that she cannot tell anything, and Clayton slaps her before beginning to instruct her in the art of Tarot. The deck is spread out in an arc with the cards face down, and Vanessa is told to concentrate on picking a card without looking. As soon as Vanessa picks the card, the witch knows what it is and what it means, even before the card is turned over to reveal that it is "the Devil." The witch then allows Vanessa to move into her home.

The viewer soon learns that Clayton had once been part of a coven of witches that had been chosen to follow "the Master" (a shadowy character who becomes increasingly important as the series progresses), but Clayton refused and became an enemy of these very evil witches known as "nightcomers." The nightcomers are now coming after Vanessa on behalf of "the Master," and they know that Vanessa is with Joan Clayton. The confrontation between the witches that follows is complicated by the fact that Joan is dying. She is hundreds of years old, and her (unstated) illness is beyond her ability to heal. The leader of the witches coming after Joan and Vanessa manipulates the local nobleman into instigating the mob of townspeople—who seem happy to oblige—into attacking Clayton. She is hung by her neck, doused in hot tar, and set on fire. As a finishing touch, they brand her with a red-hot iron cross before using the same branding iron on Vanessa's back.

Although it is made clear that the hatred of the townspeople for Joan Clayton is unjustified, Joan made it her life's work to be there for them. Before she died, Joan had asked Vanessa to take her place and became enraged when Vanessa refused. The viewer sees, among other things, that witches are portrayed in very traditional or conventional ways throughout the episode. Nonetheless, there is a range of character (in both senses of the word) reflected in the witches. They can be coarse and rough, like Joan, or they can appear upper-class and sophisticated, like Madame Kali (the leader of the "nightcomers"). They can be young and beautiful or old and ugly. They can use their abilities to do good or bad, or both. The point is that the conventions associated with creating a witch character in this episode are obvious and representative of centuries of literature, custom, and folklore that are instantly recognizable to the viewer. Simultaneously, however, the characters created by these traditional images and actions associated with witches and witchcraft can be presented to the viewers as either protagonists or antagonists.

Just as any spell, potion, or talisman presented as a prop can be seen as magical even though its use (not its nature) determines if it is good or evil, so, too, are the characters left only partially defined by the fact that they are witches. Put in more simplistic and familiar terms, one might be a good witch or a bad witch just as Glinda, the good witch, found it necessary to inquire of Dorothy when she crash-landed on the bad witch in Oz.

There is one last thing worth noting about *Penny Dreadful* that ties into *Dark Shadows*. Both series have actors who play characters who use the cards for divination and return to the show as different characters which represent scientific, objective, rational people. In the case of *Penny Dreadful*, Patti LuPone plays Joan Clayton and, later in the series, returns to play a character that strikes the viewer as a Victorian-era psychiatrist who, we learn, is a descendant of Joan Clayton. In the case of *Dark Shadows*, there is a central character named Dr. Julia Hoffman, a psychiatrist played by Grayson Hall. At various points in the series, Hall also plays other characters, two of whom read tarot cards: the Countess, Natalie Dupres, and a gypsy named Magda Rakosi. It is an interesting contrast not only to compare these two shows but to consider the character types involved. On the one hand, for the same actor to portray a doctor and a mystic in the same series allows the viewer to see the character types as opposite ends of the same spectrum. On the other hand, linking a tarot reader (albeit indirectly) to a psychiatrist might be seen as either giving some intellectual credibility to tarot or criticizing psychology as a modern form of shamanism. Of course, one might also argue that Tarot does not need any reflected legitimacy from the discipline of psychology. Suffice it to say that both character types possess a skill or have an attribute that allows them greater insightfulness than the average lay person.

Buffy the Vampire Slayer: Art Imitates Life and Life Imitates Art (If We Can Call *Buffy* "Art")

The popular *X-Files* series had two central characters who represented a dichotomy of skeptic and believer in the supernatural. A 1995 episode called "Clyde Bruckman's Final Repose" had the FBI agents Scully and Mulder (the main characters on the series) attempting to solve a series of murders of people with psychic abilities, one of which was a tarot card reader. She gets murdered by the man for whom she is reading cards. Despite the irony, the episode is written in such a way that the police rely upon a psychic to capture the criminal. The psychic they rely upon, however, can only see people's deaths. He cannot predict or visualize anything else.

The popular show *Charmed* has a (Major Arcana) tarot deck based on the characters and events from the series. This is no surprise in terms of either marketing strategy or intersecting interests of fans of the series with tarot enthusiasts. Something similar can be said about *Dark Shadows*. It is a bit stranger, however, to note that one can also purchase tarot decks associated with *Star Trek* and (God help us) *My Little Pony*. These are both television series that seem quite unrelated, even oppositional in some respects, to the social contexts in which tarot cards are situated.

Buffy the Vampire Slayer was a television series that ran from 1997 to 2003. It was based on a 1992 film that, like the subsequent series, was a Joss Whedon product. It is no surprise to see tarot cards make an appearance in a series that involves witches and demons as much as it involves vampires. The series was, in fact, an eclectic blend of darkly supernatural and mystical elements with comedy and the issues associated with the life of middle-class teenagers in the town of Sunnydale. Throw in a lot of action fight sequences and 1990s television special effects—and, well, you get the idea.

The use of tarot cards in *Buffy the Vampire Slayer* is similar to their use in other television programs. For example, they serve to forecast future events and set an ominous supernatural tone. But there are some ways in which the cards are used that deserve particular attention for the fact that they are a good example of how life imitates art and art imitates life. Let us consider the use of the cards in two, two-part episodes, and then, follow that up with the *Buffy the Vampire Slayer* tarot deck.

In season two of *Buffy the Vampire Slayer*, episodes nine and ten told a story about a vampire named Drusilla who was the love interest of a main character, a vampire named Spike. Drusilla had become deathly ill and was in need of a curative ritual. Initially, Spike and Drusilla did not even know what the ritual was or, of course, how to perform it. It turned out that they would need to capture and bleed a vampire named Angel—the vampire that had turned Drusilla into a vampire. Angel was also the boyfriend of Buffy (yes, she's supposed to slay vampires, but he's a "good" one).

At the beginning of the first of this two-part story, Spike and Drusilla are using tarot cards in an attempt to find out what is wrong with Drusilla and what needs to be done to cure her. Spike has brought in another vampire to try to interpret the meaning of Drusilla's card readings. It is an odd presentation in that someone who knows how to read the cards would not, in any typical tarot reading, have another person looking into books trying to figure out the completed reading. Drusilla explained to Spike that they would need a "key" in order to understand the meaning of the cards. That was an interesting (and probably not accidental) word choice given that "key" has a meaning for the unlocking of a code, generally speaking, but can also be a reference to the book that Arthur Edward Waite wrote in 1910 about understanding the meaning of the cards, *The Pictorial Key to the Tarot*. The layout of the reading that Drusilla does is also different than one would expect, but it appears to be a variation of the common Celtic Cross layout.

What is particularly interesting at this point in the episode is the cards themselves. The layout is obviously composed of standard cards from the most recognizable of decks, the Waite-Colman Smith deck. However, as the episode goes on, other cards are shown. These other cards are done in an artistic style very similar to the one Pamela Colman Smith used in the famous deck. The choice of colors, the framing, the portrayal of human forms, etc., are all reminiscent of the Waite-Colman Smith imagery. These other cards, though, do not have any of the suits, nor are they named or numbered like any of the Major Arcana cards in an actual tarot card deck.

The first of these other cards shows a stone building that turns out to be a mausoleum where a reliquary houses an important artifact produced by the man buried there many years ago. This artifact, shaped like a cross, will be needed in the ritual that could restore Drusilla's health. Although Spike and Drusilla are making progress in figuring out what to do for the vampire-restoring ritual, they are frustrated by their continuous opposition from Buffy. Time being of the essence, Spike makes a call to a group of elite assassins known as the Taroccha. As this is being discussed, Drusilla reads more cards, none of which are actual tarot cards. The images on the cards are portrayals of three characters who will be introduced later in the episode.

The cards, therefore, are used in a manner that foreshadows the arrival of characters, events, or changing circumstances. This is a rather typical use of Tarot on television. The cards that were designed specifically for these purposes are not actual tarot cards, but they are blended in, even camouflaged, with actual tarot cards from the most recognizable of decks. This allows the writer and props department to provide a very specific function for the cards that would not be possible had they strictly adhered to using the Waite-Colman Smith cards. Nonetheless, they maintain an association with the Waite-Colman Smith deck by incorporating those cards into the story.

The assassins sent to kill Buffy are called the Taroccha. That name seems evidently to be derived from the Italian word *tarocchi*, which, of course, is the term originally used for the game that was played with the cards in the fifteenth century, long before the cards were used for divination. The term *tarocchi* was rendered *tarot* in French and became a loan word (untranslated) for English.

In conclusion, *Buffy the Vampire Slayer* incorporated Tarot into these episodes in several ways: They made use of the iconic Waite-Colman Smith deck to create a recognizable visual authenticity while simultaneously allowing an effective "cover" through which to use their own designs in a manner

Still from *Buffy the Vampire Slayer*, 1997.

that would allow the foreshadowing of characters, events, and circumstances. They also used the terminology, that is, the name *tarocchi* to be modified for a term serving as the name of an organization of assassins.

In season four of *Buffy the Vampire Slayer*, there was another two-part story (episodes twenty-one and twenty-two) that made use of the cards. As in the earlier example, the cards are based aesthetically on the Waite-Colman Smith deck but designed for a specific purpose in the story. That purpose is a bit more sophisticated in the season four use of the cards compared to the second season's use of them. Buffy's group, who are referred to as the Scoobies, must coordinate their individual skills in a way that will maximize their ability to fight as a team against their opponent, Adam.

Doing so will involve a ritual and that ritual will involve tarot cards. The use of cards as ritual devices was certainly part of the season two episodes. Indeed, it is an actual tradition that is strongly associated with the secret organization known as the Golden Dawn in the later nineteenth century. In season four, it is the Scoobies performing the ritual. The purpose of the ritual is to take the strengths of each member of the team and combine them so that Buffy can defeat Adam, who would otherwise be able to defeat the whole team one at a time. There are four cards that are used for the ritual. Each card represents one of the team members.

The use of a single card representing a person in a tarot reading is a well-known practice. Often called a "significator," a particular card from the deck is chosen to represent a person based on factors such as age, profession, physical appearance, or even just the appeal that a given card has in the mind of the person receiving the reading. The general associations attached to a card are applied to the specific traits of the person receiving the reading. For example, the "King of Cups" might serve as the significator for a mature male who has a family and works as a professor.

In the episode "Primeval" (season four, episode twenty-one), each member of the Scoobies gets a significator card that reflects their individual strengths and character traits. As was the case with the use of Tarot in the earlier season of *Buffy*, while these cards were designed by the show, they were illustrated in a style reminiscent of the Waite-Colman Smith deck. In addition to using the color scheme and even some specific imagery from the Waite-Colman Smith deck, each of these significator cards (as I would call them) has a title written in a font comparable to the way that the Waite-Colman Smith Major Arcana cards are labeled despite the fact that the titles are not taken from the actual tarot cards. The titles on the cards represent the four characters and their key character traits as they relate to the series in general and the conflict of the episode in particular. The character of Willow gets a card that represents Spirit. The character of Xander gets a card that represents Heart. The character Giles gets a card that represents Mind. Buffy gets a card that represents Body (the image is actually made of hands), because she will be the one who physically fights against Adam.

The climactic scene of the episode involves Buffy physically beating Adam in the midst of a much larger fight between soldiers and demons. The staging and choreography of this fight scene are a bit reminiscent of a 1970s-era James Bond film, albeit with a smaller budget. At the end of the fight, Buffy kills Adam, and the friends realize their importance to one another. Simultaneously, the maniacal conspiracy that necessitated the conflict in the first place is halted. Things seem to go back to normal—but only for a little while.

The next episode, "Restless," further develops the meaning of the tarot cards in a manner that relates to the individual characters and the emotional challenges they face in life. Each character has a dream sequence in which they are forced to confront their fears and limitations. The first three die. They are killed in a manner that can be correlated to their tarot cards from the previous episode. For example, Giles, whose card was titled "Sophus" and represented his intellect, is scalped—an attack directly on his brain. Willow, whose card was "Spiritus," is killed when her spirit is sucked out of her body.

In this episode of *Buffy the Vampire Slayer*, the tarot-like cards are used to block off four separate but related stories by character and trait. It would not be an exaggeration to consider the tarot cards from the previous episode as being used for chapter headings, of a sort, in the next episode (which was a season finale).

While tarot cards certainly had a place in the series, one cannot assert that they were essential in the production of *Buffy the Vampire Slayer*. The series clearly saw tarot cards as a useful prop that served the functions mentioned above. The audience could readily identify tarot cards as an appropriate object to associate with the show's characters and supernatural storylines. Whatever aspects of Tarot that the audience members identify or imagine as having a logical place in the show, there is also an ease with which the show and its characters can be transferred into the audience's concept of the Tarot.

It would have been an enthusiastic, although not surprising, response from that audience to see a *Buffy the Vampire Slayer* tarot deck for sale. A company called Dark Horse planned to publish a deck based on the show. They hired top level figures to work on the project. Rachel Pollack was consulted in the design and commissioned to write the accompanying manual. Pollack is one of the best-known authors in the tarot community. The illustrator was Paul Lee, a well-known comic book illustrator who worked on the *Buffy the Vampire Slayer* comics.

Sadly for *Buffy* fans, the project was cancelled shortly before it was supposed to be rolled out in the summer of 2008. It had gone deep into production by then. In fact, a number of the illustrations had been publicized, and the concept was fully developed. According to a fictional backstory created to be associated with the deck, it was designed hundreds of years ago to be used by slayers (there is one slayer in each generation with Buffy being the current holder of that title). The fictional designers of the deck had visions of a future slayer (Buffy) that would "go rogue" by falling in love with a vampire and having a set of human allies.

It is an interesting product concept although it would not have been the only deck to be associated with a television series. To play upon the rhetorical question, does art imitate life or does life imitate art? The idea does suggest art, if we may consider the design of a tarot deck to be art, influencing television and, then, television influencing art in turn. Indeed, many television shows have spun off whole product lines that include everything from lunch boxes to bed sheets. The fact that we can add tarot cards to that list is an indicator of how embedded Tarot has become in American culture. Another television program, *Carnivale*, an HBO series that ran for two seasons, beginning in 2003, actually developed a downloadable game connected to the show that made use of tarot cards in a digital electronic format.

Tarot Wins an Emmy: HBO's *Carnivale* and *Game of Thrones*

Carnivale had an opening sequence that used tarot cards in an impressively artistic fashion. The first image is one of a pile of face-up tarot cards on sand. The artwork on the cards is done in a Renaissance style and even incorporates Renaissance masters such as Michelangelo. For example, the first card in the pile of face-up cards that the camera zooms in on is "the World." The design for the card is taken from Michelangelo's *Last Judgment*, the massive fresco painted on the wall behind the altar of the Sistine Chapel. It is strange that the image was used on "the World" card rather than the more logical "Judgment" card. Another Renaissance artist, Raphael, is also used in the artwork selected for the cards. His painting *Saint Michael Vanquishing Satan* appears on the "King of Swords" card (rather than "the Devil" card, as one might think more appropriate).

As the opening sequence continues, the camera moves closer to the image on the card and then passes through it. The card's image morphs into a three-dimensional form that is reminiscent of the sets used by the early twentieth-century director Georges Méliès in films such as *A Trip to the Moon* (1902) and *The Impossible Voyage* (1904). As that effect dissolves, the viewer begins to see stock archival footage of historical significance from the 1930s.

The historical archival footage creates a remarkable impression. Clips from speeches of Mussolini or Franklin Delano Roosevelt are interspersed with footage of Ku Klux Klan meetings and soup lines. All of these give a strong sense of the 1930s in America and the wider world. More than that, however, the footage complements and accentuates the themes associated with the tarot cards and the works of art that are placed on those cards. After showing one short clip of 1930s archival footage, the camera pulls back, appearing to go through a different tarot card than the one the camera had earlier passed through. In both cases, the card serves as a visual frame. The result is a wonderful in-and-out effect that is repeated as the camera pans, then zooms in on the next card, morphing into a three-dimensional form before dissolving into another piece of 1930s stock archival footage, and then zooming out before repeating the process again. The overall effect, both visually and thematically, is one in which the conflicts of good and evil register in the viewers' minds, as does the theme of struggle in life. It is a powerful visual representation of what the ancient Greek playwrights called *agon*—struggle.

Tarot cards designed for the opening sequence of HBO's *Carnivale* series, 2003–2005.

Tarot cards are used in this opening television sequence to define and contextualize *agon* in the lives and world of characters in America during the 1930s. This is accomplished partly by the simple technique of using the cards' titles in the same way intertitles were used in silent filmmaking while also using the individual cards as visual frames. These simple devices are complemented further by the imagery on each card and the imagery of the deck as a whole.

Angus Wall, the film editor who designed the title sequence, won an Emmy for it in 2004. He also won another Emmy in 2011, this time for his design of the opening sequence of the *Game of Thrones* series (also an HBO production). *Carnivale* was a brilliant piece of art and design for an opening sequence, and a brilliant montage as well.

Carnivale and Angus Wall's award-winning work on it demonstrates the potential power embedded in the imagery of Tarot at the level of popular culture. Even those unfamiliar with Tarot are instantly clued in on the meanings of individual cards (at least, of the Major Arcana) because the words are so plainly written on the cards. These are often powerful words (i.e., "Judgment," "Death," or "the Devil"). Even when they are not powerful words, as in the case of the Minor Arcana (*Carnivale* uses cards such as the "Ace of Swords," "the King of Swords," and "Three of Cups") it is clear to the viewer that a world populated with meaningful characters and images is being entered.

The show includes a scene in which the character of Ben, a young man with supernatural powers, goes to a carnival psychic and gets a tarot reading from a young woman. The deck used in the show is the Waite-Colman Smith deck, but the words on the cards are in French rather than English. As the reading begins, the woman turns over "the Moon" card and explains its meaning. Ben flashes back to memories of his childhood, when he discovered his supernatural ability to heal by raising a kitten from the dead. Another flashback, interposed with a second tarot card ("Death") being turned over in the reading, shows Ben's mother realizing what had happened with the kitten and fearing that her son is under some evil influence counteracting the will of God. The third flashback, after the third card is turned over, revealing "the Magician" card, shows Ben's mother on her deathbed rejecting Ben's desire to heal her and trying to protect herself by placing a cross between herself and her son.

It seems apparent that Ben allowed his mother to die. The tarot card reader, pointing to "the Magician" card in the inverted position, says that Ben had somehow not used his gifts and abilities. She does not know about Ben's ability to heal or about his past. Yet, the reading was quite accurate, and the accuracy disturbed Ben to such an extent that it caused him to run off. The tarot cards were used in this scene as a prop that helps to quickly establish several important aspects of the show.

The cards signify the supernatural at multiple levels because Ben and the reader both are shown to have magical abilities. At the same time, however, the reading helps to illustrate that no one has a complete understanding and that lack of understanding is a bit frightening to explore or to have exposed. The cards are also used, in a very conventional way, in order to reveal the past. As a prop, they are effective in ways that facilitate storytelling or narrative. They are also effective in establishing mood or feeling.

The HBO television series *Game of Thrones* has also gotten into the tarot game, so to speak. Craig Coss, of Petaluma, California, was selected by Chronicle Books to create a tarot deck based on the *Game of Thrones* along with Liz Dean, a tarotist from the United Kingdom, who wrote the *Guidebook* that comes with the cards. The deck went on sale in the spring of 2018. In an interview for a local news outlet, the *Press Democrat* (April 30, 2018), Coss made it clear that he hoped the deck was designed with enough depth of meaning to satisfy people who were both fans of the show and knowledgeable about Tarot (Sirdofsky).

It might be simple to choose Tyrian Lannister as "the Fool" or to choose Danaerys Targaryan as "the Empress," but Coss also intended to sprinkle meaningful objects and symbols throughout the cards that give weight to the conventional meanings of those cards as well as the identity of the characters and world of the show. This goal was fairly well executed in some respects; as in the use of red wine, so strongly associated with the character of Cersei Lannister, in the suit of cups. However, many of the images, such as "the Emperor" and "the Lovers," do not have much detail in the background and, therefore, do not strike one as being rich in attached symbolic details.

Still, for anyone who is a fan of the show and a fan of Tarot, there is no doubt that the deck achieves a dual-level rendering of one of the most important aspects of meaningful storytelling—effective use of archetypal imagery. Both Tarot and *Game of Thrones* are heavily dependent on archetypal imagery. This deck does an outstanding job of capturing that element in both senses (the show and the tarot tradition). Placing Cersei Lannister on the "Queen of Swords" card is an excellent choice, in my view, because that character from *Game of Thrones* is indeed representative of certain characteristics of the card. The iconography is even more strongly illustrated by placing her on the Iron Throne of the greatest monarchs in the fictional world of Westeros. The effect of the image is to convey the power and dangerousness of this mercurial woman who could be a decisive ally or one's worst possible enemy. The meaning of the card is perfectly illustrated by use of the *Game of Thrones* character as well as the setting in which she is placed.

Unlike many other decks, however, this one is not as strictly aligned with the poses and images of the often-imitated Waite-Colman Smith deck, although the illustrators' style and use of color does, to some degree, show an awareness of that deck's influence on most recent deck designs. For example, the "Three of Swords," "Six of Swords," and the "Nine of Cups" are all instantly recognizable as derived from the Waite-Colman Smith deck. However, the Major Arcana cards are much less likely to be recognized as being based on the imagery of Waite-Colman Smith. Having said that, they do, however, reflect the meanings (if not the appearance) very well.

Cards based on television shows have an obvious interest for any fans of the particular show, if those viewers are also fans of Tarot. Certainly, any fan of *Game of Thrones* who is also interested in Tarot will enjoy that deck. Observing how a show can inspire a deck is quite a different matter than seeing how well a show can incorporate Tarot into that show's own universe and, further, how much the use of Tarot within a television series' plot might resonate with a viewer.

What do Don Draper, Lisa Simpson, and Xena: Warrior Princess, Have in Common?

The ability to incorporate the cards as a prop and as a tool to create a psychological context or develop a theme suitable to any number of television programs is intriguing. By considering Tarot on programs such as *Mad Men*, *The Simpsons*, and *Xena: Warrior Princess*, we can develop a better sense of how broadly the social and cultural relevance of Tarot actually is while simultaneously seeing the depth of meaning made available by Tarot to writers and directors of popular television programs.

Mad Men was produced by Weiner Brothers, whose logo is actually a tarot card, "the Sun." Matthew Weiner, the creator of *Mad Men*, uses tarot readings in his own life. In fact, the tarot reading that Don Draper receives in season two, episode twelve ("The Mountain King," 2008) is, according to a *Rolling Stone* interview the following year, one of Weiner's own tarot readings. In the show, when the character Anna begins Don Draper's reading, Don says, "It's an ink blot. You see what you want to see." In the *Rolling Stone* interview, Weiner said, "I use tarot cards as a kind of Rorschach test for my life" (Maerz, *Rolling Stone*). As noted elsewhere in this book, the Rorschach is not even the best psychological test metaphor for Tarot. Consider the Thematic Apperception Test, which uses images on cards. A person is asked to arrange the cards into a dramatic story. Of course, the person's choices can reveal something about their psychology. Weiner chose the specific tarot reading on *Mad Men* because he found it both personally engaging and also generally relevant to many men because it suggests a tendency to attempt to be strong but, instead, ending up just pushing people away.

Don is asked by Anna if he wants to know what the cards say. He says "no," but Anna goes on with the reading (at least, in a partial manner, with a particular emphasis on "the World" card). When Don points to the "Judgment" card, he says, "That can't be good.... It's the end of the world." Anna responds by saying, "It's the resurrection," and goes on to point out the opportunity to start again by changing. Don responds by saying that "people don't change." But, Don Draper is, more than anybody, a person defined by change. Even his name has been changed (from Dick Whitman). He has assumed the identity of the deceased husband of the woman reading his tarot cards. In fact, the episode is largely about Don changing his life in dramatic ways. He talks about his new relationship with a woman. He is in California, and is contemplating not returning to New York. Further, the episode uses a significant number of flashbacks that illustrate the changes in Don's life while shifting back and forth to the other characters' storylines, each of which is undergoing dramatic change. One of the cards in the reading, "the World," strengthens this theme of change in the episode—indeed, in the whole series—by illustrating many ways in which Don's life is connected to the world and the people around him, just as Anna describes the card. In the end, the reading furthers the trajectory of the series (not just the episode) by raising the issues

Don Draper's tarot reading on *Mad Men*, 2008.

of Don's personal growth and self-realization juxtaposed to those whose lives are connected to his.

One of the functions provided by tarot cards in television drama is to create a field in which the viewers, like the character of Don Draper, may consider the idea of fate. Is fate something controlled by the individual or, is the individual controlled by fate? This is a theme, of course, that dates back to ancient Greek drama such as Sophocles's *Oedipus Rex* or Aeschylus's *Agamemnon*. In *Oedipus Rex*, the title character is destined to kill his father and have sex with his mother. He does all he can to prevent these prophesied events, but nonetheless, they come to pass. In *Agamemnon*, the character of Cassandra has the gift of being able to prophesy but is cursed by the fact that no one will believe her prophecies. She can see her death and the death of King Agamemnon coming but is powerless to stop either of them from being murdered. This sense that fate is sealed can be nearly as scary as any particular fate. Tarot cards, when associated with divination, have the potential to convey that frightening sense of powerlessness in the face of an ugly fate.

The use of tarot cards to predict the future raises questions about destiny. Yet, most any modern tarot reader, like Anna talking to Don, will say that one can alter—or, better yet, control—their destiny by looking into the future and modifying their actions accordingly. Tarot, like life and drama, is filled with dichotomies, ambiguities, and inconsistencies that actually add meaningfulness rather than assert meaninglessness. This may be profound or silly—maybe even both—depending on one's perspective.

One can see a glimpse of this in the 1995 episode of *The Simpsons* called "Lisa's Wedding" (season six, episode nineteen), in which the Simpsons visit a Renaissance fair. The setting of a Renaissance fair, of course, is somewhat understandable given that the cards began their history at that time.

Lisa wanders off and finds the tent of a gypsy fortune-teller who reads her cards. The stereotype of a fortune-telling gypsy, by the way, is strong in popular culture. It dates to the nineteenth century and has, as we have seen, little historical connection to the development of the cards or the use of the cards for divination. The character-type is presented in typical *Simpsons* fashion. There are recognizable elements that are twisted into a parody with some thoughtful, yet amusing, implications.

Lisa is given a five-card layout, and although each card has a member of her family drawn on it, each card is also properly named with a real tarot card title. In the center of the group is the "Death" card. This causes Lisa to gasp, but the gypsy explains that "Death" is not such a bad card. It represents transition and change. Anyone who has learned about tarot cards as a reader, or perhaps just as a person getting a reading, can identify with the experience of learning that the scary-looking "Death" card is not as frightening as an initial encounter might seem.

Then, the gypsy flips over another card, one created especially for the episode. It is "the Happy Squirrel" card. After having been relieved that the "Death" card was not so bad, Lisa's response to "the Happy Squirrel" card is one of (you guessed it) happiness. However, the fortune-teller momentarily becomes agitated to the point of near panic as if the card held terrifying implications. Lisa asks if the card is bad and the gypsy, reversing her demeanor instantly, calmly responds by shrugging and saying, "Possibly, the cards are vague and mysterious." The effect is to imply the cards appear to be meaningful but may be meaningless. This, too, reflects a familiar learning experience for card readers and the people for whom they read, even though it is presented in the form of parody. The meaning of the cards are indeed "vague and mysterious." That fact allows for the flexibility needed to get a specifically relevant meaning out of a general idea associated with the card. This is a strength or a weakness, depending on one's viewpoint. I would point out (just as a side note) that the same is true of the major prophecies given credence by adherents of the major faiths in the world for centuries.

The gypsy fortune-teller lets Lisa know that her future wedding to an Englishman named Hugh Parkfield will take place in America but that Lisa's family will be so obnoxious that Hugh will quickly leave Lisa behind and return to England. The gypsy makes it clear that these events are inevitable. Lisa will see them happen, but the gypsy tells Lisa to "try to act surprised."

Tarot reading from *The Simpsons*, 1995.

Elsewhere, the fortune-teller also says that she "specializes in relation-ships where you get jerked around." One wonders, how many people have had tarot readings on relationships where they have been "jerked around" and what does that imply (if anything) about tarot readings? One might question if people who "get jerked around" in their relationships are sup-posedly more inclined to seek the advice of fortune-tellers—but let us not take that digression.

It may be interesting to long-term viewers of *The Simpsons* to consider that this 1995 episode had a plot that took things ten years into the future via the device of the tarot cards, and that the show would indeed, in reality, last that long (quite a bit longer, in fact). The predicted events, though asserted to be inevitable by the gypsy, do not actually come to pass in the year 2005.

Another example of a tarot card reading asserting a comically tragic des-tiny can be found in the show *Schitt's Creek*. In a 2019 episode called "the Hike," there is a tarot reading set in a restaurant owned by Twyla, one of the show's secondary characters. A main character, Alexis, and her fiancé, Ted, see Twyla reading tarot cards in an attempt to raise money for a dishwasher. Alexis wants a reading. Unknown to Twyla, Alexis and Ted have been pre-paring for a trip to the Galapagos Islands. Twyla reads the cards and asks if they're going anywhere near water. She then tells them that she sees a boat capsize, a young couple sink beneath the waves, and then "it all goes black." Ted is incredulous, asking, "Surely, you can't really see all that in the cards?" When Twyla explains that she also has to interpret the cards, Ted asks her to interpret something nicer. Twyla then begins to describe what seems to be a formal party and Alexis responds by asking if it's a "black and white" party. Twyla then explains that it's a funeral.

The story has fun with the idea that tarot cards cannot tell the future by contrasting that with a scarily precise prediction that is treated by the tarot reader in an almost matter-of-fact kind of way. It is as if the viewer is being encouraged to mock the notion that the cards can predict the future while simultaneously being challenged by what seems like a real possibility that the characters' lives are genuinely in danger. The scene abruptly ends without resolving what the viewer ought to believe.

In the representation of tarot cards on *Schitt's Creek* and *The Simpsons*, the supposition that the cards can be used to divine the future is further developed in a manner that shows the future as part of an unalterable path of destiny. This notion of destiny being set in stone would be more appropriately applied to Calvinist theological doctrine than to Tarot. A very large majority of tarot readers would deny making such claims about the future or what the cards can do. Be that as it may, the use of tarot cards in storytelling is amenable to such an assertion. The fate of fictional characters, and the interest that viewers have in those characters, is controlled by writers who can, in their own way, seal the destinies of Lisa, Bart, and Homer—just as any writer can do with any of their characters. That power to determine in advance how the story will develop and end is, in some respects, how some people (mis)understand the claims of tarot readers. This creates a great opportunity for parody. It also allows a writer to make use of the mysterious powers of the cards to shape an enticing narrative and get a few laughs. If those laughs come at the expense of the tarot reader, so be it. No one, after all, is safe from parody.

Rather than being insulted by the scene and the use of tarot on *The Simpsons*, some in the tarot community have embraced "the Happy Squirrel" card. One can now buy a deck of *Simpsons* tarot cards that includes "the Happy Squirrel" card. Even more surprisingly, one can actually find "Happy Squirrel" cards designed to be added to any of several specific conventional tarot decks. While researching for an academic presentation, I found the website of a self-described "psychonaut," mystic healer, occult philosopher, and witch named Mat Auryn who came up with a detailed analysis, though half-jokingly, on "the Happy Squirrel." He examined squirrels as a symbol, squirrels in mythology and folklore, the number twenty-three (the assigned position for the card in the Major Arcana), and then discusses the Kabbalistic tree of life before offering some conclusions about the divinatory meanings one could assign to such a card. He then does a sample tarot reading incorporating the card into a popular deck (called the Shadowscapes tarot).

"The Happy Squirrel" card from *the Simpsons*.

As noted above in the discussion of *Buffy the Vampire Slayer* series and tarot deck, there is a back and forth dynamic at work between television and the art associated with the production of tarot cards. It is clear that either can influence the other. This is true even in animated series such as *The Simpsons*, which is not the only popular animated comedy series of the decade that straddles the twentieth and twenty-first centuries to incorporate Tarot.

In 2003, during its seventh season, an episode of the widely viewed animated series *King of the Hill* was called "The Witches of East Arlen," in which Bobby Hill, the son of the show's main character, Hank Hill, gets involved with some older boys—young adults, actually—with an interest in the occult. Like the child Bobby, these young men are geeky outcasts. Because of the fact that they are young adults and have a seemingly welcoming little community with an exotic identity, however, Bobby is happy to get involved with them, quickly finding himself immersed in a subculture that his parents will find ridiculous and likely to prevent Bobby from becoming a normal young man.

The episode begins with Bobby being rejected for a role in the school production of Rodgers and Hammerstein's *Oklahoma!* and becoming a little depressed. Hank has to get Bobby out of his funk and takes Bobby along on a trip to the flea market, where Bobby comes across a deck of tarot cards and a book on how to read them. Hank, unaware that they are not a regular poker deck, is encouraged that Bobby will have a new and properly masculine interest superior to that of acting in plays. Later, when Bobby is at the video rental store, he encounters Ward, the leader of a small coven of self-professed (and self-deluded) witches. When Ward sees that Bobby has a deck of tarot cards, he decides to take Bobby on as a protégé just as Ward's boss tells him to start mopping floors and mockingly refers to him as Merlin.

One of the main themes of the episode is about the formation of an identity and belonging to a group. Hank wants Bobby to be more masculine and "normal" by developing an interest in poker or sports or cars. Bobby rejects the type of identities and interests that his father has in mind (which is a recurring theme in the series), developing a sense of belonging to the new little group and furthering his interest in magic, although he never seems to take it quite as seriously as the young men in his new group of friends. The viewer is presented with the strong impression that those with an interest in magic are destined to never fit in with the rest of society or to have happy lives. Tarot, then, is presented simply as one of a few characteristics in an identity associated with being a "loser."

At one point, Bobby and his parents are called into school because Bobby's robe (which he received upon joining the coven) makes him appear to be a member of some strange religious group that will be difficult for the principal to handle in terms of political correctness. When Bobby's parents are called to the principal's office, his mother, Peggy, says that Bobby is becoming "girl repellant" and orders Hank to "fix it." The struggle to shape Bobby's identity intensifies as Hank demands Bobby get rid of the magical paraphernalia and get to work learning how to repair a carburetor. Bobby continues to resist such efforts and returns to the coven of dorks.

The coven, feeling that Bobby's experience is a perfect example of how witches are still being unjustly persecuted, as in the days of Salem, decides to "take things up a notch" by having a powerful ritual in which Bobby will drink dog blood (*caninus spiritus*, as the boys call it). Bobby ultimately refuses to go through the ritual, and the witches decide to "destroy" him using their magical spells. The effort was pathetic. This causes Bobby to laugh at them and realize that they really are as bad as his father said they were. Bobby now knows that he needs a different path in life or he will end up being a loser just like Ward, the leader of the "coven" who Bobby has now determined is a dork on the grounds that "he wears socks with sandals."

The use of tarot cards in *King of the Hill* is as an identifying trait for a character type that represents a social reject. The cards are one example of a prop that can be associated with boys who grow up to be unsuccessful in finding a good job or fitting in with "normal" kids, as well as being dependent on their mothers well into adulthood and failing to find a mate. Ward works at a video rental store, lives in his mother's basement, was regularly beaten up by bullies when he was in school, and thinks that "when the time

Bobby Hill does a tarot reading. *King of the Hill*, 2003.

is right, a maiden will be delivered up" to him, "probably from the East." It is
an interesting contrast of what tarot cards signify in a social context when we
compare *King of the Hill* with *The Simpsons*. Both shows play upon familiar
conventions with the intention of mocking them, but they do so in rather
different ways.

Popular culture, like high art, has many streams of influence. Tarot has
certainly had some detectable influences on television. So, too, can one find
the influences of television on Tarot. Shows such as *King of the Hill* and *The
Simpsons* have made use of tarot cards in ways that can mock the people and
ideas associated with Tarot or use the cards as a prop that adds a sense of
mystery and awe to a narrative associated with the supernatural.

The tarot cards themselves, as alluded to earlier, can be used to tell stories
in interesting ways. For example, the most common tarot layout, the Celtic
Cross, allows the reader to do something like this because the individual
cards and the positions in which they are placed, when read in sequence and
considered in relation to one another, is conducive to creating a narrative.
There is also an open-ended and malleable story about the Major Arcana
called "the Fool's Journey" (discussed in an earlier chapter). Starting with
card zero, "the Fool," one travels through the numerical order of the cards

considering their individual meaning in the life of the reader. This creates a narrative, but, more significantly, serves as a way to meditate on important aspects of life in both general and personal terms. Such meditation is commonly thought by users of Tarot to aid in personal or spiritual development.

The cards of the Major Arcana are used to provide a context and narrative structure for a 1998 episode of *Xena: Warrior Princess* (season three, episode twelve, "The Bitter Suite"). Just as we saw in the episode of *Mad Men* discussed above, the issue of fate is examined. A major theme of the episode, as with Greek tragedy, is the control of one's own destiny blended with the consequences of one's actions. Another distinctive element of this episode is that, for some inexplicable reason, it was written and performed as a musical.

As silly as the idea of a musical combining Tarot and Xena may be, the focus on personal and spiritual development in the context of Tarot is important. It actually represents a cultural trend that developed in the 1960s and became pervasive in the tarot community by the 1980s. That is, the use of tarot cards as a device for fortune-telling remained common, but the use of the cards as a meditative tool and a psychological or philosophical device for those seeking personal growth has also become quite typical. In a sense, this goes back to the eighteenth century and Court de Gebelin, who thought of the cards as containing hidden philosophical content. By the end of the twentieth century, such content was thoroughly grafted onto the symbols and use of the cards. Although this development originated in an artificially constructed manner, it has had profound implications (admittedly, "profound" may be an overstatement in the context of a show like *Xena*).

Rob Tapert, the show's executive producer (and the husband of Lucy Lawless, who starred as the titular character, Xena), developed the idea of using Tarot in the episode. The Waite-Colman Smith tarot deck provides extensive and obvious inspiration throughout the episode. Characters on the show are presented as figures from the tarot deck, and some of the sets or set pieces were also taken directly from the tarot deck. For example, the "Wheel of Fortune" features prominently and repeatedly. Indeed, the characters move through the fictional world of Illusia by going through the wheel, and the wheel sets in motion various changes in the characters' psychological and emotional progress. "The Tower" card was used as inspiration for a set piece and the "Judgment" card was used as inspiration for an entire set.

The character of Callisto was presented as "the Fool" in the episode. Later, she appears as "Justice," at one point saying, "Aleph am I," which refers to the Hebrew letter esoterically associated with "the Fool" card and is a quote from *The Book of Tokens*, written in 1920 by the American tarotist Paul Foster Case. The character of Xena was portrayed as "the High Priestess," "the Chariot,"

"The Fool" card from the
Waite-Colman Smith Tarot.

and "Death." Gabrielle, the series' most significant character next to Xena, was presented as "the Empress," "the Star," "the World," and "Strength."

In *Xena*, magical and supernatural aspects of the Tarot take a back seat to emotional development and the relationship of the two main characters. The Tarot is used as a means to confront and overcome problems at psychological, emotional, and spiritual levels. There is no fortune-telling component at work. The presentation of the future is one of contrasting possibilities. The reality of the future is decided by the person's free will rather than fate. Further, the present conditions of one's life are largely determined by one's past actions despite the influences of other people or general circumstances. This is at odds with popular conceptions about tarot cards, but not for those more familiar with the contemporary use of the cards.

Callisto from *Xena: Warrior Princess* dressed as "the
Fool" card from the Waite-Colman Smith Tarot, 1998.

Conclusion

I can tell you this, then, about tarot and television: they work well together.
Most obviously, tarot cards trigger certain responses associated with fear,
dread, or the presence of supernatural power, making them a valuable prop
in certain scenes and contexts. They can be used humorously to mock superstition, and just as easily, to mock those who reject the supernatural as if it
were superstition. They also help to raise questions about fate versus free will.

Furthermore, the cards are conducive to personal introspection in ways
that can define a character or touch a viewer. Tarot cards can add to and
even create a narrative for a writer or director. The place of tarot cards in
television becomes even more special when we consider the fact that television, like tarot, is itself a type of magic for those who create it as well as for
those who consume it.

CHAPTER 6

Tarot Goes to the Movies

What Tarot Can Do For A Movie . . . Any Movie

A large heart with three swords driven through it instantly evokes a feeling of heartbreak and suffering. That is what the "Three of Swords" is intended to represent. Loss and sorrow are also symbolized by this card. This card is perfectly, and simply, used for this purpose in the 2003 Walt Disney film *The Haunted Mansion*, starring Eddie Murphy as a realtor and father who moves his family into a haunted house. The opening sequence uses three tarot cards, each of which represents an element in the back-story of the eponymous house's history.

As a variety of objects float through the air and a door opens into another time period, we see the mansion as it existed during the eighteenth century (prior to it becoming haunted) and a deck of cards floating in front of the viewer, with "the Lovers" card magically pulled from the deck. This card represents Mr. and Mrs. Gracie, the original couple living in the mansion. The woman on the card transforms into a skeleton just before the card flies away. As the story within the opening sequence progresses, the next card to appear is "Death," and we see the gloved hand of a woman fall, dropping a goblet of presumably poisoned wine. Soon, we see a clock strike thirteen and a crying man embracing his dead lover. The next card to appear is the "Three of Swords." After that, we see the man has hanged himself. The cards, in conjunction with other objects floating in the foreground, the music, and the action of the characters (who have no lines in the sequence) illustrate a sad and dramatic story.

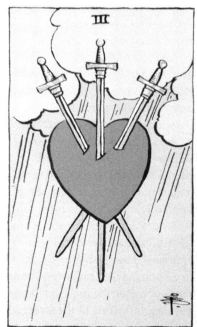

Three cards used in the opening
sequence of Disney's *Haunted
Mansion*.

The use of the cards is both symbolic and narrative in Disney's *Haunted Mansion* and in a number of other movies that employ tarot cards as a prop. The cards can even be compared to the intertitles that were used in the silent film era to provide the scenes' narration. It is a simplistic and literal process. "The Lovers" represent actual lovers, while "Death" literally represents death. These words are written on the cards and the images on the cards easily reinforce the meaning. Although the "Three of Swords" does not have a title as the other two cards do, its symbolic meaning would be clear to anyone, even without any previous knowledge of Tarot. The use of the cards in this opening sequence is clear and effective. It also makes efficient use of time and does not even require the characters to have lines.

At other times, tarot cards are used as just one prop in a grouping of items that have the connotation of spiritualism, mystery, fortune-telling, and so on. Consider the 1941 film *The Wolfman*, for example. In one scene, Lon Chaney Jr., as the character Larry Talbot, takes his date, Gwen Conliffe, and her friend Jenny to a gypsy camp for a fortune-telling session. Jenny has her fortune told by a gypsy named Bela (played by Bela Lugosi). The gypsy's room is filled with the accoutrement one would expect. He begins to do a card reading (although the viewer cannot see the cards) and abruptly stops. He then begins to read her palms but sees a pentagram, marking Jenny's impending doom from an encounter with a wolfman (Bela himself). The scene plays on stereotypes and imagery representative of gypsies and fortune-telling but also upon the idea of destiny. This is one of the more basic examples of using tarot cards as a prop. However, the cards do not play a central role in the film. They are just one of several devices used to set a stage visually or to create a mood. In the 2010 version of the film, *The Wolfman*, starring Benicio del Toro in the title role, one tarot card appears and it is only for a split-second. The card is the "Three of Swords." It is a different version of the same card used in the opening sequence of *The Haunted Mansion* yet, if the viewer knew the card was there, and knew the meaning of the card, it does serve the same function of indicating misery, loss, and heartbreak.

The 2005 film, *Monster-In-Law*, starring Jennifer Lopez and Jane Fonda, also makes use of Tarot in a manner that is incredibly brief but clearly purposeful. Early in the film, Lopez is on the beach taking a break from walking a group of dogs. She reads her horoscope, which says, "Stop looking so hard. Love is right in front of you." Then, her love interest is shown jogging shirtless on the beach (in slow motion, of course). Soon thereafter, Lopez is sitting around a patio table with her friends talking about a tarot card reading they are doing. The only card shown is not a genuine tarot card. It appears to be the "King of Spades," except the number fourteen is on the card. At that point, the opening credits have very nearly finished. A few scenes later, after Lopez's and Fonda's characters have just met and Fonda's son has just proposed to Lopez, we find Fonda going off into a room to perform a cleansing ritual so she can cope with what she perceives to be the traumatic idea of her beloved son marrying a woman who is simply not good enough for him (indeed, no woman could be good enough for this mother's son).

The cluster of events and associated props—the horoscope, tarot reading, and cleansing ritual with a large feather and incense—all signify a certain spirituality. Indeed, Lopez's character says at one point in the film that she is more spiritual than religious. Perhaps more significantly, all three devices serve the function of showing that a higher power is at work in people's lives. The viewer can certainly take this as an implicit nod to the concept of destiny.

In the few seconds spent on the tarot scene, we begin by hearing one of the characters saying that he doesn't really know anything about Tarot, but this doesn't deter the little group. He looks at the card somewhat quizzically and says, "I don't know. The knight in shining armor?" With that, Lopez grabs the card and says, "That's mine." She then begins to tell her friends about the man she saw at the beach and how she bumped into him later at the coffee shop. Two brief encounters seemed to create a sense of destiny when contextualized with the tarot card and the hopes of the character. Similarly, the horoscope clearly indicated the destiny of the main character and her romantic interest. To this, we can add that Jane Fonda's ritualized efforts to regain her composure after hearing the marriage proposal show a spiritual, somewhat supernatural effort to accept the things that fate will not allow her to change, and eventually she does accept (and will learn to love) the woman who marries her son.

Although I am using the terms interchangeably, as people often do, there is a bit of a distinction between fate and destiny. We shall look at that distinction here only as a side note and, then, quickly move on. The word "fate" is that power which controls the course of events. This power may be seen as God, another deity (or deities), or it may be an ambiguous and inanimate force of nature operating at a supernatural level. Destiny properly refers to the idea of a predetermined outcome. The word "destiny" is derived from the Latin root *destinata*, which also gives us the English word "destination." Despite the distinction, the words are often used interchangeably because context often merges the two ideas of direction and result.

The 1993 Western *Tombstone* not only had a star-studded cast, it also provided another example where Tarot was used very briefly but to significant effect. During a stormy night, the wives of Wyatt Earp and his two brothers, Virgil and Morgan, were sitting in their parlor with a deck of tarot cards. Allie Earp (Wyatt's wife) turns over three cards in quick succession and names them; "Death," "the Devil," and "the Tower" (which she refers to as "the Tower of Babel"). These three cards have great significance and a frightful connotation.

Although there are certainly other ways of interpreting these cards, "Death" and "the Devil" can (and in this case do) represent the obvious characteristics of death and evil. The third card, "the Tower," represents chaos, confusion, and destruction. The viewer only gets a glimpse of the "Death" card. As soon as the cards are named, chaos ensues. Josephine Marcus (Allie's rival for the affections of Wyatt Earp) enters the house as lightning strikes outside. An instant later, the women think that Virgil Earp is about to come inside from the rain, but it turns out to be a gunman who fires into the house. No one is hit. The camera then moves to a room in another location where Virgil walks in having just been shot and is very seriously wounded. Next, the viewer sees Morgan Earp at a saloon, playing pool, when yet another gunman barges in and shoots Morgan, who dies just after Wyatt and some other people arrive.

The most dramatic point in the movie, setting aside the famous gunfight at the OK Corral (a scene which had occurred earlier in the film), is this scene, sparked by the mention of these three tarot cards. Death and chaos immediately follow the mention of the cards, and the life of the main character, Wyatt Earp (played by Kurt Russell), is turned upside down. Indeed, his entire family is under attack and it seemed as if there was nothing that could stop or prevent the attack.

The scene represents the forces of evil arrayed against the "good guys" and their loved ones. The dramatic intensity of the scene is introduced with the names of the three tarot cards. In other settings, each of these cards might be given meaning and significance that is not so scary or ugly. That does not exclude such possible meanings, however, and the dark meanings of the cards are readily absorbed by the viewer. The use of the cards in *Tombstone* creates a rapid and ominous revelation as the climactic stage in the narrative unfolds. This effect is achieved with the cards as a prop whether or not the viewer has a full appreciation of the conventional meanings of these three tarot cards.

Sherlock Holmes: A Game of Shadows

We have seen how the use of gypsy characters in the *Wolfman* films incorporate Tarot. In both versions of the film (1941 and 2010), the cards are props that help to define gypsy characters in conventional ways along traditional stereotypes that a viewer might instantly recognize. The year after the

Wolfman film starring Benicio del Toro and Anthony Hopkins, another film with a subject and character history of its own was released: *Sherlock Holmes: A Game of Shadows*, starring Robert Downey Jr., as the title character and Jude Law as his friend and sidekick, Dr. Watson. Another major character in the film was a gypsy named Madam Simza Heron, played by Noomi Rapace.

Madam Simza and the other gypsy characters in the film are tied to the conventions typically used to illustrate such characters and their settings. Music, dancing, stealing, traveling, and the stereotypical costume of nineteenth-century gypsies are used in presenting the character and her community. So, too, of course, are tarot cards.

The tarot cards in Madam Simza's possession are the ones designed by Oswald Wirth from Switzerland. Wirth's fame and contribution to Tarot rests on his cards being labeled with Hebrew letters and being used to illustrate Gerard Encausse's (aka Papus's) book, *Tarot of the Bohemians*, which was published along with Wirth's deck in 1889. Additionally, Eliphas Levi's work was an influence upon Wirth in terms of the use of Zodiac symbolism and a Christianized Kabbalah. Wirth developed a theory of astrology for his cards that went beyond his predecessors. So, Wirth's deck is an important one in the history of Tarot, and its placement in this film is significant for a few reasons.

For one, the title of the book written by Holmes's arch-rival, Professor Moriarty, is *The Dynamics of an Asteroid*—the sort of book that Wirth might have been interested in reading, had it been a real book. But, this is less important than some other matters for our consideration. Most significantly, Wirth's deck, published in 1889, would have been available to people living at the time in which the movie was set, 1891. Thus, there is not necessarily an anachronism in using the deck as a prop for the film. However, Wirth's original deck consisted only of the Major Arcana. In the movie, one of the cards that appears is the "Two of Cups," a Minor Arcana card that would not have been part of the deck until years later. It was not until 1909, in the illustrations done by Pamela Colman Smith for Arthur Edward Waite, that more detailed imagery was put on the Minor Arcana cards. In 1891, Sherlock Holmes and Simza would most likely have encountered cards with a simpler illustration for the "Two of Cups." They would have just seen two cups.

The artwork for this particular card is clearly based on the 1909 Waite-Colman Smith deck. It shows two people, each holding a cup, standing under a caduceus (the medical symbol), and above that is the winged head of a lion. It is a more impressive image, of course, than just two cups. However, the two figures on the card are, in this case, representative of two characters in the film. In order to create visual and artistic cohesion for the film, the card is stylized to fit the color scheme and features of the Wirth deck. That is to

Madam Simza prepares to read Sherlock Holmes's tarot cards from *Sherlock Holmes: Game of Shadows*, 2011

say, the Waite-Colman Smith "Two of Cups" card is modified to reflect the style of the Oswald Wirth deck. So, the tarot cards in the movie are partially anachronistic despite good reason for the anachronism.

The scene in which the cards are used is the same scene where Holmes and Simza meet. When we first see the gypsy woman, she has her back turned to the viewer and to Holmes. After having Holmes place some money on the table, she turns around and begins to put on a little show before reading the cards. Perhaps it would be more fair to say that she was creating the appropriate atmosphere for Tarot. She was, after all, in a parlor decorated to look like what one might imagine a gypsy fortune-teller's room to be. She lights a candle and says that, the Tarot "can illuminate your past, clarify your present, and show you the future." As she says this, she waves the match with which she had lit a candle and creates a swirling circle of smoke while she stares at her new client.

Simza then sits down across the table from Holmes and prepares to read his cards when he suddenly grabs the deck from her hands and says, "Actually, I prefer to read your fortune." In the moment that Holmes seizes the cards, he has begun to assert himself over the gypsy by dramatically revealing personal and imperative information about her and her brother. He does this in a manner that is reminiscent of how one would expect a (disreputable?) fortune-teller to do their reading. That is, he demonstrates an understanding

Tarot layout from *Sherlock Holmes: Game of Shadows*, 2011.

of how the cards are properly used, but beyond that, he incorporates what he knows of the person's life and what he can intuitively discern from their cues—their facial expressions, posture, verbal responses to the card reader, and so on. It is somewhat like a poker player trying to read their opponent's face to gain insights before placing bets.

Holmes does not choose at random the cards he sets on the table, but he locates them and places them on the table so rapidly it implies a practiced efficiency. The first of four cards that Holmes draws is "Temperance," which he notes is inverted. He says that it is "indicative of volatility" which may not be a typical way of describing the card, but neither is that an inaccurate description. Holmes knows what he wants to say in this conversation, and he is simply using the cards to deliver his statements in a way that not only conveys the information he wishes but also shows he has the same skill sets as gypsies who might use the cards in a cunning way to make money. He continues talking, revealing that he knows she had recently taken a drink. The viewer, knowing the incredible abilities of the character to use deductive reasoning, suspects that Holmes was not relying on the cards for that particular statement of fact.

Madam Simza, too, has quickly assessed that Holmes is toying with her. Holmes, feigning to ponder the cards, rhetorically asks, "What does she not wish to see?" To this, Simza curtly suggests, "A fool embarrassing himself?" At that point, Holmes smiles and quickly turns over "the Fool" card, giving an ostensible reading of the card in conventional terms while simultaneously informing Simza a little bit more about the fact that her brother is in mortal danger and that he (Holmes) knows something about it. Still, he does not wish to reveal too much to her because he is also trying to assess if

Simza is a potential ally or an enemy. For her part, Simza continues to suggest that Holmes is not as impressive as his smugness and self-satisfaction would indicate.

Holmes says he can do better. As he then turns over the "Two of Cups" (as mentioned above), he says, "A powerful bond, but between who?" Pretending to think aloud, he suggests a brother and sister. At this point in the scene, it is evident to Simza that Holmes knows something about the disappearance of her brother. The viewer will learn later that the reason Simza was in London was to try to find her brother. Holmes's interpretation of the "Two of Cups" is, again, ostensible in terms of conventional meanings, but more important, it also reveals his knowledge of the person on the other side of the table. Furthermore, Holmes has not yet tired of displaying his abilities as a person who can read people while appearing to read cards.

Simza's facial expression indicates immediately that she knows Holmes is holding some important secrets, and when Holmes pretends to have a vision in which he sees the name "Rene," it becomes clear that Holmes knows something about her brother. Simza asks him, "What do you want?" Holmes, looking at Simza rather than the deck of cards, replies, "The Devil," while laying that card down on the table. Simza asks, "Why are we playing this game?" (a great line, given the subtitle of the movie). At that point, Holmes stops playing the game. He hands her a letter that had been written by Rene, and it becomes clear that the two of them will need to work together in order to try to rescue Rene and put an end to the evil plans of Holmes' archenemy, Professor Moriarty, who is now identified with "the Devil" card.

What makes the use of the cards in this film so interesting is not merely that they can be placed in the historical context or used as props in developing and defining a character who is a gypsy. It is interesting to see the cards used in a way that asserts the aphorism associated with Sir Francis Bacon and John F. Kennedy that "knowledge is power."

In the scene where Simza and Holmes meet, one sees the mental prowess of Holmes on full display, but we also learn that the character of Simza is quite impressive. Up until this point in the movie (twenty-four minutes has passed when the scene starts), the story has seemed to be about Irene Adler, who fans of Sherlock Holmes (whether in the books or in film) will recognize as the most important woman in his life. She is both beautiful and intellectually brilliant. Adler's adventures had been followed throughout the film until that point, and a series of action sequences and mysterious revelations ended in her death by the design of Professor Moriarty. In this sense, Madam Simza comes to replace Irene Adler as the female protagonist of the film. For those viewers who saw the first film (*A Game of Shadows* is a sequel), in which Irene Adler was a main character, it begins to become evident that the character of Madam Simza is quite important for the current movie.

The tarot reading provided a background for the plot and the gypsy character. That character turns out to be smart and tough. She is a worthy partner for Holmes and Watson, and will be a worthy adversary of the villains in the film. Immediately after the card reading, Holmes and Simza encounter a Cossack assassin who is hell-bent on killing Simza. Although Holmes certainly helps her survive the ordeal, she demonstrates an ability to think and fight her way through adversity. In a later scene, she will help Holmes and Watson find and get to the location of an arms depot that is well-defended by a group of bad guys working for Moriarty. When an urgent need to escape is upon the heroes, Simza and several gypsy men have to run for their lives, along with Holmes and Watson. The men chasing them are heavily armed with automatic weapons and artillery. Simza shows she can survive as well as any man under the physical demands of the chase. In yet another scene, late in the film, Simza and Watson are at a peace conference with a number of diplomats, soldiers, spies, and others. She and Watson must use the methods of observation and deduction that Holmes is famous for, in order to identify her brother Rene who had been surgically altered to look like one of the diplomats at the conference. Simza's deductive abilities seem as good as Watson's in this scene.

If the stereotypes of gypsies are simplistic or even negative, the character of Simza is not (at least in the context of an action-adventure film) either simplistic or negative. She is portrayed as intelligent, physically and mentally strong, cool under pressure, and a worthy "replacement" for Irene Adler. The development of this character is not dependent upon any particular use of the Tarot by the movie's writers or director. Nonetheless, the cards are used in such a way as to contribute to developing the character and the tenor of the film in general. They are even used to demonstrate another facet of Holmes's brilliance. Like his disguises, Holmes's use of the cards shows him to be something of a showman as well as a sleuth.

Nightmare Alley

Tarot cards are notorious for providing accurate, though ambiguous, predictions for the future. This certainly applies to the way they are used in the 1947 film *Nightmare Alley*. The first time the cards appear in the movie, the fate of the character Pete is revealed. Pete is a washed-up drunk whose alcoholism is about to kill him. The cards are used by Joan Blondell's character, Zeena, who is Pete's longtime girlfriend and partner in their carnival psychic act. Zeena's method of using the cards, as we shall see, is interesting, as is her understanding of the cards' meanings, but her understanding would cause many tarot readers to cringe. Historians of Tarot might also cringe, but for somewhat different reasons. She does a reading for Stan, the main character of the movie (played by Tyrone Power) who, at that point, wants to have an affair with Zeena. Stan is also interested in trying to steal the code that Zeena and Pete once used in a popular and entertaining circus act in which they would speak using coded language so as to make Zeena appear to be psychic.

Zeena begins by telling Stan to cut the deck into three stacks, a common practice for many readers (although there are numerous customary variations). She then tells Stan that the Tarot originated in ancient Egypt (a popular misconception). The future of Pete, Stan, and Zeena is accurately revealed as Zeena reads the cards. However, the reading that Zeena gives is much more detailed than the conventional meanings of the cards would actually allow. More to the point, she makes statements that are definitive as if they were derived clearly and directly from the cards, when actually such a reading would not be possible to one whose interpretation of the cards is based directly on any number of tarot instruction manuals. Having said that, tarot readers do, in fact, develop a narrative as they go through the displayed cards. The narrative is built from the meaning given to the cards (through convention and intuition) and also from the context provided by whatever (or whomever) motivated the reading. In this case, Zeena wanted to do a reading that informed her about the relationship she was having with Pete and Stan, as well as how that relationship would affect their overlapping careers. On the one hand, it might be acceptable to see the character of Zeena as having insights that allow for such a detailed expertise in applying meaning to the cards for the viewer of the film. On the other hand, it might be unrealistic to the viewer of the film (even supposing that the viewer is familiar with Tarot) to have a character who can see so much, and in such specific ways, from a tarot reading.

Nonetheless, Zeena sees a lot in the cards. She identifies the "Hanged Man" as Pete. That card does not even show up in the layout. She pulls it from the deck later as she explains something to Stan. Stan had noticed that a (different) card had fallen on the floor, and he picked it up and gave it to Zeena. The card that had fallen to the floor was the "Death" card. Zeena became apprehensive, asking Stan if the card had been face up or face down on the floor. When Stan said that the card had been faced down, Zeena became certain that Pete was going to die and that his death would be soon. How Zeena connected it to Pete, and why Pete was the "Hanged Man," is unclear.

Joan Blondell and Tyrone Power in *Nightmare Alley*, 1947.

The fact that Pete's card wasn't part of the layout and the fact that the reading was about all three people makes Zeena's conclusions questionable, to say the least, but she is certain and she turns out to be correct. She knows that the new psychic act that she and Stan are planning will be successful and that Pete won't share in that success. She decides not to work with Stan in a desperate attempt to stop something bad from happening to Pete because she knows that the carnival act and Pete's death are linked. Yet, Zeena also knows that Pete's fate is somehow sealed. She speaks as if the cards make this plain and obvious as she shows Stan the "Death" card and the "Hanged Man" card next to each other and asks him in an angry and worried voice, "Do you see what it means? Are you satisfied?"

The impact of the cards in this scene are to demonstrate the certainty of Pete's fate as well as Stan's and Zeena's. The viewer soon realizes, as does Stan, that the cards are absolutely correct. Stan doubts the accuracy of the cards from the beginning, but he is plagued by their apparent predictive abilities. Yet, Stan is a man who considers the supernatural to be nonsensical and foolish, as he does psychic abilities. The lucrative career that he is about to embark upon is predicated on the supposition he makes that people are gullible and can be manipulated because of their foolish belief in things like spiritualism and fortune-telling.

In some ways, the cards and the card reader in *Nightmare Alley* fit an enduring character type. Calista Flockhart, for example, plays a tarot reader named Christine who can use tarot cards to vividly read people in *Things You Can Tell Just by Looking at Her*. In that film, the tarotist is able to go into great detail describing the personal flaws of another character, a doctor played by Glenn Close. Tarot cards being used to go into such specific detail about a person or about events can be found in movies such as *Things You Can Tell Just by Looking at Her* or *Nightmare Alley*, but this would not be expected in an actual tarot reading. Nor would such a powerfully precise ability be developed from reading books on Tarot. In film, however, this can be done to depict the power of psychics, the inevitability of destiny, or to reveal personal aspects of characters. Tarot cards have a resonance with the viewer and in the culture that makes them useful to writers and directors for such purposes.

It is intriguing that tarot cards are used in *Nightmare Alley* as a reliable and verifiable form of the supernatural because the entire film is about the fraudulent use of supposed psychic abilities. Stan gets rich by learning how to take advantage of people's faith in the supernatural, whether that involves religion, stagecraft, the belief in the afterworld or any other form of inexplicable supernatural phenomenon. The Tarot, however, serves as an exception that lets the viewer know, and eventually forces Stan to accept, that the supernatural is genuinely real even though it remains true that human gullibility can be exploited.

The death of Pete follows quickly after Zeena reads the cards. Stan, intending to share some of the moonshine he had just bought with Pete, accidentally mixes up the bottle with wood alcohol. Pete is found dead the next morning. Stan never takes responsibility or reveals his mistake. Stan soon begins working with Zeena on building up an act based on the code Pete and Zeena had developed a few years before. The two never do establish a long-lasting intimate relationship. Instead, Stan becomes intimate with Molly, a beautiful young performer at the carnival (played by Coleen Gray). In a very awkwardly scripted scene, Stan is forced into marrying Molly although he soon comes to view the circumstances as a great opportunity to start his life over again and take the psychic act to another level, replacing Zeena with Molly and focusing on high-class, wealthy venues. Eventually, Stan and Molly become wealthy with their act. Stan, knowing that he has not yet neared the limits of the fortune he could make, continues plotting an even more financially successful future, but he does so without regard to the moral implications of deceiving so many people for so much money.

It is at that time that Zeena reappears in Stan's life. She shows up with Bruno, another one of the carnival people. Zeena and Bruno are visiting with Molly when Stan arrives home at his upscale apartment. Zeena has just laid out some tarot cards on the table, and Stan says, "Are you still monkeying around with those things?" Stan opens up his mail and hands a letter to Molly, who tells the group that the letter is a lucrative offer from New York. Molly quickly adds that Stan is unsure what to do. Suddenly Zeena interjects by telling Stan he's making a big mistake with his business plans. Stan becomes angry with Molly, thinking she had told Zeena about their plans which were supposed to be secret. Zeena then insists that she knows from the cards. Molly says nothing. It was in the cards "plain as day," says Zeena.

Stan begins to argue with Molly and Zeena about the cards. Molly becomes certain that the plans she and Stan had been making were unethical and dangerous. After another tarot reading, Stan tries to get Molly to reject the cards' revelations, saying, "Don't be a sap. This is the stuff she feeds the chumps. It's nothing but a deck of gypsy cards." The viewer, however, can tell that Stan is fighting off his own internal worries. Then, Zeena sets one last card face down without looking at it and demands that Stan turn it over. Stan refuses, still trying to assert that the cards are phony, but the expression on his face shows genuine concern. Molly intervenes by turning the card over to reveal the "Hanged Man" card. Stan realizes the meaning. "Wasn't that Pete's card," he says. Zeena replies, "It's your card now." Although Stan continues to verbally dismiss the cards as nonsense, when Molly says that Zeena believes them, Zeena insists, "So does Stan." Stan then becomes enraged and kicks Zeena and their fellow circus performer, Bruno, out of the apartment.

Stan knows that he is headed down the exact same path that Pete once went down. He will get wealth and fame for a little while, but the cost will require wading into a moral quagmire that will make his life miserable and inevitably ruin his finances. It will also destroy the relationship with the woman he loves.

Film noir conventions require a *femme fatale*, and in this particular film, that role is played by Helen Walker. The character's name is Lilith Ritter. Both Lilith and Stan are scam artists of a similar type, although they appear to be at opposite ends of a spectrum. Lilith is a psychologist who makes her living by comforting people who have confided personal information in her. The same could be said about Stan. The two first meet while Stan was performing his psychic act before a wealthy audience in an upscale Chicago lounge. Lilith, wishing to expose the psychic scam to her companions, asks a misleading question: "Will my mother recover from her present illness?" Stan, however, responds by saying he believes her mother is dead and that the woman is trying to trick him. Lilith is impressed, and the encounter leads to the two working together to exploit several of Lilith's wealthy clients by arming Stan with their personal information taken from Lilith's records.

In the end, we learn that Lilith is actually manipulating Stan to a much greater degree than Stan had ever manipulated his victims. The two launch an ambitious scam to get $150,000 from a wealthy man by fooling him into thinking Stan can bring back his dead wife. Lilith is able to hold the money, and once she has it in her possession, she sets up Stan for a fall by presenting evidence of Stan's guilt, simultaneously expunging all evidence of her part in the scam. Stan soon finds his life in a downward spiral and goes back to the circus where he gets the most menial of jobs and drinks himself into oblivion just as Pete had done.

As an interesting historical side note, there was a magician who went by the name Zanzic in Chicago (the city where *Nightmare Alley* is set) in 1893. He made a significant amount of money running a parlor where people could supposedly contact the dead. The parlor was set up to demonstrate some supposedly supernatural tricks such as floating furniture and disembodied voices. One of Zanzic's clients was a man who was fooled into believing that several contacts were made with his deceased wife. He wanted Zanzic to arrange an actual physical contact with his wife. Zanzic hired a prostitute to play that role with the intention that the man would be able to make love to his deceased wife. The man died of a heart attack while having intercourse with his "wife," and Zanzic placed his body out in the alley. He then told the police that the man had died before arriving for his appointment. Zanzic bribed the police, but eventually, people found out what had actually happened.

It is interesting that *Nightmare Alley* includes a number of different scams based on the belief in magic or the supernatural. The characters use fake psychic abilities, crystal balls, religion, and even psychological counseling to demonstrate that there are myriad ways to take advantage of people for amusement and money. They assert their intellectual superiority by manipulating the gullibility of people who place their hopes in some force greater than human reason. One would think that tarot cards would be just one of the props in such endeavors. Yet, they are used in the film to demonstrate to the reader that fate is certain and that taking advantage of people will ultimately be punished as an act of hubris. That is, the cards get it right. And, while it is certainly true that several of the ways in which tarot cards are used in this film are not consistent with their "proper" use in conventional or traditional ways, the film does place Tarot above the various con games that are used by Stan, Lilith, Zeena, and other characters. It is quite surprising to see a movie about psychic con games using Tarot to show that such scams are immoral and will have catastrophic results. Perhaps this is one reason why the film *Nightmare Alley* is a popular favorite with members of the tarot community such as Mary Greer, a prominent writer and tarot instructor.

The Red Violin

Tarot serves, yet again, as a device for framing the narrative in the 1998 Francois Girard film, *The Red Violin*. Although the film's subject is the eponymous violin, there are four tales that are woven within two central stories. One of those stories belongs to an expert appraiser of musical instruments whose occupation and obsession take him to an auction in Montreal in 1998, when the violin goes up for sale. The other story is set in Cremona, Italy, in 1681, when the violin was created. Anna Bussotti, the pregnant wife of the master violin maker, requests a tarot card reading for her unborn child from a servant who is, perhaps, a *strega* (an Italian witch) named Cesca (played by Anita Laurenzi).

Cesca explains that she cannot tell the future of an unborn person, but, nevertheless, she lays out a spread of five cards and proceeds to tell Anna (played by Irene Grazioli) her future. A key element of the film is that the fortune being told belongs, in fact, to the violin rather than to Anna, who dies in childbirth. Her husband adds her blood to the lacquer used to make the violin, brushing it onto the instrument using a brush made from his dead wife's hair. This accounts for the confusion in the tarot reading. Each time the reader flips over a card, she accurately foretells events. Even though she believes she is describing the future of Anna, she is actually describing the future of the violin. When she completes her reading of an individual card, the film transitions to another place and time and the viewer follows the story of the violin. Each of these vignettes concludes by cutting to the Montreal auction house in 1998 and then flashes back to Cremona in 1681, where the tarot reader goes on to the next card before the next vignette begins and repeats the cycle.

A number of film critics who reviewed *Red Violin*, including Roger Ebert, noted the idea of following an object through geographical space and time as an effective storytelling device. This is part of what won justifiable acclaim for the film upon its release (Ebert 1999). Yet, it might be more appropriate to consider how the device of the tarot cards is used in the film. It, too, provides a narrative structure that links the various times and places of the film, conflating the lives of the characters from seventeenth-century Italy (especially Anna, with the violin). It is also possible to see the late twentieth-century character, Charles Morritz, being contrasted with the violin as well as being connected to the story of destiny told in the tarot reading. The tarot reading is, in some respects, as important to the plot as is the violin itself.

Angus Fletcher, writing about allegory in a 1964 book called *Allegory: The Theory of a Systemic Mode*, discussed using double plots in order for allegorical stories to demonstrate magical causation. When "the major plot is mirrored by a secondary one, and the mutual mirroring is felt to have a magical force, as if one plot brought the other into existence, since the other was its double, this is magical causation through doubling. Each plot recreates the logic, the coherence, the persuasive force of the other, and the result is that we get something like a miraculous reduplication of two worlds that belong together" (182). This is exactly the device being used in *The Red Violin*. It is all the more intriguing considering that Tarot itself can properly be viewed as an allegorical system. Thus, the cards have several levels of functional and representational meaning within the film. Further still, they may even serve the purpose of providing a contour to the seventeenth-century Italian setting of the film.

Tarot cards do indeed come from Italy and had, in fact, existed for some time prior to 1681 (when the reading in the story takes place). As I indicated in an earlier chapter, however, there is simply no conclusive evidence to support the notion that the cards were being used to tell fortunes at that time. Thus, this narrative does have an anachronistic element to it despite the historical accuracy of placing tarot cards in seventeenth-century Italy. To be even more critical, I point out that none of the woman's readings of the five individual cards would line up with the established conventional interpretations assigned to those cards. For example, the first card that Cesca draws is "the Moon," which, Anna is told, signifies a long life. It does not, although the violin will certainly have a long life. "The Moon" is generally associated with the unconscious and things hidden in the mind and the self. The second card drawn is "the Hanged Man," to which Cesca ascribes the meaning of illness and that those around her will suffer. Again, this is not a conventional meaning ascribed to "the Hanged Man." Common interpretations include suspension, waiting, indecision, and sacrifice. Cesca's interpretation of these cards sets the themes for the vignettes they introduce. In fairness, the use of "the Devil" card is more appropriate. Becoming too attached and being restricted by one's desires is a traditional reading of the card. The vignette attached to this card in the film is appropriate. A gifted musician named Frederick Pope gets the violin from a band of gypsies, becoming so obsessed with it that it interferes with his relationship with the woman that had been his muse and her frustration with the circumstances leads her to try to shoot him. The attempt results in the violin being damaged.

One might be generous and point to the fact that many tarot card readers base their interpretations on personal and intuitive responses to the cards rather than on traditional and conventional meanings. Just as we saw in *Nightmare Alley*, so, too, in *The Red Violin*, the conventional and traditional meanings of the cards do not match their supposed meanings in the film. However, the function of the cards is to effectively assert to the viewer that the reader does see future events with clarity and can foretell disaster. In a 2013 online review of the film, Jessica Lynn Norman wrote, "Bussotti adding his wife's blood to the varnish was a detail thought up by the director, which ties in perfectly to the film being weaved together by a tarot card reading done for his wife" ("Red Violin: A Feast for the Senses").

The use of Tarot in film and television allows a writer to have a narrative device with eerie and prophetic powers capable of exposing the destiny of a character, as well as their strengths or flaws. A writer might choose to use the conventional meanings of the cards in shaping the story that they write (as we saw in the previous chapter on television with *Mad Men* and *Xena: Warrior Princess*). But, in *Nightmare Alley* and *The Red Violin* the writers are making use of the powerful mysteriousness and reputation of the cards to convey strong emotions and a sense of certainty about the future. This is done both oddly and quite effectively in *The Red Violin*.

To add artistic weight to the force with which the cards are used, the imagery of each card is a combination of traditional style associated with Tarot and added visual elements that hint at, and tie into, the individual stories that are represented by the specific cards. For example, at one point in the film the violin has made its way to Shanghai, China, during the so-called Cultural Revolution of the 1960s. Introducing this vignette, the tarot card that was shown was the "Justice" card. The theme of justice is central to the phase of the story about to be told. The "Justice" card used in the film is stylistically comparable to recognizable genuine tarot cards available in the public market. If one looks closely at the card, however, one will notice a Chinese flag in the background. In these ways, the cards' subjects and visual elements tie into the tales being told about the violin's journey through time and around the world. This is a bit different than the modifications made to tarot cards in cases such as *Sherlock Holmes: A Game of Shadows* that was discussed earlier in this chapter. In that example, the viewer sees several cards from an actual historical deck designed by Oswald Wirth. One card, though, is based on a deck that did not exist at the time in which the film was set. Yet that card, the "Two of Cups," was slightly modified to reflect the style of the Oswald Wirth deck.

While those who are knowledgeable about the traditional meanings of the cards, their history, and the way that they are used will find inconsistencies

Tarot card layout from *The Red Violin*, 1998.

and anachronisms, they will also see in this film an excellent use of Tarot as a prop for filmmakers who wish to shape a narrative, add symbolic strength to the film's imagery, and make effective use of the sense of foreknowledge popularly associated with Tarot. The film has flashbacks and flashforwards, elements that could cause annoyance or confusion for the viewer, but they do have a structure and a pattern that is formed, in large part, by the tarot reading. The meanings of the cards, however inaccurately detailed, provide meaning to the narrative of the story as a whole, as well as in the context of the numerous vignettes that make up the story of the violin. Thus, the Tarot helps to provide structure to the film as well as aiding in the development of the film's themes. These are the same functions that Tarot serves in *Nightmare Alley* and several other films.

Live and Let Die

The 1973 James Bond film *Live and Let Die* is another example of Tarot bringing something to films revolving around action heroes. As in the case of *Sherlock Holmes: Game of Shadows*, Tarot is used here in a way that helps to define a character or create a mood within a scene. Unlike *Game of Shadows*, however, *Live and Let Die* uses tarot cards as a major component in defining a main character. Further, *Live and Let Die* uses the cultural reputation of the cards to define a social milieu just as *Game of Shadows* or, more significantly, *Nightmare Alley* had done, although in a much different way. Both

Nightmare Alley and *Live and Let Die* create contexts in which Tarot is only part of what makes up an environment where the supernatural is viewed by some as real, others as a hoax, yet by all as having some significance in terms of good and evil or right and wrong.

Live and Let Die is much more of a parody or spoof of the "blaxploitation" genre of the early 1970s than it is an exploration of magic or the supernatural. The use of voodoo in the film is quite prominent, and the tarot cards themselves feed into that milieu. Early on in the movie, Bond enters a small store called the Oh Cult Voodoo Shop, which turns out to be a front for the villain of the film, Mr. Big (played by Yaphet Kotto). The voodoo element actually fortifies the "blaxploitation" features of the movie more than the tarot features. The connections between Tarot and voodoo on the cultural or historical level are not, in fact, very significant. Having acknowledged that, it still remains obvious that the connections between voodoo and Tarot are actually significant in terms of shaping both the attitude of the viewer and the social context(s) of the story. In addition to the popularity of the "blaxploitation" genre, the early 1970s was a period of significant social upheaval related to feminism.

The topic of feminism in Bond films, in general, and in *Live and Let Die*, in particular, is worthy of attention and can also be connected to the use of Tarot in the film in some interesting ways. The film came out in 1973 which was the same year that the Supreme Court issued its *Roe v. Wade* decision. Despite that decision, by 1973 the feminist movement was beginning to lose ground in important ways and was, in fact, experiencing a backlash. Consider, for example, that the Equal Rights Amendment was faltering through the process of ratification. Phyllis Schlafly, rather prophetically, was arguing against the ERA, saying it would "establish unisex public facilities, permit unlimited abortions, recognize homosexual marriages, send women into war, and absolve men from any obligation to support their spouses" (Caplen, 247–51). Anti-feminist groups, including one known as "the Pussycats," emerged in the early 1970s. These groups sometimes likened women's liberation to communism, describing liberationists as "'malcontents' who failed to comprehend or acknowledge that women had already achieved total equality" (Caplen, 247).

It is certainly true that the women's movement had solidified some gains by 1973. Yet, the level of opposition and ridicule that it sustained at that time is indicative of how far it truly was from being mainstreamed. As Robert Caplen writes of this period, "The feminist and Women's Liberation movements ultimately influenced the world of James Bond, which entered the 1970s with a refined Bond Girl archetype that would serve as its own unique response to new conceptions of gender rights and equality" (251).

There were three Bond films produced during this period; *Diamonds Are Forever, Live and Let Die*, and *The Man with the Golden Gun*. It is quite easy to make the case that, with the introduction of Roger Moore as James Bond at this moment in the Bond franchise, the rugged masculinity of Sean Connery had become less relevant. Perhaps that transition has some implications for feminism or for the Bond Girls. Moore's first film, *Live and Let Die*, brought forth a new style for the famous character. But, the changes for the female characters might not have been quite as drastic. In all three of these films, the Bond Girls that exhibit traits associated with the women's liberation movement (strength, independence, assertiveness) typically found themselves "put in their place" or revealed to be out of their "natural" and "proper element" (as critics of feminism might have expressed it). Simultaneously, some of the other Bond Girls in these films are portrayed as timid and naïve. Yet, they are strongly objectified, along with the more "liberated" Bond Girls.

This is certainly the case with the lead Bond Girl of *Live and Let Die*, Solitaire, played by Jane Seymour. Her naïveté about sexuality and the world in which she lives is prominent and obvious. Her dependence on Bond is comparable to any other "damsel in distress" (as one would expect with an objectified young woman whose purpose in a story is to create an opportunity for the lead male to play the hero in a traditional—albeit comically—sexualized, manner). This is another element to consider in terms of how the franchise wished to portray women in the early 1970s. It is worth considering here that, at twenty years of age, Jane Seymour was the youngest Bond Girl in the history of the Bond film series. Roger Moore, who was playing James Bond for his first time, was forty-six when the film was made. I leave the implications of that age difference to the reader.

The scene in which Solitaire and James Bond meet is set in a hidden backroom behind the wall of a Harlem nightclub. Bond sees her reading the tarot cards and, ignoring the gangsters in the room, introduces himself to her. She says, "I know who you are, what you are, and why you've come. You have made a mistake. You will not succeed." Mr. Big then enters the room, asking Solitaire if Bond is armed. This demonstrates both Solitaire's psychic prowess and the extent to which Mr. Big may confidently rely upon her abilities. She answers Mr. Big with a "yes," and Bond's gun is taken away and destroyed by the henchmen that Mr. Big did not use to search Bond. When Bond walks back to Solitaire, he sees "the High Priestess" card as one of several cards laid out on the table and identifies it as Solitaire, saying, "That's you, obviously. An amazing resemblance." (It doesn't look like her.)

When Bond asks if he is in there as well, Solitaire tells him to pick a card and turn it over. Bond randomly chooses "the Fool" card, leading Solitaire

Jane Seymour reading
the cards in *Live and Let
Die*, 1973.

to answer: "You have found yourself." Just then, Mr. Big walks up to Bond
for the first time and Bond tries to introduce himself by saying, "My name
is . . ." But, before Bond can finish, Mr. Big says, "Names is for tombstones,
baby. Take him outside and waste him." Mr. Big then walks out of the room
leaving Bond alone with several henchmen and Solitaire. Bond walks back
to Solitaire and says, "'Waste him.' Is that good?" Then Bond asks Solitaire to
tell him his future. She indulges him by having him pick a card. He draws
"the Lovers" and asks, "Is that us?" Solitaire gets a surprised look on her face
as the henchmen take Bond outside to kill him. Of course, Bond escapes.

In this and other scenes, the viewer sees that Solitaire is able to give very
specific details from her card readings. For example, she knows when Bond
arrives at a particular location and she knows whether he travels by land, sea,
or air. By the way, there actually are cards that indicate travel by land or sea.
In one scene, however, she is confused on this score because Bond happens

to be using a hang glider that is tethered to a boat cruising along the coast of Dr. Kananga's island. Dr. Kananga, incidentally, is the true identity of "Mr. Big." They are one and the same, although, this remains unknown until later in the movie. In that same reading, Solitaire warned Kananga that he was at fault for misinterpreting an earlier prediction of death. He had thought that the cards indicated Bond would be killed. In fact, Rosy, an American CIA agent who was working with Bond, was the person who got killed. She had been forced to work undercover for Kananga and had been used as bait to lure Bond to Kananga's island hideout.

At the point in the film when Bond sneaks onto Dr. Kananga's island, Solitaire finds him waiting for her in her parlor. He was seated at her table, wearing her elaborate robe and playing with her cards. By the time that Solitaire entered the room, Bond had laid down three cards ("the Chariot," "the Fool," and "the High Priestess"). She demands that he put the cards down, insisting that it is a blasphemy for him to be using them and that "they tell nothing to those that cannot see." Bond, claiming that the cards on the table indicate they are to be lovers, begins to make his case that the cards reliably indicate destiny, and if she believes that to be true, she knows they are destined to be lovers. He then asks her to pick a card from the deck and she draws one at random. She turns it over and sets it down, revealing "the Lovers." Cue the music and cut to the love scene! Bond tells her that she knew the answer before it was given, and he says, "Strangely enough, so did I." Bond then lets the deck of cards fall as he begins kissing Solitaire and the viewer sees that the entire deck was composed of nothing but "the Lovers" cards.

As the film progresses, and Bond and Solitaire are both captured by Mr. Big, who is by that time revealed to also be Dr. Kananga, there is a scene in which Solitaire must use her cards to demonstrate psychic ability while Bond is at risk of having a finger cut off if she fails to answer Kananga's question about the number on the back of Bond's wristwatch. She answers correctly. Kananga was trying to establish if she had had sex with Bond, which would cause her to lose her psychic powers. Just like her mother and grandmother, Solitaire's psychic abilities were linked to her virginity. The viewer had previously heard that Solitaire's mother had some vaguely defined but clearly bad outcome several years before because she lost her virginity and, consequently, became useless to Kananga. That was when Solitaire became Kananga's reader.

The main point of this scene was for Dr. Kananga to prove to himself that Solitaire had sex with Bond, and thus, she would lose her psychic powers. Additionally, the issue of jealousy arouses the villain's anger. Kananga had said earlier in the movie that he would take her virginity if and when she

"The Lovers" cards. Bond must have gone through a lot of trouble to get an entire deck of "Lovers" cards.

ever lost it. Indeed, he certainly treated her as a possession. This relationship is indicative of the character's status as well as the status of Bond Girls in the early 1970s. After Bond has been removed from the room so that Kananga can confront Solitaire, who has stood up from her cards and walked to the other side of the room, Baron Samedi (played by Geoffrey Holder) enters. Baron Samedi is a character based on a voodoo figure of the same name. He is a loa (a spirit or minor deity) of the dead. In *Live and Let Die*, he is also a man associated with Kananga. One sees in this character a major blurring of the lines between the reality of the world in which Bond lives and the mythology of the supernatural world in which this particular film is set.

It is interesting to see Baron Samedi enter the room and begin to handle Solitaire's tarot cards. He picks up "the High Priestess" card and sets it on fire before handing it to Dr. Kananga. Remember, of course, that the card represents Solitaire. After Kananga slaps Solitaire, knocking her down to the floor, and begins to indicate his plans to kill her, Baron Samedi picks up the "Death" card, shows it to Solitaire, and starts to laugh maniacally.

The scene is also interesting from the perspective of sharp-eyed people who are familiar with tarot cards. All through the film, the deck used was one called the "Tarot of the Witches." It was created by Fergus Hall and is a Major Arcana-only deck (it does not have the numbered suit cards). In the scene where Dr. Kananga decides to kill Solitaire, after verifying that she had sex with Bond, the cards used as props are from the Waite-Colman Smith deck. The change in decks is unexplained. It should be noted, though, that the backs of the cards in both decks look the same. The backs are red with a design that incorporates several lines of "007" in swirling script.

Fans of Bond and Tarot can find these cards for sale. They are sold by US Games Systems and can be purchased with a booklet called "The James Bond 007 Tarot Book," written by that company's president, Stuart Kaplan. The booklet was published and put on sale to coincide with the release of the movie. Fergus Hall made the "Tarot of the Witches" deck for the movie. He also did artwork for the British rock band King Crimson. The fact that the producers had created a deck specifically for the film makes it surprising that they would have switched to a different deck for a prop in a major scene and yet camouflaged the other deck by using the same card backs. At any rate, *Live and Let Die* provides us with an intriguing example of a film franchise being connected to the tarot community in a way that capitalizes on the card industry. It was an interesting merchandising and product placement opportunity.

The scene where Dr. Kananga confronts Bond and Solitaire illustrates the use of the young woman as object and possession. That is, she is portrayed as the object of competition between the men. She is also the trophy to be possessed by the winner of that competition. She is not really an independent actor with her own mind. Both Dr. Kananga and James Bond exploit and possess Solitaire. She serves as a tool in the plans of both men and does so in ways that she has no influence, much less control. The two men discuss Solitaire as "*something*" that belongs to Dr. Kananga. She is not referred to, in the scene, as *someone*, and she is not allowed to participate in the conversation although she is in the room. Kananga slaps Solitaire, deciding that her betrayal, as he deems it, will be punished by sending her to the Caribbean, where she will be sacrificed in a voodoo ritual that involves tying her up to two poles while Baron Samedi dances around her with poisonous snakes intended to be the instrument of her death. Of course, Bond saves her. Robert Caplen argues that she "actually represents the ideal woman in the Bond mythology: obedient, subservient, impressionable, and an overall object of visual and physical pleasure" (293). The message that *Live and Let Die* conveys about the Bond Girl archetype generally, and Solitaire specifically, is that "women are best kept away from the real world. Injecting these characters into Bond's world only causes harm to befall them" (295).

While one might interpret the role of women in this film (or Bond Women in general) in different ways, this particular interpretation has merit. From that basis or foundation one can then contemplate the role that Tarot has as a tool to be used in developing such a character as Solitaire. It might be argued, on the one hand, that the association of Tarot with superstition, allows a context of ignorance, gullibility, naïveté, and foolishness to be illustrated. On the other hand, Tarot is sometimes associated (properly or not) with feminine power, or to borrow Betty Friedan's terminology, feminine mystique. Both of these interpretations could be, to varying degrees, applied to the character of Solitaire. Yet, in either case, Solitaire and her powers are controlled by the primary men in the film: Bond and Kananga. Her abilities may be characterized as feminine by virtue of the fact that they are an aspect of the particular (female) character, and also feminine to the extent that the viewer associates Tarot with females. In either sense (or both senses), Solitaire and her abilities, despite being powerful, are ultimately under the control of men. Bond manipulates her both sexually and for information, while Kananga, too, manipulates her sexually in his control of her virginity. He also, like Bond, uses her for providing information.

A feminist reading of the character or the movie is, ultimately, dependent on how one wishes to define feminism. It is even more subjective when one takes into account the additional interpretational possibilities within the context of the film. Interpreting the actions of characters or the contexts of the scenes allows for enough subjectivity to lead our discussion away from the topic of how Tarot is used in movies. At the same time, this depth of possibility is itself evidence of a meaningfulness associated with Tarot.

Moving on, it is certain that the screenwriters and others associated with producing the movie had the intention of creating depth and meaning by using the cards and the context of the supernatural or psychic phenomenon. They did not, however, intend to make some specific or profound statement about Tarot in the movie. Be that as it may, it is interesting to know that the screenwriter Tom Mankiewicz developed a familiarity with the cards while working on the movie. He would take the cards to parties and, according to the Internet Movie Database's *Live and Let Die* trivia page, predicted the marriage of Michael Caine and his future wife, Shakira, who felt that Mankiewicz had a supernatural ability with the cards.

Conclusion

When a series of tarot cards is laid down on a table, one sees a sequence of pictures. Some of these pictures represent obvious things in a film. Other pictures have flexibility of meaning. Think of the value that this simple set of pictures might have for a filmmaker or any other storyteller. It could be used to foreshadow, as in *Nightmare Alley*. It could be used to frame a narrative both topically and chronologically, as in *The Red Violin*. It can be used to define a character or a set of characters. It can also be used to assert the power of magic or to attack superstition-based con games. In fact, films such as *Sherlock Holmes: Game of Shadows* and *Live and Let Die* used Tarot in both ways, even within a single scene.

The 2019 Netflix comedy film *Wine Country* exemplifies several of the ways Tarot can be used in filmmaking. The tarot card reader enters as a bit of a stereotype with her quirky desire to smudge the room with smoke from burning sage, exhibiting a sense that there is a bad aura all around the home (which is actually a rental). Lady Sunshine, as the character is improperly and ironically named, will read the cards in a manner that shows she is, on the one hand, insightful about the individual characters' lives and personalities, while, on the other hand, bossy, in charge, even domineering while simultaneously telling the customers their fortunes in an all-business, nononsense manner. When the group of ladies spontaneously sing a line of music together, Lady Sunshine, played by Cherry Jones, says, "Oh my God! Are you a singing group?" The ladies answer, "No. We're just friends." The tarotist then says, "We'll see," and prepares to do the card reading.

Lady Sunshine begins the reading by flipping one card over and talking to the main character, played by Amy Poehler. The card is identified with the character. Each character, in turn, gets a new card and is identified with that card. In this way, the ladies each get an individual one-card reading. Lady Sunshine at first speaks of the cards in a way that is accurate in terms of the traditional meanings associated with the cards she has flipped. Further, the cards she flips are, indeed, accurate representations of the characters to which they are linked. Within each card reading Lady Sunshine becomes increasingly specific and predictive, revealing herself to be incredibly accurate.

She then lays out a few cards that provide the reading for the group of ladies as a whole. Again, she is accurate and insightful. The women are celebrating the fiftieth birthday of one of their group and are also on a trip to the Napa Valley wine country in order to work on their friendship. The tarotist concludes the reading by telling the ladies, "Get over all your shit, 'cause it is later than you think." Immediately after that she tells the ladies, "That will be $475."

In a short and humorous scene, Tarot is used to clarify the personalities and circumstances of all the main characters, to define certain aspects of relationships, to foreshadow certain conflicts and events in the film, and to elucidate the moral of the film (that enduring friendship requires struggling together, accepting one another, and remaining aware of the value of friendship even as life interferes with it). The characters, of course, don't quite realize just how important the reading was until later in the film. It is a bit of a time-delayed revelation—as are all prophecies, I suppose.

Wine Country is not the only film that employs the tendency for the cards to be misunderstood, yet, accurate. The tarotist can be silly or serious; often, they are both. A death may be predicted, but whose death? A victory may be foretold, but what sort of victory? This ambiguity makes for good drama and good comedy. It is also inherent in the cards because of the fact that the cards are symbols with a great depth of meaning. For storytellers, this allows the cards to be used as much more than a prop. The cards are a valuable narrative device and they are a vast reservoir of symbolic and cultural meaning that can be called upon to perform any number of functions in any kind of movie.

CHAPTER 7

Tarot and Comics

Introduction

In comics, as well as Tarot, pictures are used to tell a story. Will Eisner, who began writing comics in the 1940s, popularized the term "graphic novel" in the 1970s and helped to create comics studies as a topic for university courses. He wrote about what he called "sequential art." Sequential art, put simply, is the dramatization of a narrative or idea conveyed by the juxtaposition of images. The layout of a tarot card spread and the arrangement of a comic book are both sequential art narratives. In the eighteenth century, Antoine Court de Gebelin came to the conclusion that the Tarot was, in fact, an ancient Egyptian book on magical philosophy. He argued that each card was actually a page that could only be read by those who understood the meaning of the symbols in the artwork.

It might be argued that tarot cards are (typically) randomly drawn, and therefore, the narrative is not one designed by the storyteller. There is something to that criticism. Interestingly, some comics have been created with the intention of being read in random order. Others have been written in such ways as to allow them to be read back to front or in reverse order or even upside down. Such comics are, by their design, intended to defy a conventional linear sequence. The same can be said of the Tarot. Just as each panel in a comic book is a distinct drawing, so, too, is each tarot card in a layout. Yet, in both cases, there are several ways to juxtapose the images and allow a story to develop. Of course, it does not need to be so complex. Sequential

A portion of the Bayeux Tapestry. It exemplifies sequential art narrative in the eleventh century.

art narrative actually goes back to the Bayeux Tapestry (which illustrates the medieval French conquest of England) or, even further, to the hieroglyphics of ancient Egypt.

The point here is simply that both the medium of Tarot and the medium of comics use artistic imagery in sequence to create a narrative. A tarot card and a comic frame are analogous units. The analogy can easily be extended to a layout of three tarot cards and a typical comic panel sequence. A more extensive layout of cards is, then, analogous to several pages or an issue of a comic book. It is not the numerical ratio that matters so much as the development of a narrative based on a sequence of images. Clearly, both use sequential art and imagery to create a narrative.

Tarot and comics have a lot more in common. Consider how the Major Arcana can be divided into three groupings: the first of these is a collection of archetypes. "The Fool," "the Lovers," "the Devil," "the Empress," etc., are all archetypes and, as such, provide inspiration for the stock characters found in comic books (or, for that matter, many other literary categories). The second grouping for the cards of the Major Arcana is a set of virtues or characteristics such as "Strength," "Justice," and "Temperance." These virtues are relevant as the traits that help to define characters. A third grouping of cards provides a number of themes which also appear in comics. For example, "the Tower" is representative of chaos and a downfall. "The World" represents fulfillment and success. And the "Wheel of Fortune" represents the tendency toward sudden and dramatic change.

The Major Arcana can be seen as containing some of the raw ingredients needed to construct a comic—and in a form that is already quite familiar to readers and writers of comics. The Minor Arcana does much the same thing, although one could interpret its functionality as allowing for some additional depth of meaning, or perhaps, some less dramatic variations on the categories mentioned above in association with the Major Arcana cards. Another possibility is to view the Minor Arcana cards as additional pages (or panels) that can be used to broaden the spectrum of literary possibilities already present with the Major Arcana. For example, the "Six of Swords" can indicate a transition or a rite of passage, an important topic in the narrative of many myths and comic books. However, one may choose to flesh out the analogy: a deck of tarot cards is a small library of comic books waiting to be pieced together into myriad narratives with a full cast of characters, villains and heroes, as well as adventurous circumstances and all the emotional, psychological, and spiritual elements needed for an absorbing drama.

None of the figures in the Tarot meet the definition of a superhero. At least, if we rely upon scholars in the field of comic studies, such as Peter Coogan, the Tarot lacks characters (if you will) who have the "mission, powers, and identity," all of which Coogan considered essential elements in defining the comic book superhero ("Definition of a Superhero"). The Major Arcana figures of the Tarot cannot be equated with superheroes even liminally, as with examples such as Marvel's Nick Fury or DC's John Constantine who occupy a sort of "demi" space halfway between regular people and superheroes. Instead, the Tarot offers a collection of archetypes that can be used to populate a comic landscape just as capably as they might populate a novel, a myth, or a movie. Nonetheless, archetypes are as critical to comics as they are to other narrative media. The superheroes of comic books are developed by using some of the same concepts and images associated with Tarot.

The Minor Arcana's court cards are often associated with actual people in the lives of the person who is the subject of the reading. Kings, Queens, Knights, and Pages are figures who can easily be seen as analogous to certain figures in everyone's life, such as a parent, child, teacher, boss, friend, and so on. Thus, the court cards provide yet another resource for finding the elements needed to create a narrative.

Scott McCloud, another comics scholar, argued that the imagery of the superhero uses simplification to lead to amplification. Moving from realism to simplification in the artwork accomplishes something. A smaller number of specific details focuses the viewer's attention on essential details (as opposed to a variety of details). Those few essential details, then, amplify whatever they represent in the context of the character or story. The result is that the world of the comic can be the world of concepts and ideas (30–41). The same use of simplification tending toward amplification of an essential element is accomplished with color by comic book artists limiting themselves to a small number of basic colors. The very same approaches are found in the artwork of Pamela Colman Smith, the artist of the most popular and most influential tarot deck. Smith was representative of the symbolist movement in art (discussed in an earlier chapter), which, like the better known and contemporaneous movement of fauvism, has conceptual and philosophical commonalities with McCloud's notion that simplification leads to amplification.

Let us now move forward by examining a few comic characters that incorporate Tarot. This is usually done in fairly superficial ways. We shall also consider a tarotist with a background in writing comics. Then, we will go a little deeper by examining a slightly more sophisticated use of Tarot in comics. Finally, we will consider tarot decks that incorporate comic characters.

Comic Characters Associated with Tarot

In the same ways that Tarot works well for television and movies, it also works for comics. Tarot cards are often used as a prop in television and movies. The deck, as an object, has certain cultural connotations that can be evoked through visual display. That is, the viewer sees the cards and has certain expectations such as the future could be revealed, something supernatural is about to happen, and so on. In addition to the visual display of the cards as a prop designed to trigger a reaction or create a mood, the cards are also frequently used as a narrative device. For example, three or four cards might be laid on a table and used by a character who will shape the scene by reference to the interpretation of the cards. The interpretation of the cards can be tied to characters and their actions or to circumstances which surround the characters. We saw examples of all of this in earlier chapters on television and movies.

These same uses of Tarot can be found in comics along with additional, but related, elements. So, while tarot cards can be used in many ways as a prop, in comics they can be attached directly to the powers of a particular hero or villain. They might physically be thrown at someone or used in some other physical way that demonstrates the character's power. Another similarity that gets modified in the way that comics can use tarot cards is that a character's superpowers might be powers that are associated with the cards. Obvious examples of this would include having foreknowledge, or being a sorcerer or witch.

In issue 3 of Marvel's *Dr. Strange and the Sorcerers Supreme*, there is a character named Kushala who appears on the cover of the issue while levitating in a sitting position. She is surrounded by a variety of what might be described as magical paraphernalia. Most prominent on the cover art, beside the character herself, are the numerous tarot cards floating around her in the foreground and background. The cards are clearly recognizable as tarot cards. Yet, they are labeled with characters from the comic rather than with the traditional images and titles. For instance, one of the cards is titled "the Doctor," which bears the image of Doctor Strange, the main character of the series and a prominent Marvel superhero.

Tarot is only one device (although quite prominently displayed) used to develop the sense of the character Kushala's powers and personality that is displayed in the cover art. There are several Sorcerers Supreme, each is associated with a certain time frame, even though they occasionally move through time. Kushala is a Native American from the nineteenth century whose family and tribe are viciously attacked by the United States Army. She survives the massacre and seeks revenge only to find herself becoming possessed by a spirit of vengeance. She then becomes known as the Demon Rider. She embarks upon a quest, as all heroes do, and learns to master numerous sorts of magic becoming the greatest sorcerer of her time period. The display of tarot cards sets up the character's persona as a master magician. More than that, the images on the deck connect her to the same magical stature as other Sorcerers Supreme characters, including Doctor Strange and Merlyn (yes, that Merlyn—the one from Arthuriana is also a Marvel character).

The manga and anime series *Sailor Moon* also makes use of tarot cards as a prop. A character named Balm uses the cards in a manner different than for telling fortunes, although she can do that too. The cards are used as actual physical weapons in a couple of ways. For one, Balm uses "the Devil" card to cause some of the characters to behave mischievously in school. Elsewhere, Balm throws tarot cards at Sailor Moon, and as the cards fly through the air, they turn into knives.

The character of Balm is a clairvoyant. Her ability to tell the future is what makes her an attractive choice to be employed by her leader, Jadeite, in the task of trying to "harness the rebellious energy" of youth to be put toward some evil purpose. Balm is also one of a number of characters who are actually monsters that can appear in human form. She is referred to as a Youma, a type of monster. Thus, the tarot cards in this series are associated with evil as well as clairvoyance.

In at least two instances, superheroes have been named "Tarot." In both of these instances, the characters are female. The first character named Tarot

Example of the use of tarot in Marvel's Sorcerers Supreme comic series.

Marvel character named Tarot who uses the cards as her superpower.

appeared in Marvel Comics' *The New Mutants* in 1984 ("Away Game"). Her actual name is Marie-Ange Colbert. She was the granddaughter of a woman who could see the future by using tarot cards. The grandmother passed this talent on to Marie-Ange along with a genetic legacy (the characters are empowered by genetic mutations which the world at large considers to be bad) that grows in power over the generations. That is, she becomes even more powerful than her grandmother. As a child, Marie-Ange becomes separated from her family somehow and lives in a convent school where she increasingly relies upon her tarot cards. She is recruited to join a special school for mutants called the Massachusetts Academy. The academy is actually a front for training the next generation of mutant superheroes known as the Hellions and led by Emma Frost, who will mentor Tarot.

Tarot would use her cards to fight by calling out the characters on the cards. She could take out "the Devil" card, for example, and call forth the Devil to be used in battle. This and precognition were her main superpowers.

Over a period of years, the good-natured character died, came back from the dead, and later died again. During her resurrection, she appeared as the "Death" card. She remained throughout her run as a minor character in a comic series that was about a sizable team of heroes interacting with other teams of heroes and villains. Most interestingly, perhaps, Tarot appeared in the 2016 *Spider-Man/Deadpool* comic (issue 11), "Change Partners," which included the famous stage magicians Penn Jillette and (Raymond Joseph) Teller. Harry Houdini also makes an appearance. The theme of magic was obviously important to the issue, and Tarot was an appropriate selection to add to the list of characters. Yet, Tarot cannot be considered a significant member of the Marvel Comics population.

The other superhero with the name Tarot is the main character of her own comic series. However, the publisher is not one of the major comic publishers. *Tarot: Witch of the Black Rose* is published by Broadsword Comics, which is owned by Jim Balent and Holly Golightly. Tarot is the flagship creation and character of Broadsword. The character's name obviously signals a connection with the cards. Yet, the cards are not a particularly prominent feature of the comic. The character of Tarot is a witch, and witches are associated with Tarot—which is itself, of course, associated with magic in popular culture. Magic, the supernatural, and neopaganism are generalized elements throughout the comic's topics and settings, as well as its characters.

What *Tarot: Witch of the Black Rose* is really about, to a significant degree, is sexuality. The main character is hypersexualized in terms of her body, her clothing (or lack thereof), and her behavior. The same may be said of the other characters. Tarot has two lovers: one, a male named Jon Webb who works in a cemetery and communicates with the world of the dead, and another, female, named Boo Cat, a werecat (not werewolf) who has another lover that is a vampire named Licorice Dust. If all of this sounds weird, it's because it is. The themes and tropes of the comic's world of the supernatural contest of good versus evil, with humans caught somewhere in the middle, is not particularly unique.

What gives the comic its own identity is less the supernatural aspects, of which tarot cards are hardly relevant on the list, and more the sexual escapades of the main characters. In both visual and narrative terms, sexuality is the subject matter, and witchcraft, the supernatural, and the liminal realms of the afterlife largely serve as a backdrop. One web page devoted to the comic describes it this way: "The series is a mixture of action, tits, magic, tits, neopagan propaganda, tits, Author Tracts [*sic*], and tits" (tvtropes).

As with the other eponymous comic character, Tarot's name signals a specific magical skill set that, while not normally associated with a superhero,

Spider-Man/Deadpool comic by Penn Jillette, 2016.

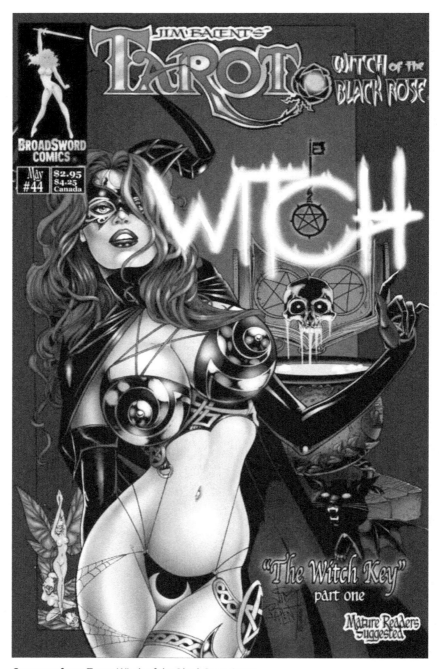

Cover art from *Tarot: Witch of the Black Rose*, 2007.

is readily associated with a superpower. The name also suggests links to the supernatural and the occult. The deck of cards is an obvious prop and capable of being used in several ways. In both cases involving superheroes named Tarot, the cards do not define narrative as we have seen elsewhere. The next example of tarot cards being used in comics will illustrate their effectiveness in functioning as a tool for shaping a narrative.

Batman Who Laughs

The DC Comics publication *Dark Nights: Metal* takes place in an alternate world known as the Dark Multiverse. Later, a series of tie-in issues was created to develop the characters created from this alternate world. The series includes several one-shot issues, each with an evil variation of Batman. In one of these, a character called the Batman Who Laughs is created when Batman kills the Joker in such a way as to cause chemical nanotoxins within the Joker's body to infect Batman with the sinister traits that make the Joker evil. These chemical nanotoxins had been used as a weapon against many people in the Gotham City of that particular alternate world in which the comic issue is set. In fact, it is evident that the Joker planned his own death at the hands of Batman for the purpose of infecting Batman and thereby creating the ultimate supervillain. This character, the Batman Who Laughs, then goes on a killing streak against his "Bat family" and against the other members of the Justice League as his condition deteriorates over the time it takes for the nanotoxins to completely corrupt his brain.

The story is partly told by having the Batman Who Laughs sitting at a table across from an unidentified man who is bound and covered with bandages. The Batman Who Laughs pulls out a set of tarot cards and provides the narrative of the comic, as well as an interpretation of previous events and a forecast of future catastrophe. The cards that he uses are unique to the comic, but they are also stylistically recognizable as the Waite-Colman Smith deck. So, for example, the card with Batman on it is clearly styled upon "the Hermit" card from the Waite-Colman Smith deck. Just as plainly, the Superman card is based on "the Magician" card of the Waite-Colman Smith deck. There is also a Wonder Woman card, but it seems to be a composite, or one loosely styled like the Waite-Colman Smith deck.

The Batman Who Laughs pulls out one card at a time and, as he displays them, provides more and more narrative detail. Part of his tale is that things may seem familiar, the cards are recognizable, and one might think that they know how the hand will be played out, but something ends up happening to upset the plan and to confuse the player. The character is one who wishes to sew chaos, violence, and misery. At a certain level, the writer seems to want to use the setting of a tarot card reading as a way of conveying some sense of dread in the person whose fortune is being told. At another level, the reader is unaware exactly what type of harm is coming while the person reading that fortune is both aware of the forthcoming disaster and diabolically amused by it.

There is no "Joker" card in the Tarot. Given that the Joker is the name of one of the principal villains in Batman's world, it would seem almost obligatory to wedge in the "Joker" card into the story despite the fact that the Tarot is being used as a narrative device. There is a "Fool" card, of course, in Tarot, but its meaning is substantially different than a "Joker." In this comic, the author decides to incorporate the "Joker" card and juxtaposes it with a "King." While there are "Kings" in tarot decks, the Batman Who Laughs talks about the "King" and the "Joker" in a way that is more implicit of a standard playing card deck (even though his monologue is visually presented as a tarot reading). He refers to the "King" as the most powerful card and the "Joker" as having all of its potential defined by what it is played against. What is being alluded to here is that the Joker and Batman (represented by the "King") are being bound together in the story, and in the character of the Batman Who Laughs. This combines the evil force of the Joker with all of the power of Batman. Rather than being opposed forces as they are typically understood and presented, we now have Batman and the Joker combined and driven by evil motives.

Cards are used to convey this narrative in symbolic and textual form. Tarot cards are given center stage, so to speak, but the reference to the "Joker" card breaks with a proper use of Tarot (although for understandable reasons). In an online article, Thelonia Saunders makes a very good point that Tarot is being used in this story not in order to tell the future "but rather to expose the past" (Saunders). Indeed, much of the narrative is in the form of flashback or backstory. Other parts of the story are, however, forward looking. Such an approach is actually typical of Tarot. Consider, for example, that a simple three-card layout would have cards in positions representing past, present, and future. Many layouts for tarot cards have positions designated to represent both the past and the future. This provides yet another similarity between Tarot and comics (or other literary genres) and narrative style.

Saunders makes an interesting point about the imagery on the cards. She notes that tarot cards traditionally do not represent anyone in particular because they convey symbols (or, one might say, types). By placing particular superheroes on the cards, Saunders argues, this comic uses those heroes

Tarot was used in several ways for *The Batman Who Laughs*, 2017.

as symbols, replacing whatever symbols are conventionally used for any given card. Put differently, the traditional meaning associated with the card (and the symbols on that card) can convey something about the hero. But, at the same time, the opposite effect can be established: the hero on the card becomes a symbol representative of that card's meaning. For those familiar with the heroes, but less familiar with the cards, the cards become a bit more understandable because of what the heroes already represent symbolically in the mind of the comic reader.

With the Batman Who Laughs, author James Tynion was able to incorporate elements of Tarot to create a narrative device. He was also able to use the symbolism associated with tarot cards to enrich that narrative at a visual and symbolic level. Tarot has been used in this way even more effectively in DC comics featuring the character Madame Xanadu.

Madame Xanadu

In Matt Wagner's 2009 graphic novel *Madame Xanadu: Disenchanted*, one finds an in-depth treatment of a character who was introduced in the 1970s and has appeared and reappeared numerous times ever since. Madame Xanadu has been featured in several different comic series, including a run of eponymously titled comics. She has also appeared, or is referenced, in television and video games associated with DC, as well as the 2017 animated movie *Justice League Dark*. In the various series in which she appears, Madame Xanadu interacts with other characters from DC's gallery of mystical characters including Merlyn, Death, the Spectre, John Constantine, Zatanna, and the Suicide Squad.

In *Madame Xanadu: Disenchanted*, Wagner and illustrator Amy Reeder Hadley provide an origin story while also creating or developing a number of connections between the main character and other DC characters. Her origin story is set in Camelot. She is the sister of Morgan Le Faye and Vivien (aka the Lady of the Lake). Her name was Nimue Inwudu, an Arthurian character found in Sir Thomas Malory's *Le Morte d'Arthur* from the fifteenth century. Nimue Inwudu becomes Madame Xanadu after she spends time at the court of Kublai Khan with Marco Polo in the late thirteenth century. Madame Xanadu, it turns out, has been around for centuries and been just about everywhere, including in France with Marie Antoinette at the dawn of the French Revolution, and in nineteenth-century England with Jack the Ripper. Along the way, she developed her skills as a sorcerer and a psychic (Gross). Reading tarot cards is just one of the many things she does which are characteristic of a great magician.

By the time *Madame Xanadu: Disenchanted* finishes, Madame Xanadu ends up in a present-day location familiar to readers who have encountered her in other comics, television shows, or video games. She resides in a parlor in New York City. The setting is one that might be stereotypically associated with a modern-day gypsy, psychic, or mystic. The parlor is where she encounters guests and clients, all of whom are having some sort of problem that requires a supernatural approach to its resolution. Madame Xanadu will diagnose the problem using tarot cards, advising her clients on how to resolve the matter. After consulting a book on an occult subject, she may equip them with some magical device or weapon she has hidden away in her parlor. At that point, the story moves to another scene, focusing on the characters who had been her clients and their journey to overcome whatever obstacle they were facing that caused them to go to Madame Xanadu in the first place. Thus, the visit to Madame Xanadu's parlor for a tarot reading is often the introduction to the main story (rather than the story itself). It could also be a scene within the central story. This is a literary approach well-suited for Tarot.

At the conclusion of the story, the characters are likely to return to Madame Xanadu's parlor having captured the essence of some supernatural entity which she will then place in a mason jar and keep in the back of her parlor. She has, over the years, built up an incredible inventory of demons

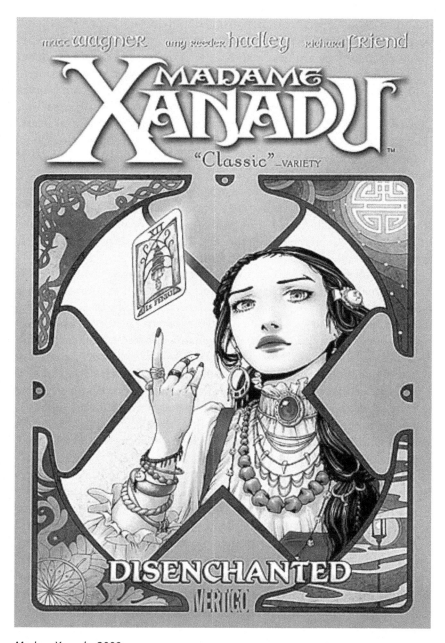

Madam Xanadu, 2009.

and other malevolent creatures imprisoned in these jars. Between the tarot readings, the jars filled with evil supernatural creatures, a library of occult literature, and the magical paraphernalia kept on hand to assist her clients in their quests, Madame Xanadu's parlor emerges as a fascinating setting.

Madame Xanadu is a DC character. The character Tarot is from Marvel Comics. Both characters are illustrated as conventionally physically attractive. They are, however, no more hyper-sexualized than other female characters. Their association with tarot cards goes a long way in defining the characters' images. The same is not true of the other character named Tarot, the witch from Broadsword Comics by Jim Balent and Holly Golightly. That character is unapologetically hyper-sexualized. Yet, despite her name, Tarot the witch is a fictional character that is not as thoroughly defined by Tarot as are the other two. It should be noted, though, that all three of these characters are attractive females, and that the literary and illustrative use of Tarot is linked to social conventions associated with femininity.

Laura Mulvey's work on film theory as expressed in her coining of the term "the male gaze" in 1975 has been effectively applied to comics. Mulvey asserted that there is a psychological element of a power relationship expressed in the male gaze based on heteronormative gender roles with an assumption of masculine control. The woman in the frame is objectified for the male's visual pleasure. This structure is a reflection of the social construct of heterosexual masculine power in both an internalized fashion and as a functionalist social construct. One sees this played out in comics, perhaps, even more strongly than one sees it in film (the area of Mulvey's interest). In full agreement with Mulvey's model of the male gaze, I would add that Michel Foucault's work on examining relationships of power and the social dynamics of power as applied to the human body also merits some consideration in this context. Foucault asserted that, in order to understand the dynamics of social power, one had to examine the subjects upon which that power was applied at a micro-level—the individual body. These dynamics certainly manifest in comics as they do in any other entertainment medium.

A more recent feminist critique called the Hawkeye Initiative was launched in the online community. The Hawkeye Initiative gets its name from the Marvel superhero of that name. He was drawn in ways that copy the poses of females as depicted in comic panels. The point was to illustrate the unnatural, nonsensical, hypersexualized posing of the female form by applying that same convention to the masculine form. There is an infinite amount of material to be mined, and through the display of fan art, the initiative has certainly made its point in quantitative and qualitative ways. Nonetheless, "boys will be boys" (so to speak), and circumstances have, arguably, changed very little, at least with regard to the depiction of female characters displayed in and for the male gaze. In other respects, gender and sexuality have been addressed in more progressive ways within the sphere of comics and graphic novels. Let us consider, as an example, transgender characters.

Rachel Pollack: Tarotist and Comic Writer

One leading light in the tarot community who has had an impact in the comics community is Rachel Pollack. In addition to being an author and designer of tarot decks, Pollack also has a solid background in writing, with a master's degree in English and a successful history of writing science fiction. Pollack wrote a run of the DC Vertigo comic *Doom Patrol* in the early 1990s. Pollack said, "Tarot is like comics in a way, a story constructed in pictures. When I first encountered Tarot it struck me as so like a comic, in the best way" (*Tarot*). Elsewhere, she said that she sometimes uses tarot cards to get inspiration for stories although the cards are not *in* the stories (Doom). Although the series of comics did not draw upon Tarot as a theme, Pollack did make use of the Kabbalah in certain ways during the writing of *Doom Patrol*.

Pollack did, however, bring her life experience as a trans woman to the comic by introducing themes of gender and transsexuality into the storylines. Pollack was the first trans writer for a major American comic publisher. She created a character that was the first trans superhero. That hero was named Kate Godwin, which is a compound of trans activists Kate Bornstein and Chelsea Goodwin. The superhero name of the character is Coagula. Her powers are the ability to liquefy or solidify things—that is, she can transmute the physical substance of things. At one point in the storyline of *Doom Patrol*, Coagula defeats Codpiece, a villain who is representative of toxic masculinity.

The character of Kate Godwin, aka Coagula, gave voice to issues and attitudes of importance for the LGBTQ community. The mere fact that she could be so open about her sexuality and her gender in the first place was a significant social step. Her criticism of heteronormative social conventions had the potential to empower and hearten the community. Comics have often been a forum for social commentary in a positive way. Pollack clearly wanted to be able to tap into that power, and she did. When I interviewed Pollack for this book, the conversation moved from Tarot to her comic writing. Pollack told me that she had received a letter from a teen reader who was struggling with psychological, social, and familial issues that challenge trans people. She had pondered suicide but found comfort and relief in the character of Kate Godwin and the stories in *Doom Patrol*. Pollack achieved her goals as a writer in bringing a positive trans presence into popular culture through comics and reaching a community seeking to overcome a unique set of troubles.

In the years since Pollack wrote *Doom Patrol*, the presence of various queer people within the tarot community has continued to grow in an open cultural environment. One example of this can be seen in the 2017 comic anthology *Tabula Idem*, edited by Iris Jay and Hye Mardikian. It contains twenty-two stories by different authors. Each story explores one of the Major Arcana cards in an LGBTQ context.

Pollack's contributions to the world of comics went beyond writing a run of *Doom Patrol*. In 1995, she served as a writer for the fourth volume of *The New Gods* comics series, which had been started back in the 1970s by Jack Kirby. She has also played a consultative role for other authors and she has been involved in the development of a tarot deck based on comic characters. Her work with Neil Gaiman is significant and also deserves some attention.

Neil Gaiman

In Neil Gaiman's four-issue run that started off *Books of Magic*, there is a scene involving the character of Madame Xanadu in which she does a tarot reading. In researching the topic before writing the scene, Gaiman consulted with Rachel Pollack. Both Pollack and Gaiman have deep interests in esoterica, mythology, and storytelling. All of these interests are distilled and harnessed in an impressive way in the *Books of Magic* as they are in Gaiman's popular *Sandman* series. Tarot plays a significant part at various points in the narrative for *Books of Magic*, aside from the reading by Madame Xanadu. Both Gaiman and Pollack consider comic books to be a delightfully effective vehicle by which esoterica can travel through popular culture ("Gods of the Funny Books").

Gaiman's *Books of Magic* contains extremely good examples of Tarot being put to use in all of the ways that one can properly expect. The symbolism of Tarot, the narrative elements, the cultural mystique, and, of course, the cards themselves are all utilized in a story about a boy named Timothy Hunter who must decide if he is to take the path of becoming the greatest magician ever or remaining in a simple and obscure life. Yes, that sounds like a no-brainer of a choice, but, like Achilles in the *Illiad*, the path of greatness will also lead to a troubled, sad, and tormented existence.

Timothy Hunter is a twelve-year-old British boy with round glasses who looks too much like Harry Potter. That is what strikes the viewer of the comic's first cover, but the reader should realize that this comic was actually

Books of Magic, by Neil Gaiman, issues 1–4, 1991–92.

written before J. K. Rowling's masterpiece (which is certainly not to say that Rowling imitated Gaiman).

The story is a quest, as well as an origin story. Gaiman obviously draws upon the style that Dante used in the *Divine Comedy*. There are four different guides. Instead of Virgil and Beatrice, there are the DC mystic characters of John Constantine, Mister E, Dr. Occult, and the Phantom Stranger. Instead of Hell, Purgatory and Paradise, there are other realms. Well, actually Hell is one of the realms that Timothy Hunter visits. There are also past, present, and future journeys. In this respect, *The Books of Magic* is stylistically somewhat reminiscent of Dickens's *Christmas Carol*. In fact, the main characters in both tales, go through their journeys in order to be prepared to choose how they shall live. The Fool's Journey of Tarot is also an introspective quest drawing upon archetypes, and *The Books of Magic* can certainly be read through that lens. It could also be read as a "coming-of-age" story. In Roger Zelazny's introduction, Gaiman's work is characterized as sharing many of the traits of Joseph Campbell's *The Hero with a Thousand Faces*. This vast mixture of influences and styles provides the ingredients for an interesting recipe which Gaiman cooks up rather deftly.

Gaiman also incorporates an incredible number of DC characters besides the "Trenchcoat Brigade" consisting of his four guides, John Constantine, Mister E, Dr. Occult, and the Phantom Stranger. As stated above, the character of Madame Xanadu is used in the story, and so is just about every other character in any way associated with magic that might be familiar to DC readers.

In book one of *The Books of Magic*, "The Invisible Labyrinth," John Constantine, Mister E, Dr. Occult, and the Phantom Stranger confront Timothy about magic. Timothy's yo-yo is turned into an owl (a witch's familiar) that is then given the name Yo-Yo. The Phantom Stranger takes him on a journey through time. Each of the members of the Trenchcoat Brigade will individually escort Timothy on a journey. Each of these journeys is the subject of one of the four books in the series. Timothy sees the fall of Satan from Heaven. He goes to Atlantis where he is first told that a life of magic is not worth its cost. They then pass through ancient Egypt, China, and Greece. Then he meets Merlin and learns that the way of the magician might be desirable even if one cannot control destiny. The 1600s is shown as a time of killing witches because of a failure to "understand" on the part of their persecutors. Witches disappear in a way that makes me think that Gaiman is influenced by the views of Gerald Gardner and Margaret Murray.

Murray was an anthropologist that argued medieval and Early Modern witches were actually vestiges from pre-Christian religions whose forms of worship were demonized once they were viewed through a Judeo-Christian cultural context. Gardner was a contemporary of Murray's who, in the 1930s, claimed that he had encountered and joined a "coven" in Lancashire. This "New Forest Coven," as it was called, was never actually located, and it is easy to doubt its existence. Gardner, however, spoke of it as a chronologically uninterrupted continuation of a pre-Christian religion. He and the movement that he started are seen as the origin of modern Wicca.

Returning to Gaiman's "The Invisible Labyrinth," Timothy encounters magicians from the DC Comics world—Dr. Fate, Zatarra, Sargon the Sorcerer—and is offered the Ruby of Life, but doesn't know if he should take it. The character Boston Brand makes repeated appearances throughout the issue, possessing a different body each time. He informs Timothy of ongoing threats to his life.

In book two, "The Shadow World," John Constantine takes Timothy to meet still more DC characters. Madame Xanadu in Greenwich Village is among the first. She reads Tim's cards. He draws "the Hermit," "Wheel of Fortune," "the Empress," and "Justice." The cards represent aspects of Tim's journey and the people around him. Constantine is represented by the "Wheel of Fortune." Madame Xanadu doesn't have quite enough time to interpret the cards, but she does tell Timothy to "beware Justice." Before Timothy leaves, Madame Xanadu (who said the querant would normally give her a gift) gives Timothy his owl, which he had lost earlier.

A number of assassination attempts are made on Timothy. Other boys are killed in the attempts to do away with him. After one such attempt, Dr. Fate tells Timothy that true magic is "the imposition of order on formless chaos, the release of joyous chaos on the gray monotony of order." Constantine then tells Timothy that "there's no chaos, no order; just patterns of different levels of complexity." After meeting Doctor Terrence Thirteen, Timothy is told that magic doesn't exist. Constantine rebuts that magic is real only if you believe in it. If you don't, it isn't. All of these viewpoints are interpretations that have actually been debated amongst occultists for countless generations.

The next person they meet is Zatanna, who shows Timothy some fun aspects of magic (like making clothes or meals). She takes him to a party with a bunch of magical characters. Timothy learns that the world of magic is connected to the regular world but is distinct from it. Again, this reflects the views of various occultists.

In book three, "The Land of Summer's Twilight," Dr. Occult takes Timothy to Fairyland. Dr. Occult changes form when they enter Fairyland, aka The Land of Summer Twilight. He becomes a woman that Timothy chooses to call Rose (which turns out to be a correct name). Timothy meets a dormant Arthur under the hill. Then, he is temporarily captured by Baba Yaga.

Madame Xanadu reads Timothy Hunter's tarot cards in "the Shadow World," 1992.

Timothy encounters Queen Titania who sends them to different realms of the imagination which are, in addition to being imaginary, also strangely quite real. One such realm is Hell. Timothy briefly meets Gaiman's most famous character, the Sandman, in the realm of Dreaming.

In book four, "The Road to Nowhere," the last of the series written by Gaiman, Timothy goes into the futures (deliberately plural) with Mr. E as his fourth and final guide. Timothy learns that there are many possibilities for the future, and he sees some of them unfold as if they are real events. For instance, he sees Zatanna getting hurt in a battle, and when he wants to intervene, he is told that there is no point because it hasn't happened yet and it may not happen at all. Timothy sees himself fifteen years older and fighting on the evil side against John Constantine. Mr. E wanted to show Timothy the triumph of evil as a future possibility.

Mr. E tells a story of how his father cut his eyes out when E was a child looking at a picture of "a shameless woman with concupiscent lust" in his heart. He then quotes Matthew 18: 9: "If thine eye offend thee, pluck it out, and cast it from thee: It is better to enter into life with one eye, rather than having two eyes to be cast into Hell." Mr. E explains that he can now only see good and evil.

The two travel one thousand years into the future, where Doctor Fate reappears (having been in an earlier part of the story) and says that order and chaos are actually the same thing and all is meaningless. They then go on to the sixtieth century and find a world where science and magic are blended. Then they go millions of years into the future. Meanwhile, back in the present, the others worry that Mr. E has taken Timothy dangerously far into the future.

When Timothy and Mr. E enter the end of time, they meet several characters based on tarot cards from the Major Arcana. The first of these is "the Hierophant." He refers to "the Hermit," saying that "the Hermit claims that we do not exist at all." "The Lovers" are mentioned as having left to look for food and never having returned. "The Hierophant" said that there are no more journeys to be taken. When asked by the Empress who he would be if he went back to his time, Timothy says, "Maybe a Magician. I'm not sure yet." "The Hanged Man" is mentioned. He had said that "we were everything." These Major Arcana tarot beings debate what they are, if they are, where they are, etc. At this key point in the narrative, Gaiman chose to insert the archetypal figures of Tarot as the characters to populate the setting of the end of time. They serve as characters who are also symbols. They also seem to represent the very essence of categories of people and, simultaneously, the essential traits of humanity in their most basic form as they philosophically wrestle with the meaning of life.

John Constantine, who (along with Yo-Yo the owl) pursued Timothy and Mr. E to the end of time in an attempt to rescue the boy, reappears as "the Fool." Mr. E tries to kill Timothy but is blocked by Yo-Yo. Then, two of the "Endless" family, Destiny and Death (who calls Mr. E Eric) appear just at the close of time. Destiny dies, having fulfilled all his purposes, but Death sends E back to travel through the long passage of time in reverse before she herself comes to an end. Timothy, however, gets instantly sent back to his present time. The remaining three Trenchcoat Brigade guys are left thinking he chose to reject the life of magic. Timothy goes home to his dad and their boring apartment. He sits alone on his bed and plays with a yo-yo that turns back into his owl before finally choosing magic as his path in life.

Neil Gaiman's *Books of Magic* makes use of Tarot in numerous ways. He incorporates the character of Madame Xanadu (one of several characters he borrows from the world of DC Comics) to serve a number of purposes. One of the things she does is to provide foreshadowing and context for various events in the story, as well as to supply other characters with the tools and information needed to fulfill their quests. Another function that she serves is to contribute significantly to the overall mystical atmosphere of the universe created in the story. There are many mystical people and magical moments that make up the story, and she is certainly one of these. The tarot card reading that she gives Timothy encapsulates, entirely, the four issues that Gaiman wrote, the four characters of the Trenchcoat Brigade, the four parts of Timothy's quest, and so on. She serves a unique function in these ways. Simultaneously, she serves a more general function by being representative of the mystical and occult characters that make up the comic series.

Gaiman uses the Tarot's Major Arcana to populate the setting of the end of time with characters that represent archetypes. This is an appropriately placed trope that gives the main character a better sense of the magnitude and significance of the decision he must make. Archetypes provide metaphor and analogy not only for characters but for circumstances as well. By the time Timothy gets to the end of time in his journey, he is prepared to learn from these Major Arcana figures the lessons to be applied in his own life and choices.

Tarot Card Decks Based on Comic Books

Neil Gaiman and Rachel Pollack worked together on a project to design a tarot deck in 1995 that was based on DC/Vertigo comic characters. The deck comes with a 128-page book written by Pollack and featuring an introduction

A sampling of cards from the DC/Vertigo deck.

by Gaiman. It is illustrated by Dave McKean, who worked with Gaiman on *Sandman*. The deck features John Constantine as "the Fool" and Timothy Hunter as "the Magician." It is a full, seventy-eight-card deck and is packaged with a velvet bag in which to store the cards.

One gets a sense of how popular the deck is by looking a little at its sales history. It has been republished, reformatted, and restyled. Its original

A sampling of cards from the Italian company, Lo Scarabeo, maker of the *Tarrocchi Marvel*.

pricing was not radically higher than other decks, but it is not a "cheap" deck, either. The availability of the decks never seemed to meet market demand. Consequently, one sees these decks sold online by individuals in settings such as eBay and Etsy where they sell for quite a bit more than manufacturer suggested retail price, if one can even find an available deck. They are clearly a successful collectors' item.

Marvel Comics has a deck made by the Italian publisher Lo Scarabeo. The *Tarocchi Marvel*, as it is called, is a Major Arcana-only deck. It features Wolverine as "the Fool" and, of course, Dr. Strange as "the Magician" card.

This deck does not have the popularity of the Vertigo deck, whether that is because of the fact that it isn't a full seventy-eight-card tarot deck or some other reason. The cards were not published in large quantities. So, although demand for this deck may not be as high as the Vertigo deck, the limited supply means that collectors who want the *Tarocchi Marvel* will also have to pay a high price (if they can get it at all).

Fan art is strongly associated with comics. Individually drawing one's own tarot cards is a tradition that dates back many generations. Consequently, it would not be surprising to see that comic fan art and tarot cards can be found together. A recent example of this is with Julia Cross's *Art Deco Avengers Tarot*. It is fan art based on the *Avengers* movies franchise. It is a partial deck and includes only a portion of the Major Arcana. The popularity of this type of fan art in an area of the online world is easy to understand. It draws on a collection of characters with an obvious association—superheroes and villains—and links that with the collection of iconic images associated with Tarot.

On the one hand, there is a unique dynamic established by the large collections of heroes and villains to be found in a major comics publisher such as DC or Marvel, with the collections of concepts represented by the Tarot, on the other. It is simple to draw from a large roster of comic characters and start to make associations about where one might position them in the categories of the Tarot. It is enjoyable to ponder which hero might best represent "Justice" or "Strength." It can be easy and enjoyable to think about which villain to label as "the Devil" or which location to choose for "the Tower." Thus, it is easy to understand how there would be interest and demand for comic-based tarot decks.

Problems for creators can begin to occur as they contemplate filling in the less obvious slots in the list of cards as the remaining roster of characters is stripped of the most popular figures. Once the deck's designer has made all of the fun or obvious choices and still has several cards left in the seventy-eight-card deck to complete, the difficulties might become significant enough to account for the fact that only a small number of decks have actually been completed. The exercise of creating such a deck becomes more challenging as it goes along. It might be fun and obvious to start off saying, for example, that the Hulk would be a good choice for the "Strength" card. Yet, after forty or fifty characters have been assigned and the artist still needs to come up with a "Three of Swords" or a "Five of Pentacles," the task becomes a difficult one. Yet, once completed, the task will be seen as rewarding to the artist and desirable for the collector. Tarot and comics make for an intriguing blend.

Conclusion

Comics, as narrative and art form, are incredibly conducive to the incorporation of Tarot. As we have seen, both comics and Tarot use sequential art to create a narrative. Tarot supplements comics in other ways. Much the same as with movies and comics, tarot cards can be used to perform the function of narration, but they can also serve to reveal plot twists or shape storylines, reveal character traits or events, and perform a number of other actions and serve as a device for numerous story elements. The cards can be props and, as we have repeatedly seen, they can even provide characters. The cards themselves might serve as symbols while elsewhere the symbols on the cards might be utilized in shaping the context of the story or providing meaning to an event.

We also saw that people from the world of magic as entertainment or people from the tarot community have become directly involved with comics as in the cases of Rachel Pollack or Penn and Teller writing comics. Finally, the use of comic book characters as inspiration for tarot decks illustrates the depth of linkages between the two media. As in the case of the other chapter topics on movies and television, the relationships between comics and Tarot is an area for further fruitful exploration in the scholarly research of popular culture.

Conclusion

By their very nature, esoteric subjects cannot be mainstream and, therefore, cannot be part of the popular culture as it is typically conceived. Yet, many areas within popular culture do draw upon the esoteric, as well as the occult, for a number of reasons. It is in this way that Tarot has found a place in popular culture. In art, for example, Tarot has served as inspiration for many artists. Tarot can also be used by artists for purposes of social commentary whether that is in painting, sculpture, or other visual media. When tarot cards appear in television, movies, and comics, social commentary sometimes accounts for the reason.

More often than not, however, the reason that tarot cards appear in television, movies, and comics is because of the cultural context that can be identified with (or created by) the cards. When the cards are seen, the viewer or reader can be expected to have an almost visceral reaction. The cards contribute to (or create) a sense of drama simply because they symbolize something in the imagination of the general population—although exactly what is symbolized depends on the particular presentation.

Because of the esoteric and occult nature of the cards, the viewer (or reader) can be prodded to think in terms desired by the storyteller. For example, if foreshadowing is needed, the use of the cards allows the creation of a narrative that reveals something about the future, and only to the extent desired by the writer. Another example of contextualization commonly used by employing tarot cards in television, movies, and comics is a character's archetype—simply put a deck of tarot cards in the hands of a woman and the viewer recognizes her as a mystic. If a set needs to be established that evokes a sense of the occult in the mind the viewer, tarot cards are a tried-and-true prop for contributing to developing such an aura. As an object, they can serve a function similar to any other dramatic prop, such as a knife or a set of keys. Beyond that, however, they can also function something like an intertitle in an old silent film, a road sign, or some other brief written statement.

The cards have so much cultural recognition that, simply as a visualized object, they can easily help create a context for understanding a character, a setting, or a moment in time. They are a highly effective prop. They can be used with greater precision or increased effect by focusing attention on a single card or a small set of cards. In this respect, the "Death" card is commonly deployed because it is so easy to use for a dramatic impact. Other cards, however, can contribute just as effectively. The "Justice" card or "Three of Swords" card, with its image of a pierced heart, can elicit an immediate response and that response can function on more than one level. For example, a single tarot card such as these might simultaneously define a character's personality, actions, or experiences.

The cards have an incredible narrative capacity, too. By laying out a series of cards, a character or narrator tells a story. We saw how this was done in comics with the example of the Batman Who Laughs, and we discussed another example of it being done in a movie with *The Red Violin*. Tarot is often used as a narrative device to quickly inform the viewer (or reader) of past events. This can allow a summary of sorts in the narrative or it can allow a backstory to be created without taking up much time. This tactic can also be used to verify something about the storyline, to raise questions, or to establish something about a character's function. Tarot cards are also used to set the stage for various sections of a story, or to reveal a dramatic outcome.

The point to be made here is that the cards are incredibly versatile because they are understood to be charged with a range of meaning that can be tapped instantly. Further, they can do this at a conscious or subconscious level. Recognition of the cards, and a variety of traits symbolized by the cards, permeates the entire popular culture. The esoteric element of the cards simultaneously maintains the mysterious nature of their meaning even as they are capable of instantly creating a more obvious reaction. This all happens without creating any confusion. Rather, it draws upon the sense of wonder and awe that can be associated with magic in any of its forms.

The occult aspect of Tarot can make it frightening and suspicious to the viewer when they are encouraged to associate the cards with evil. This, too, makes tarot cards an effective device in art, television, movies, and comics. This connotation of evil associated with the cards is not built into the mindset of everyone in the same way. Some may exaggerate it while others may find it laughable, and there is a spectrum of reactions in between. Regardless of how one responds to the occult element of Tarot, it is quickly recognized throughout popular culture. This fact gives writers an opportunity for further contextualization. For example, we saw in our discussion of the movie *Nightmare Alley* the ways in which Tarot could be presented as the one "true" form of occult knowledge in a world full of supposedly psychic swindlers. However, the television show *Dark Shadows* provided an example of tarot cards feeding a narrative of the supernatural that is filled with mystery and danger.

In the introduction of this book, I defined "occult" not so much in terms associated with evil or Satanism (as is often done colloquially) but, rather, with the more precise meaning of something hidden and charged with some sort of supernatural power. Although both definitions are employed in popular culture, the latter definition, I would argue, allows for a broader and deeper use of the cards in creating a narrative for television, movies, and comics. This aspect of the occult, and its association with Tarot, also provides a broad and deep power in terms of the imagery that can be used in comics or other art forms.

Tarot has not received much attention from scholars of popular culture. However, scholars of the esoteric and occult traditions in Western civilization have given it significant attention. But, for them, it is more often than not a subtopic rather than a topic in its own right. The place of Tarot in popular culture has only recently become a focus of scholarly research and it remains a field with much to investigate. Scholars with an interest in film studies, comics, and other areas that come under the scope of popular culture should be encouraged to look further into the areas covered in this particular book. More in-depth examinations, such as thesis and dissertation work, should be conducted.

The bulk of books on the subject of Tarot are from practitioners and intended for the tarot community. Scholarly research by sociologists, anthropologists, historians, and others would be met with an abundance of primary source material from tarotists over the centuries, but very few secondary sources from the scholarly and academic presses. This should be understood as an indication of the need for research rather than a lack of importance.

Members of the tarot community began producing a significant amount of material in the form of books, articles, decks, blogs, and other sources beginning in the 1970s with what became known as a Tarot Renaissance. It would be a mistake to view this as a cultural fad in the sense of pet rocks or the Macarena. Tarot's origins, as we have seen, go back hundreds of years. There are peaks and valleys in its popularity, but its cultural presence has proved enduring. I suppose that if one traveled to their local tarot reader and asked them to do a reading on the future of the cards in American culture, the fortune-teller would speak of an important but mysterious future.

Timeline

_____⚬⚬⚬_____

Suggested Reading List

The following books are a combination of those found in the cited sources and other books that would be useful for readers and researchers on the topics covered in this book. This is by no means an exhaustive bibliography. It does, however, give a good sense of the literature in the field as well as a reflection of the writing that I found to be important for developing an appreciation for (primarily) Tarot and some of the related aspects of popular culture that have been explored here.

Auger, Emily. *Cartomancy and Tarot in Film, 1940–2010*. Intellect, 2016.

Auger, Emily, ed. *Tarot in Culture*. Two vols. Valleyhome Books, 2014.

Auger, Emily. *Tarot and Other Meditation Decks: History, Theory, Aesthetics, Typology*, McFarland, 2004.

Beaty, Bart. *Comics versus Art*. University of Toronto Press, 2012.

Betts, Raymond F. *A History of Popular Culture: More of Everything, Faster and Brighter*. Routledge, 2004.

Bongco, Mila. *Reading Comics: Language, Culture, and the Concept of the Superhero in Comic Books*. Garland, 2000.

Brandt, Jenn, and Callie Clare. *An Introduction to Popular Culture in the U.S.* Bloomsbury, 2018.

Crispin, Jessa. *The Creative Tarot: A Modern Guide to an Inspired Life*. Simon and Schuster, 2016.

Danesi, Marcel. *Popular Culture: Introductory Perspectives*, fourth ed. Rowman and Littlefield, 2019.

Daniels, Kooch N., and Victor Daniels, *Tarot at a Crossroads: The Unexpected Meeting of Tarot and Psychology*. Schiffer, 2016.

Decker, Ronald, and Michael Dummett. *A History of the Occult Tarot*. Duckworth, 2002.

Decker, Ronald, Thierry Depaulis, and Michael Dummett. *A Wicked Pack of Cards: The Origins of the Occult Tarot*. St, Martin's, 1996.

Duncan, Randy, Matthew J. Smith, and Paul Levitz. *The Power of Comics: History, Form, and Culture*, second ed. Bloomsbury, 2015.

Eisner, Will. *Comics and Sequential Art*. Poorhouse Press, 1985.

Farley, Helen. *A Cultural History of Tarot: From Entertainment to Esotericism*. L. B. Tauris, 2009.

Flowers, Stephen F. *The Magian Tarok: The Origins of the Tarot in the Mithraic and Hermetic Traditions*. Bear, 2019.

Giles, Cynthia. *The Tarot: Methods, Mastery, and More*. Simon and Schuster, 1996.

Giles, Cynthia. *The Tarot: History, Mystery and Lore*. Paragon, 1992.

Gray, Eden. *A Complete Guide to Tarot*. Bantam, 1970.

Greer, Mary K. *Tarot for Your Self: A Workbook for the Inward Journey*. Weiser, 1984.

Harvey, Robert C. *The Art of the Comic Book: An Aesthetic History*. University Press of Mississippi, 1996.

Heline, Corine. *The Bible and Tarot*. New Age Press, 1969.

Jorgenson, Danny. *The Esoteric Scene, Cultic Milieu, & Occult Tarot*. Routledge, 1992.

Kaplan, Stuart. *The Encyclopedia of Tarot*. Four vols. US Games Systems, 2002.

Kaplan, Stuart, ed. *Pamela Colman Smith: The Untold Story*. US Games Systems, 2018.

McCloud, Scott. *Understanding Comics: The Invisible Art*. Harper Collins, 1993.

Moakley, Gertrude. *The Tarot Cards Painted by Bonifacio Bembo for the Visconti-Sforza Family: An Iconographic and Historical Study*. New York Public Library, 1966.

Monaco, James. *How to Read a Film*. Oxford University Press, 1977.

Mulvey, Laura. "Visual Pleasure and Narrative Cinema." *Screen*, 1975.

Nichols, Sally. *Jung and Tarot: An Archetypal Journey*. Weiser, 1980.

Place, Robert K. *The Tarot: History, Symbolism and Divination*. Penguin, 2005.

Pollack, Rachel. *Seventy-Eight Degrees of Wisdom: A Book of Tarot*. Weiser, 2007.

Pustz, Matthew. *Comic Book Culture: Fanboys and True Believers*. University Press of Mississippi, 1999.

Rosengarten, Arthur. *Tarot and Psychology: Spectrums of Possibility*. Paragon House, 2000.

Roszak, Theodore. *Fool's Cycle, Full Cycle: Reflections on the Great Trumps of the Tarot*. Broadside, 1988.

Snow, Cassandra, and Beth Maiden. *Queering the Tarot*. Weiser, 2019.

Storey, John. *Cultural Theory and Popular Culture: An Introduction*, seventh ed. Routledge, 2015.

Tiryakian, Edward. *On the Margin of the Visible: Sociology, the Esoteric, and the Occult*. Wiley, 1974.

Versaci, Roco. *This Book Contains Graphic Language: Comics as Literature*. Continuum, 2007.

Wagner, Wynn. *Tarot for Christians: Lessons from Christ's Fool*. Mystic Ways, 2012

Wanless, James, and Angeles Arrien, eds. *Wheel of Tarot: A New Revolution*. Merrill-West, 1992.

Wen, Benebell. *Holistic Tarot: An Integrative Approach to Using Tarot for Personal Growth*. North Atlantic Books, 2015.

Works Cited

Chapter One

Alliette, Jean-Baptiste. *Cartomancy: The Art of Card Reading*. 1783.

Court de Gebelin, Antoine. *The Primeval World*. 1781.

Decker, Ronald, Thierry Depaulis, and Michael Dummett. *A Wicked Pack of Cards: The Origins of the Occult Tarot*. St. Martin's, 1996.

Farley, Helen. *A Cultural History of Tarot: From Entertainment to Esotericism*. L. B. Tauris, 2009.

Greer, Mary K. "Origins of Cartomancy (Playing Card Divination)." *Mary K. Geer's Tarot Blog*. www.marykgreer.com/2008/04/01/origins-of-divination-with-playing-cards/. Accessed July 7, 2018.

Levi, Eliphas. *Dogma and Ritual of High Magic*. 1854.

Levi, Eliphas. *A History of Magic*. 1860.

Moakley, Gertrude. *The Tarot Cards Painted by Bonifacio Bembo for the Visconti-Sforza Family: An Iconographic and Historical Study*. New York: New York Public Library, 1966.

Papus. *Tarot of the Bohemians*. 1889.

Papus. *Tarot Divination*. 1909.

Vincenzo, Sofia di. "Sola-Busca and Alchemy." *Sola-Busca Tarot Meyer*. 1998. www.solabusca tarot1998mayer.wordpress.com/sola-busca-alchemy. Accessed July 7, 2018.

Chapter Two

Auger, Emily. *Tarot and Other Meditation Decks: History, Theory, Aesthetics, Typology*, McFarland, 2004.

Auger, Emily, ed. *Tarot in Culture*. Two vols. Valleyhome Books, 2014.

Blavatsky, H. P. *The Secret Doctrine: The Classic Work, Abridged and Annotated*, ed. Michael Gomes. TarcherPerigee/ Penguin, 2009.

Book T: The Tarot. Samuel L. MacGregor Mathers. www.tarot.org.il/Library/Mathers/ Book-T. Accessed July 19, 2018.

Case, Paul Foster. *An Introduction to the Study of Tarot*. 1919.

The Cipher Manuscript. Several theories and significant debate exist about the authorship and origin of this document. William W. Westcott is the most likely candidate.

Crowley, Aleister. *The Book of Thoth: A Short Essay on the Tarot of the Egyptians*. 1944.

Crowley, Aleister. *Diary of a Drug Fiend*. 1922.

Crowley, Aleister. *Liber 777*. 1909.

Decker, Ronald, and Michael Dummett. *A History of the Occult Tarot*. Duckworth, 2002.

English, Jane. "A Scientist's Experience with Tarot." In *Wheel of Tarot*, 1992.

Farley, Helen. *A Cultural History of Tarot: From Entertainment to Esotericism*. L. B. Tauris, 2009.

Giles, Cynthia. *The Tarot: History, Mystery and Lore*. Paragon, 1992.

Ginzburg, Carlo. *The Night Battles: Witchcraft and Agrarian Cults in the Sixteenth and Seventeenth Centuries*. Johns Hopkins, 1966.

Gray, Eden. *A Complete Guide to Tarot*. Bantam, 1970.

Greer, Mary K. "Eden Gray's Fool's Journey." *Mary K. Greer's Tarot Blog*. www.marykgreer .com/2008/03/27/eden-grays-fools-journey. Accessed July 20, 2018.

Greer, Mary K. "1969: The Tarot Renaissance," *Mary K. Greer's Tarot Blog*. www.marykgreer .com/2008/05/20/1969-the-tarot-renaissance. Accessed July 20, 2018.

Greer, Mary K. "Permutations: On the Celtic Cross Spread." In *Wheel of Tarot*, 1992.

Greer, Mary K. *Tarot for Your Self: A Workbook for the Inward Journey*. 1984.

Heline, Corine. *The Bible and Tarot*. New Age Press, 1969.

Kaplan, Stuart. *The Encyclopedia of Tarot*. Four vols. US Games Systems, 2002.

Katz, Marcus. "Tarot on the Threshold: Liminality and Illegitimate Knowledge." In *Tarot in Culture*, volume 1, ed. Emily Auger. Valleyhome Books, 2014.

Libenson, Bess. "How a Passion for Tarot Cards Led to a Full-Time Business." *New York Times*, October 1, 2000.

Pollack, Rachel. *Seventy-Eight Degrees of Wisdom: A Book of Tarot*. Weiser, 2007.

Regardie, Israel. *The Golden Dawn*. 1940.

Rodriguez McRobbie, Linda. "The Strange and Mysterious History of the Ouija Board." *Smithsonian Magazine*, October 27, 2013. www.smithsonianmag.com/history/the -strange-and-mysterious-history-of-the-ouija-board. Accessed July 19, 2018.

"Sola Busca Tarocchi." www.wopc.co.uk/italy/sola-busca. Accessed 19 July 19, 2018.

Waite, Arthur Edward. *A Handbook of Cartomancy, Fortune-Telling, and Occult Divination*, 1889.

Waite, Arthur Edward. *The Pictorial Key to the Tarot*. 1911.

Wanless, James, and Angeles Arrien, eds. *Wheel of Tarot: A New Revolution*. Merrill-West, 1992.

Wen, Benebell. *Holistic Tarot: An Integrative Approach to Using Tarot for Personal Growth*. North Atlantic Books, 2015.

Yates, Frances. *Giordano Bruno and the Hermetic Tradition*. University of Chicago Press, 1964.

Zain, C. C. *The Sacred Tarot*. 1936.

Chapter Three

ABC News. "Convicted Killer Says he admitted to Murder Because Tarot Cards Said Guilt 'Would Destroy' Him." *20/20*, October 21, 2016. www.abcnews.go.com/US/convicted -killer-admitted-murder-tarot-cards-guilt-destroy/story?id=42972129. Accessed September 30, 2018.

Bursten, Lee A. www.tarotpassages.com/occhist-lb.htm. Accessed October 14, 2018.

Crispin, Jessa. *The Creative Tarot: A Modern Guide to an Inspired Life*. Simon and Schuster, 2016.

Daniels, Kooch N., and Victor Daniels, *Tarot at a Crossroads: The Unexpected Meeting of Tarot and Psychology*. Schiffer, 2016.

DiMatteo, Dante. "Personality Types: The Tarot Court Cards, and the Myers-Briggs Type Indicator." *78 Revelations Per Minute: Tarot in the Digital Age*, July 8, 2015. www.78revelationsaminute.wordpress.com. Accessed September 15, 2018.

Farley, Helen. *A Cultural History of Tarot: From Entertainment to Esotericism*. L. B. Tauris, 2009.

Graham, Billy. *Billy Graham Evangelistic Association*. "There's Nothing Innocent About Occult Games." www.billygraham.org/answer/theres-nothing-innocent-about-occult -games. Accessed May 18, 2018.

Heline, Corine. *The Bible and the Tarot*. New Age Press, 1969.

Jorgenson, Danny. *The Esoteric Scene, Cultic Milieu, and Occult Tarot*. Routledge, 1992.

Jung, Carl. *Psychological Types*. 1923.

Jung, Carl. *Synchronicity: An Acausal Connecting Principle*. 1955.

Katz, Marcus. "Tarot on the Threshold: Liminality and Illegitimate Knowledge." In *Tarot in Culture*, vol. 1, ed. Emily Auger. Valleyhome Books, 2014.

Liebenson, Bess. "How a Passion for Tarot Cards Led to a Full-Time Business." *New York Times*, October 1, 2000.

NewsOK. "OKC Psychic Charged with Rare Fortune Telling Offense," February 2017. https://newsok.com/article/5538393/okc-psychic-charged-with-rare-fortune-telling-offense. Accessed September 30, 2018.

Nichols, Sally. *Jung and Tarot: An Archetypal Journey*. Weiser, 1980.

Pollack, Rachel. Personal interview, July 1, 2015.

Record Courier." Psychic Arrested in Sting," July 23, 2014. www.recordcourier.com/news /crime/psychic-arrested-in-sting/#.WuueDP0x68Q.email. Accessed September 30, 2018.

Robertson, Pat. "Bring It On: Tarot Cards." Christian Broadcasting Network. www1.cbn.com /video/bring-it-on-tarot-cards. Accessed May 18, 2018.

Rosengarten, Arthur. *Tarot and Psychology: Spectrums of Possibility*. Paragon House, 2000.

Telegraph. "Tarot Card Reader Kept Murderer Talking for an Hour While Waiting for Police after Dealing Him Death Card," May 27, 2016. www.telegraph.co.uk/news/2016/05/26 /tarot-card-reader-kept-murderer-talking-for-an-hour-while-waitin. Accessed September 30, 2018.

Wagner, Wynn. *Tarot for Christians: Lessons from Christ's Fool*. Mystic Ways, 2012

Chapter Four

Auger, Emily, ed. *Tarot in Culture*. Two vols. Valleyhome Books, 2014.

Auger, Emily. *Tarot and Other Meditation Decks: History, Theory, Aesthetics, Typology*. McFarland, 2004.

Campbell, Joseph. *The Hero with a Thousand Faces*. Pantheon, 1949.

Crowley, Aleister. *Book of Thoth*. 1944.

Farley, Helen. *A Cultural History of Tarot: From Entertainment to Esotericism*. L. B. Tauris, 2009.

Fletcher, Angus. *Allegory: The Theory of a Symbolic Mode*. Princeton University Press, 1964.

Gray, Eden. *A Complete Guide to the Tarot*. Bantam, 1970.

Greer, Mary K. Personal interview, August 13, 2017.

Katz, Marcus. "Tarot on the Threshold: Liminality and Illegitimate Knowledge." In *Tarot in Culture*, vol. 1, ed. Emily Auger. Valleyhome Books, 2014.

Kaplan, Stuart, ed. *Pamela Colman Smith: The Untold Story*. US Games Systems, 2018.

Levy, Ariel. "Beautiful Monsters; Art and Obsession in Italy." *New Yorker*, April 18, 2016.

Sefer Yesirah or *Book of Creation*.

"The Tarot Card Deck Designed by Salvador Dali." *Open Culture*. www.openculture.com /2016/12/the-tarot-card-deck-designed-by-salvador-dali.html. Accessed July 28, 2018.

Waite, Arthur Edward. *The Pictorial Key to the Tarot*. Rider, 1911.

Willshire, William Hughes. *A Descriptive Catalogue of Playing and Other Cards in the British Museum*. British Museum, 1876.

Wright, Glenn. "Cartofeminism: The War to Make Tarot the Exclusive Domain of Women." www.http://glennfwright.com/Tarot/cartofem.html. Accessed October 15, 2018.

Chapter Five

The Andy Griffith Show. "Three Wishes for Opie." CBS, 1964.

Auryn, Mat. "The Happy Squirrel Card in the Tarot." *Patheos*, December 28, 2017. www. patheos.com/blogs/matauryn/2017/12/28/happy-squirrel-tarot. Accessed July 29, 2018.

Bones. "Harbingers in a Fountain," season 5, episode 1. 20th Century Fox Television, 2009.

Buffy the Vampire Slayer. "What's My Line?" parts 1 and 2, season 2, episodes 9 and 10; "Primeval" and "Restless," season 4, episodes 21 and 22. Warner Brothers, 1997–2003.

Carnivale. HBO, 2003.

Charmed. TNT, 1998–2006.

Dark Shadows. ABC, 1966–71.

King of the Hill, "The Witches of East Arlen," season 7, episode 23. Fox, 2003.

Lawman. "Tarot," season 4, episode 14. ABC, 1961.

Mad Men, "The Mountain King," season 2, episode 1. AMC, 2008.

Maerz, Melissa. "The Mind Behind 'Mad Men.'" *Rolling Stone*, June 17, 2009. www.rollingstone .com/culture/culture-news/the-mind-behind-mad-men-60817. Accessed July 29, 2018.

Penny Dreadful. "The Nightcomers," season 2, episode 3. Showtime, 2015.

Schitt's Creek. "The Hike," season 5, episode 13. Canadian Broadcasting Company, 2019.

The Simpsons. "Lisa's Wedding," season 6, episode 19. Fox, 1995.

Sirdofsky, Dylan. "Petaluma Artist Scores 'Game of Thrones' Deal for Tarot Card Deck." *Press Democrat*, April 30, 2018. www.pressdemocrat.com/lifestyle/8179597–181/petaluma -artist-scores-game-of. Accessed July 29, 2018.

The X-Files. "Clyde Bruckman's Final Repose," season 3, episode 4. Fox, 1995.

Xena: Warrior Princess. "The Bitter Suite," season 3, episode 12. NBC, 1998

Chapter Six

Caplen, Robert. *Shaken and Stirred: The Feminism of James Bond*. Xlibris, 2010.

Ebert, Roger. "Red Violin Movie Review." June 18, 1999. www.rogerebert.com/reviews/the -red-violin-1999. Accessed August 5, 2018.

Fletcher, Angus. *Allegory: The Theory of a Systemic Mode.* Princeton University Press, 1964.

The Haunted Mansion. Directed by Rob Minkoff. Performance by Eddie Murphy. Walt Disney, 2003.

Live and Let Die. Directed by Guy Hamilton. Performances by Roger Moore, Jane Seymour, Yaphet Kotto, Geoffrey Holder, Gloria Hendry. Eon Productions, 1973.

Monster-In-Law. Directed by Robert Luketic. Performances by Jennifer Lopez and Jane Fonda. New Line Cinema, 2005.

Nightmare Alley. Directed by Edmund Goulding. Performances by Tyrone Power, Joan Blondell, Coleen Gray, Helen Walker, and Ian Keth. Twentieth Century Fox, 1947.

Norman, Jessica Lynn. "The Red Violin: A Feast for the Senses." *James River Film Journal,* November 30, 2013. www.jamesriverfilm.wordpress.com/2013/11/30/the-red-violin-a -feast-for-the-senses. Accessed August 5, 2018.

The Red Violin. Directed by Francois Gerard. Performances by Anita Lorenzi, Carlo Cecchi, Irene Grazioli, Samuel L. Jackson, Jason Flemyng. Rhombus Media, 1998.

Sherlock Holmes: A Game of Shadows. Directed by Guy Ritchie. Performances by Robert Downey Jr., Noomi Rapace, Jude Law, Rachel McAdams, Jared Harris, and Laurence Possa. Warner Brothers, 2011.

Things You Can Tell Just by Looking at Her. Directed by Rodrigo Garcia. Performances by Glenn Close and Calista Flockhart. MGM, 2000.

Tombstone. Directed by George Cosmatos and Kevin Jarre. Performances by Val Kilmer, Kurt Russell, Sam Elliott, Bill Paxton, Paula Malcolmson, and Dana Delaney. Hollywood Pictures, 1993.

Wine Country. Directed by Amy Poehler. Performances by Amy Poehler, Rachel Dratch, Maya Rudolph, Ana Gasteyer, Cherry Jones. Netflix, 2019.

The Wolfman. Directed by George Waggner. Performances by Lon Chaney Jr., Evelyn Ankers, Fay Helm, and Bela Lugosi. Universal, 1941.

The Wolfman. Directed by Joe Johnston. Performances by Benicio del Toro and Anthony Hopkins. Universal, 2010.

Chapter Seven

"Away Game." *The New Mutants.* Marvel, June 1, 1984.

Balm (from *Sailor Moon*). http://villains.wikia.com/wiki/Balm. Accessed November 19, 2018.

Coogan, Peter. "The Definition of a Superhero." In *A Comics Study Reader,* eds. Jeet Heer and Kent Worcester. University Press of Mississippi, 2009.

Dark Nights: Metal. "The Batman Who Laughs," issue 5. DC, 2017.

Davis, Erik. "Gods of the Funny Books; An Interview with Neil Gaiman and Rachel Pollack." Gnosis, 1994.

Doctor Strange and the Sorcerers Supreme, issue 3, February 2017.

"Doom Patrol: The Rachel Pollack Interview." *DC Comics News.* www.dccomicsnews.com /2017/10/22/doom-patrol-the-rachel-pollack-interview. Accessed December 15, 2018.

Eisner, Will. *Comics and Sequential Art.* Poorhouse Press, 1985.

Foucault, Michel. *The History of Sexuality,* volume 1. Penguin, 1976.

Gaiman, Neil. *The Books of Magic,* issues 1–4. DC Comics, 2014 [1991,1992].

Gross, Melinda-Catherine. "Vertigo Book Club: Madame Xanadu Unites a Universe." June 19, 2018. www.dccomics.com/blog/2018/10/30. Accessed December 14, 2018.

Jay, Iris, and Hye Mardikian, eds. *Tabula Idem: A Queer Tarot Comic Anthology*. Fortuna, 2017.

McCloud, Scott. *Understanding Comics: The Invisible Art*. New York: Harper Collins, 1993.

Mulvey, Laura. "Visual Pleasure and Narrative Cinema." *Screen*, 1975.

Saunders, Thelonia. "Reality Check: The Tarot Cards of the Batman Who Laughs," February 11, 2018. http://www.adventuresinpoortaste.com. Accessed November 19, 2018.

Spider-Man/Deadpool. "Change Partners," vol. 1, issue 11. Marvel, November 9, 2016.

"Tarot, Trans-Gender Robots, and Friendly Bandage-People." www.sequart.org/magazine/53227/doom-patrol-interview-rachel-pollack December 28, 2014. Accessed December 15, 2018.

TV Tropes. "Tarot: Witch of The Black Rose." www.tvtropes.org/pmwiki/pmwiki.php/Comic Book/TarotWitchOfTheBlackRose. Accessed November 19, 2018.

Wagner, Matt. *Madame Xanadu: Disenchanted*. Illustrated by Amy Reeder Hadley. DC Comics, 2009.

Index

References to illustrations are in *italics*.

About the Author

Photo by Bonnie Maille

Patrick Maille has a PhD in history from Texas Tech University and is a professor of history at Oklahoma Panhandle State University, where he teaches various courses including one on the history of magic.

Printed in the United States
By Bookmasters